WITHDRAWN BY THE
UNIVERSITY OF MICHIGAN

D1521744

WITHDRAWN BY THE
UNIVERSITY OF MICHIGAN

Nation and Identity

'*Nation and Identity* is well organised, well written, carefully argued and at the cutting edge of the relevant literature. In addition, and most importantly, it has a striking and important set of conceptualisations and arguments about nation, national identity and nationalism, and some probing conjectures about "the future of nationalism" in an increasingly globalised world. Ross Poole writes persuasively and with force.'

Kai Nielsen, University of Concordia

'*Nation and Identity* is a beautifully written, timely and thoughtful engagement with nationalism. It eschews the conventional pieties so often offered on the subjects of nationalism and cultural pluralism, and gives admirably clear expression to the view that nationalism is a creature of modernity whose day may yet be seen to be over. Ross Poole argues his case persuasively and elegantly using his philosophical, political and historical sources judiciously.'

David Archard, University of St Andrews

Ross Poole is Associate Professor of Philosophy at Macquarie University, Australia. His previous book, *Morality and Modernity* (Routledge, 1991), was selected by *Choice* as an outstanding philosophy book in 1991.

Ideas
Series Editor: Jonathan Rée
Middlesex University

Original philosophy today is written mainly for advanced academic specialists. Students and the general public make contact with it only through introductions and general guides.

The philosophers are drifting away from their public, and the public has no access to its philosophers.

The Ideas series is dedicated to changing this situation. It is committed to the idea of philosophy as a constant challenge to intellectual conformism. It aims to link primary philosophy to non-specialist concerns. And it encourages writing which is both simple and adventurous, scrupulous and popular. In these ways it hopes to put contemporary philosophers back in touch with ordinary readers.

Books in the series include:

Getting What You Want?
Bob Brecher

Morality and Modernity
Ross Poole

Children
Rights and Childhood
David Archer

The Man of Reason
Genevieve Lloyd

Philosophical Tales
Jonathan Rée

Freedom, Truth and History
Stephen Houlgate

Nation and Identity

Ross Poole

London and New York

GRAD
JC
311
.P6621
1999

First published 1999
by Routledge
11 New Fetter Lane, London EC4P 4EE

Simultaneously published in the USA and Canada
by Routledge
29 West 35th Street, New York, NY 10001

Routledge is an imprint of the Taylor & Francis Group

© 1999 Ross Poole

Typeset in Times by Routledge
Printed and bound in Great Britain by Biddles Ltd, Guildford
and King's Lynn

All rights reserved. No part of this book may be reprinted or
reproduced or utilised in any form or by any electronic,
mechanical, or other means, now known or hereafter
invented, including photocopying and recording, or in any
information storage or retrieval system, without permission in
writing from the publishers.

British Library Cataloguing in Publication Data
A catalogue record for this book is available from the British
Library

Library of Congress Cataloging in Publication Data
Poole, Ross
    Nation and Identity / Ross Poole.
    Includes bibliographical references and index.
    1. Nationalism. 2. Liberty. 3. Multiculturalism. I. Title.
    JC311.P662   1999   99-23022
    320.54–dc21   CIP

ISBN 0–415–12622–3 (hbk)
ISBN 0–415–12623–1 (pbk)

GRAD
32443043
POLSC
02-14-00

For Nicholas and Alexander

For Nicholas and Amanda

Contents

Preface

Although this is a rather short book it has taken me a long time to write it, and I have incurred many debts on the way. It is easiest to begin with the institutional ones. In 1994, I spent a productive and enjoyable period in the stimulating environment of the Humanities Research Centre of the Australian National University. The University Center and Graduate School of the City University of New York provided me with an academic base during the very exciting year I spent in New York in 1995. My thanks are due to the staff of both these places for their friendliness, helpfulness and efficiency. At my own University, my fellow members of the Philosophy Department have always been supportive of my research, tolerant of my absences, and understanding of the conflict between the demands of research and those of administration, particularly in the period when I was Head of Department. I could not imagine a better group of colleagues. Over a long period, the Philosophy Department's Administrative Officer, Sandra Dunn, has taken on burdens well beyond her formal responsibilities in order to make the academic life of myself and my colleagues easier. More recently, this tradition has been continued by Jane Farquhar. My very great thanks to both of them.

The Research Office at Macquarie, the Research Committee of the School of History, Philosophy and Politics, and the Australian Research Council, have all shown faith in my work by supporting research assistance, teaching release and travel. I hope this book justifies that faith.

Over the years in which I have been thinking about nationalism, I have given seminars and courses, read papers at and attended conferences, and participated in formal and informal discussions on most of the topics discussed in this book. I cannot now remember all the people from whom I have learned something which has found its way into this book. I am uncomfortably aware that some of the views

presented here were probably first put to me by others in circumstances I have long forgotten. To the many – now anonymous others –
who have contributed to my thinking about nationalism, I can only
express my thanks and apologise for the lack of a more individual
acknowledgment.

I have been very fortunate to have had friends and colleagues who
have been prepared to read and criticise drafts of this book or to spend
time talking about the issues discussed in it. These include Jack
Barbalet, Jocelyne Couture, Omar Dahbour, Philip Gerrans, Winton
Higgins, Peter Hill, Barry Hindess, Ian Lennie, Genevieve Lloyd, Kai
Nielsen, Paul Redding, John Roberts, Michel Seymour, Nicholas
Smith and John Sutton. In 1995, David Miller was kind enough to
send me a proof copy of his (then) forthcoming book. At various
times, Andrew Mason, Bernhard Ripperger and Rebecca Ripperger
have carried out research for this or closely associated projects.
Insightful comments on a penultimate draft by an anonymous reader
were responsible for a number of improvements. Sandra Lynch played
a key role in finalising the manuscript. As Editor of the 'Ideas' Series,
Jonathan Rée has always been immensely supportive of the project,
despite his strong disagreement with my evaluation of nationalism. He
has been just the right reader for various drafts of the manuscript.
Lisabeth During has been involved from the beginning, and has
striven hard – I hope not unsuccessfully – to improve my style and
broaden the focus of my arguments.

To all these people, many, many thanks.

Nicholas During, Alexander Poole and Lisabeth During have all
had their own important commitments and projects while I have been
writing this book. I suspect that they have made greater concessions to
mine than I have to theirs. Each of them has contributed, not merely
to the book, but also – more significantly – to the well-being of its
author. I owe them more than I can say.

Nation and Identity draws on material which first appeared in the
following published articles (though in almost all cases there are
significant changes):

'On national identity: A response to Jonathan Rée', *Radical Philosophy* no. 62
(autumn 1992), pp. 14–19.
'Nationalism: The last rites?' in Aleksandar Pavkovic, Adam Czarnota and
Halyna Koscharsky (eds), *Nationalism and Postcommunism*, Dartmouth,
Aldershot, 1995.
'On being a person', *Australasian Journal of Philosophy* vol. 74 (1996),
pp. 38–56.

'Freedom, citizenship and national identity', *Philosophical Forum* vol. 28 (1996/97), pp. 125–48.
'National identity, multiculturalism and aboriginal rights: An Australian perspective', *Canadian Journal of Philosophy* supp. vol. 22 (1996): *Rethinking Nationalism* (eds Jocelyne Couture, Kai Nielsen and Michel Seymour), Calgary, University of Calgary Press, 1998.

My thanks to the publishers for permission to make use of the material here.

Ross Poole
Macquarie University
7 January 1999

Introduction

Nationalism has played an enormous role in world history over the past few hundred years. It continues to do so. For many – I suspect for most who open this book – it is indelibly associated with some of the worst aspects of modern history. Large numbers of otherwise decent people have carried out unbelievable atrocities for no better reason than their nation required them to. Authoritarian and totalitarian regimes have crushed dissent, eliminated opposition and trampled on civil liberties in the name of the nation. The rhetoric of national identity is used to stand in the way of civilised policies towards refugees and immigrants. Yet, as we recount the horrors, we should also be – perhaps uncomfortably – aware how much we take the nation for granted in our day to day life. Without thinking about it, we pick out one stretch of territory and one collection of historical narratives as ours, and we recognise one group of people as fellow members of our nation. And even the horrors have another side. Nations have called forth heroism and sacrifice as well as murder and torture. People have risked their lives to restore democracy and civil rights in their own country, when they could easily have chosen comfortable exile elsewhere. Programmes of health reform, social welfare and environmental repair have gained political support because they appeal to a sense of national identity.

Nationalism has always been of interest to historians and social theorists. In the eighteenth and nineteenth centuries, it also received considerable attention from philosophers. But for most of the twentieth century, it has been all but ignored by philosophers. Students of moral and political philosophy might attend lectures, read the recommended texts and complete their degrees without coming across the concepts of the nation, national identity and nationalism. The overwhelming consensus among philosophers was that nationalism was not worth talking about. For example, Robert E. Goodin and

Philip Pettit's *A Companion to Contemporary Political Philosophy* (published in 1993) was intended to provide – in the editors' words – a 'synopsis of the "state of play" in contemporary political philosophy'.[1] The second of its three sections was entitled 'Major Ideologies' and it included articles on Anarchism, Conservatism, Feminism, Liberalism, Marxism and Socialism. There was no article on Nationalism. Goodin and Pettit differed from most of their predecessors in that they felt it necessary to explain this omission:

> Nationalism – still less racism, sexism or ageism – does not figure, on the grounds that it hardly counts as a principled way of think-ing about things.[2]

That nationalism was lumped together with racism, sexism and ageism, together with the claim that it 'hardly counts as a principled way of thinking about things', suggests that it is the expression of prejudice, a form of unreason, not a coherent – let alone morally defensible – outlook on the world.[3]

   However, even at the time Goodin and Pettit made the claim, the collective wisdom was crumbling. Yael Tamir's *Liberal Nationalism* (Princeton, Princeton University Press, 1993; second edition 1995) was published that very year, and David Miller's *On Nationality* (Oxford, Clarendon Press, 1995) and Margaret Canovan's *Nationhood and Political Theory* (Cheltenham, UK, and Brookfield, VT, Edward Elgar, 1996) followed close on its heels. All these books argued that some forms of nationalism were morally defensible, and, indeed, that a form of national community was presupposed by much of the liberal thinking which dominated mainstream political philosophy. While these arguments have not received universal assent, there is no doubt that nationalism is back on the philosophical agenda. Very few would now claim that nationalism was not worthy of philosophical discussion. In the past five years there have been a number of anthologies, special issues of journals, and articles and chapters by distinguished philosophers on nationalism and related subjects.[4]

   In retrospect, it is clear why nationalism was emerging as a central issue for political philosophers, even before Goodin and Pettit compiled their *Companion*. The debate between liberals and their opponents on the meaning and value of 'community' had reached a point where it was almost inevitable that *someone* was going to notice that nationalism was the form of communitarian thinking most influential in the modern world. Multiculturalism had already emerged as a significant political issue within all liberal-democratic countries, and political philosophers had become uneasily aware of the extent to which mainstream political and legal institutions operated through an established public culture. Nationalist movements, claiming the right of self-determination, emerged in the United Kingdom, Canada, France, Italy and Spain, as well as in Eastern Europe, Africa and Asia. Philosophers were forced to consider, not merely the constituents of a liberal and democratic order, but how the borders of that order were to be determined. Indeed, despite the editors' rejection of nationalism as a 'Major Ideology' worthy of philosophical attention, at least two of the contributors to the 'Special Topics' Section of Goodin and Pettit's *Companion* offered some discussion of nationalism.[5]

However, if the letter of Pettit and Goodin's judgement was being overturned even as they wrote, something of its spirit lives on. Mainstream political philosophy remains dominated by various forms of liberalism. In the debate about nationalism, those who remain sceptical of its philosophical and moral credibility do so on the grounds that even the most benign forms of nationalism offend against some central tenets of liberalism, whilst those – such as Tamir and Miller – who argue *for* nationalism make it clear that the form of nationalism they defend is one which is compatible with liberal principles. If nationalism is to gain an invitation to the companionable world of political philosophy hosted by Goodin and Pettit, it will be because it has shown itself to be acceptable to the already invited guests. Tamir puts this bluntly: her project is 'to "translate" nationalist arguments into liberal language'.[6] No doubt this reflects the balance of power within academic philosophy (if nowhere else). However, it is not at all clear that it is the most appropriate approach. Despite the best intentions of some authors, it draws a line between those nationalisms which are compatible with liberalism (the good 'civic' nationalisms) and those which are not (the bad 'ethnic' ones), and focusses on the former.[7] However, it may be that we will better understand the variety of nationalisms – including the 'good' ones – if we approach the phenomenon as a whole. It is also one of the strongest arguments presented by pro-nationalist theorists – and one which will find echoes in this book – that many characteristic liberal positions presuppose the existence of a political order based on the nation. If this argument is correct, then it is not only nationalism which must present itself in a form acceptable to liberalism, but liberalism which must also find a form appropriate to its nationalist underpinnings. If liberal principles are dependent upon the nation, then liberalism is hardly the appropriate tribunal to assess its moral credentials.

There is another respect in which liberalism does not provide the appropriate perspective from which to view nationalism. Liberals take for granted a certain conception of the moral agent – the *person* – who may be held responsible for what he or she chooses to do, possesses certain rights and obligations, is the subject of certain moral emotions, and enters into relations with other agents on the basis of mutual recognition and respect. Other identities – citizenship and nationality, for example – are treated as derivative, to be justified, if at all, from the perspective of the person. Where this perspective defines our conception of morality, the responsibilities which go with other moral agendas – those of national membership, for example – may well seem alien and unjustified. Even Yael Tamir, who is concerned to emphasise the importance of national identity in our lives, does not question the priority of personhood.[8] Yet it is only when we recognise that liberal personhood is only one of the moral identities which are available to us, that we can come to terms with the significance of these other identities. Membership of the nation, for example, is a specific form of *individual* existence and carries with it a certain conception of agency, of relationship with others, and appropriate forms of activity. From this perspective, the demands of the nation are not alien intrusions, but forms of individual commitment and, indeed, of individual fulfilment. If we are to come to terms with the moral force of nationalism, we must take seriously not only the likelihood that it involves values which are different to those of liberalism, but also the possibility that our national identity may be no less fundamental than our identity as persons.

One way to diminish the temptation to give liberalism priority over nationalism is to conceive of them both historically. They are in fact almost coextensive. Both doctrines emerged in a self-conscious form in the late eighteenth and early nineteenth centuries in Western Europe and the European colonies in the Americas. In both cases, it is possible to trace the roots a few centuries earlier, liberalism to the sixteenth century and nationalism perhaps a century earlier.[9] In the nineteenth century and later, both were exported to the rest of the world, nationalism with rather more success than liberalism. That both liberalism and nationalism originated in early Western modernity has suggested to some that they are the effects of more basic causes – capitalism, the market, industrialisation, or whatever. Marxists, for example, are tempted to conceive both liberalism and nationalism as mere epiphenomena of the market, while Ernest Gellner – as we shall

see in Chapter 1 – conceived of nationalism as an effect of industrialisation. There is, however, no good reason to draw the connections as
tightly as this, and many reasons not to. All we need to recognise is
that both doctrines developed as men and women tried to make sense
of the changes which were taking place and to work out how to
respond to them, how to organise social and political life, what
responsibilities men and women had to each other and to the State,
and so on. These ways of conceiving the world have been embodied in
the institutions and practices of almost all Western societies – and a
good number of non-Western ones as well. Neither liberalism nor
nationalism are comprehensive moral doctrines (in the way that some
religious codes aim to be comprehensive); both leave large areas of
human life for the operation of choice or other moral codes. It is for
this reason that both liberalism and nationalism have proved
remarkably flexible in their choice of partners – including, occasionally, each other.

By and large, I will not be concerned to discuss the historical
conditions which have engendered liberalism, though I will make some
gestures in this direction in Chapter 3.[10] But I do wish to look at the
historical conditions which have encouraged and sustained the
nationalist project. Indeed, I do not think that it is possible to evaluate
any form of morality without some understanding of the social
context within which it is practised (I provide a justification for this
approach in Chapter 2, in the section entitled 'National identity and
moral philosophy'). For this reason, this book contains a much more
explicit encounter with historical and sociological theories of
nationalism than is usual in works of philosophy, even those of Tamir,
Miller and Canovan which are explicitly concerned with nationalism. I
will suggest in Chapter 1 that in the conditions of the modern world,
nationalism became an almost inescapable political project. It was not
a historical accident which more enlightened political strategies might
have avoided: it was the very condition of a coherent political and
social life. This argument has profound implications for the moral
evaluation of nationalism. It may be that we wish to reject the changes
which have engendered nationalism. But failing heroism of this
magnitude, the onus is placed on the critic of nationalism to propose
an alternative. However, this is not the end of the story. For I will
suggest in Chapter 5 that the conditions which have sustained
nationalism are themselves undergoing transformation, and that it is
now possible to envisage – however tentatively – the end of nationalism. If, as I will have argued, nationalism has been central to the social
and political life of modernity – and also the unacknowledged

foundation of much political theory – this is no small matter, and I end the book by speculating briefly on the future.

However, the main role of the first and last chapters of this book is to characterise the historic moment of nationalism and thus to define the conceptual space within which it is possible to pursue a number of philosophical questions about it. Which is not to say these chapters do not raise philosophical questions of their own. For example, the concepts of imagination and culture employed by theorists of nationalism are not ones which philosophers can afford to neglect or take for granted, and I try to say something about these in my discussion. A discussion of globalisation in Chapter 5 leads naturally to the issue of cosmopolitanism. However, the bulk of the philosophical discussion takes place in Chapters 2, 3 and 4. In Chapter 2, I address the concept of identity. This term is inescapable in discussions of nationalism (indeed, in social and cultural studies generally), but is employed in a variety of different senses, none of which bear much resemblance to the way in which the term is deployed in philosophy. Part of my project in this chapter is to construct a concept of identity which does justice both to the requirements of social theory and those of philosophy. My other aim in this chapter is to bring out the centrality of this concept to issues of moral commitment, responsibility and agency, and ultimately to the question of moral justification. That the concept of identity is important for social theory and political philosophy is relatively uncontroversial; what I hope to establish in this chapter is that it is also central to moral philosophy.

In Chapter 3, I take up the relationship between liberalism and nationalism in terms of a concept which is central to both, that of freedom. Here it is convenient to introduce another player, the tradition of civic republicanism. This tradition is in fact a good deal older than both liberalism and nationalism, so its conception of freedom can reasonably claim a historical priority, if nothing else. But more significant to my argument is the issue of political priority. I argue, following Philip Pettit and Quentin Skinner, that some version of the republican emphasis on active citizenship is necessary for a liberal society; but also, and here disagreeing with Pettit and Skinner, that the only viable form of republicanism in the modern world is a nationalist one. I further suggest that a serious concern with the negative freedom valued by liberals should lead them to a consideration of the political and cultural conditions of this freedom, and thus ultimately to a more positive – and nationalist – understanding of this concept.

In Chapter 4, I put some of my own nationalist cards on the table, and discuss multiculturalism and indigenous rights, especially as these issues have surfaced in my own country, Australia. I argue, against currently fashionable views, that there are good liberal and democratic reasons to subordinate the claims of multiculturalism to those of national identity. However, I sharply distinguish the issue of multiculturalism from that of indigenous rights. I argue for a much stronger form of recognition of indigenous people than of other cultural minorities not only on the grounds that it is due to them, but also because our national identity demands it of us. This issue is perhaps the most morally significant issue confronting postcolonial societies today. It presents a challenge to the national self-understanding of the countries involved; but it also requires that self-understanding if we are to marshal the moral resources necessary to confront it.

As this book engages with the work of historians and social theorists as well as that of philosophers, it runs the risk of leaving readers from all sides unsatisfied. The historian's demand for revealing detail will not be satisfied by the schematic history of nationalism offered here; the sociologist may well find the explanation of nationalism lacks the nuance and caveat necessary to deal with troublesome counter-examples; while the philosopher will be aware that I move quickly over issues which have received enormous attention in the professional journals and often use a house-painter's brush where a draftsman's stylus would be appropriate. I try to make some amends in the Bibliographical Essay at the end of this volume where I indicate where the issues discussed may be pursued further (though this may well risk further irritation by its failure to mention some favoured authors). However, a synoptic approach is essential to the enterprise. I see no adequate way of dealing with the moral issues of nationalism which is not informed by a sociological and historical understanding of the phenomenon. On this issue – as almost all others – philosophers must be prepared to incorporate something of the historian's, anthropologist's or sociologist's understanding into their approach. Nationalism arose in certain specific circumstances, and, if we are to assess its claims to provide a way of organising social and political life, we need to know what these circumstances were. However, historians, anthropologists and sociologists also have much to learn from the concerns of philosophers. The reason that nationalism has proved such a potent force in the modern world is that it has been experienced by many as a moral imperative. Even the social scientist will not get very far in understanding nationalism unless he or she is prepared to understand and evaluate that imperative. Unless the investigation of nationalism is also informed by a moral concern, it will not yield an adequate understanding of it.

1 The coming of nationalism

> Nationalism is primarily a political principle, which holds that the political and the national unit should be congruent.
>
> (Ernest Gellner)[1]

In its most familiar and historically potent form, nationalism is the principle that the nation is the ground of political sovereignty and that political sovereignty is the right and destiny of the nation. This principle is satisfied when and only when nation and State come together as the nation-state.

Nationalism has played an enormous role in modern history. World maps have had to be redrawn – and are still being redrawn – in the effort to make state borders coincide with what are conceived to be the boundaries of the nation. Large numbers of people have been prepared to make great personal sacrifices – up to and including life itself – in the struggles needed to achieve or defend the political sovereignty of their nation. At the end of the twentieth century, it does not need emphasising that many have been prepared to commit unspeakable atrocities in the name of the nation. However, it should also be remembered that those of us who go about our business in politically stable countries rely on this principle when we draw a comfortable moral line between the claims of our compatriots and those outside our national boundaries.

But what is the nation? And what is it about the nation which supports – or has seemed to support – the claims made on its behalf? If the nation is the source of political authority, what is the source of *its* political authority? Why is it our nation, rather than our class, religion or political commitment, that demands political recognition?

The nation: imagination and culture

> In an anthropological spirit...I propose the following definition of the nation: it is an imagined political community – and imagined as inherently limited and sovereign.
>
> (Benedict Anderson)[2]

Benedict Anderson's characterisation of the nation as an 'imagined community' has become unavoidable in recent discussions of nationalism. And for good reason. Prior to Anderson's work, too many theorists – especially liberals and Marxists – had dismissed the nation as a collective illusion or form of false consciousness, as a pathology unworthy of serious engagement, let alone sympathetic attention. The term 'imagined community' provided a way forward. In suggesting that the nation is an object of the creative imagination, a cultural product analogous to a work of literature or music, it encouraged more sensitive investigations of the kind of imagination involved in the nation. Anderson's own work was exemplary in this respect. The term also allowed theorists to entertain the idea that the nation might be a creative response to economic and political changes, rather than a rationalisation or mystification of them. It lessened – though it has never quite removed – the temptation to conceive of the nation as a mere epiphenomenon of more fundamental economic and political causes.

These consequences have been entirely beneficial. However, the enthusiasm with which the term has been taken up has obscured the fact that it also has major problems and limitations. Anderson's own account of the term is quite confused. A 'nation', he writes:

> is *imagined* because the members of even the smallest nation will never know most of their fellow-members, meet them, or even hear of them, yet in the minds of each lives the image of their communion.[3]

This passage implies that the notion of an 'imagined community' comes into play when a group becomes too large for its members to know each other personally. This suggestion is reinforced when Anderson goes on to say that 'all communities larger than primordial villages of face-to-face contact (and perhaps even these) are imagined'.[4] But the suggestion – albeit half-hearted – that 'face-to-face' contact might do without imagination is highly misleading. It is after all a hermeneutic truism that *all* social relations – even those between 'primordial' villagers – work through the shared understanding (and misunderstanding) of those involved. 'Face-to-face contact' is hardly a substitute for imagination. If the concept of an 'imagined community' is to mark an important *distinction* among social relations, it is not because of the presence of imagination in some and its absence in others.

In the final clause of the passage cited, Anderson hints at a different reading. Here he says that the notion of an 'imagined community' comes into play when the members of a community *'live the image of their communion'*. I take this to mean both that people conceive of themselves as belonging to the community, and also that the conception of the community informs the way in which they live, relate to others, and so on. This suggests a different way in which the distinction between imagined communities and other forms of social relation might be drawn. We can – and should – recognise that *all* social relations work through the reciprocal understandings of those involved. However, *some* social relations require a shared understanding of the social whole – the community – which makes the relationship possible. A representation of the community is a constitutive presence in the relations. These are the relationships which involve the idea of an imagined community.

This distinction is *not* based on size. As Anderson himself allows, there are extensive networks of social relations which do not depend upon an understanding of the network as a whole. He suggests, for example, that Javanese villagers think of themselves as connected with people they have never met by 'indefinitely stretchable nets of kinship and clientship', and that they do not have the idea of a 'society' to which they all belong.[5] Or, to take a more familiar example, people may conceive of themselves as related to others through an extensive web of exchange relations without forming the concept of the 'market' as the social whole which makes these relationships possible. The relevant concepts – of society and of the market – are the inventions of theorists, and need not be part of the conceptual equipment of the participants in social or market relations. On the other hand, relations between members of the nation are mediated by their mutual recognition that they belong to the same nation. Nations are not, of course, the only imagined communities. For example, the relationships between Islamic or Roman Catholic co-religionists may well depend upon a shared conception of the church to which they belong. In cases of this kind, where it is the representation of the community which makes the relationship possible, the representation is not a merely theoretical category, but is a component of the consciousness of its members. If we are to understand such 'imagined communities' we must explore the ways in which they are conceived by those who belong to them.[6]

It may be that Anderson's confusion of size with the need for imagination is one of presentation rather than of substance.[7] It is, however, very important to clear it up. The distinction, between those social relations which depend upon a shared conception of the social whole and those which do not, is of considerable importance to the understanding, not merely of the nation, but of a range of other kinds of social relationship and community. It is also, as we shall see in the next chapter, crucial for the understanding of the different forms of *identity* involved in social life.

A second problem for Anderson's account concerns the *limitations* of the concept of imagination. Though the concept of the nation as an imagined object provides a place for the creativity involved in conceiving the nation, it does not help us understand the extent to which we find ourselves subject to an object we have ourselves created. It is one of the great strengths of Anderson's own account that he recognises the strength of the hold of the nationalist imagination on us. Indeed, this forms his starting point:

No more arresting emblems of the modern culture of nationalism exist than cenotaphs and tombs of Unknown Soldiers...[V]oid as these tombs are of identifiable mortal remains or immortal souls, they are nonetheless saturated with ghostly *national* imaginings.[8]

The various commemorations of war – cenotaphs, tombs of the unknown soldier, and the like – play a central role in the iconography of the nation just because they symbolise the sacrifices that men and women have been willing to make on its behalf. As Anderson emphasises, if we are to understand the moral presence of the nation in our lives, we must come to terms with its capacity to demand and be freely given these sacrifices. However, it is at this very point that the notion of imagination fails. It does not explain why the object we have imagined can make these claims on us. The first steps towards this explanation are made when we realise that when we imagine the nation we do not merely construct an *object* of consciousness, but *we also form a conception of ourselves as existing in relation to that object.* The nation is not just a form of consciousness, it is also a form of *self*-consciousness. As members of the nation recognise each other through the nation, they also recognise themselves. If the nation is an imagined community, it is also a form of *identity*. As an imagined community, it exists as an object of consciousness. It is the public embodiment of the nation's conception of itself. As a form of identity, it exists as a mode of individual self- and other-awareness. In order to understand this dual form of existence, we need to go beyond the concept of imagination to that of *culture*.

This may not seem much of an advance. The concept of culture is a notoriously difficult one. As Raymond Williams commented, '*Culture* is one of the two or three most complicated words in the English language.'[9] However, it is inescapable in a discussion of nationalism. Of its many senses, three are especially important here.

In one significant sense, a culture consists of a gallery of meaningful or representative objects which those with the appropriate cultural knowledge and identity can interpret and evaluate. In this sense, culture exists as a public realm. However – and this is the second sense – the concept of culture also refers to the way in which these objects are created, recreated and modified. In this sense, culture is process rather than product. A culture is not made once and for all. It is continually being remade, reaffirmed and sometimes changed. Cultural objects may change their meaning or become less central; new objects may be introduced. Even the most static culture is the scene of contestation, reinterpretation and criticism, and these are all aspects of the process by which a culture is produced and reproduced. In a third sense, the concept of culture refers to the process by which people acquire the knowledge which allows them to understand the various cultural artefacts and to recognise them as their own. It is the process by which members of the culture come to understand the meaning of the objects which form the culture and, crucially, find their *identity* in these objects. In this final sense, culture is '*Bildung*' – education or formation.[10] It is the process by which an individual is inscribed within a particular form of life. This is not a passive acquisition of pre-existing patterns of behaviour ('socialisation') but a process in which the individual fashions and finds him- or herself within the forms (or images – *die Bilder*) which are socially available. It is a process of *self*-formation, not merely formation of the self; it is the process by which human individuals acquire various social identities.

In order to understand the nation, we need to make use of the concept of culture in each of these related senses. The nation is a specific cultural object. It exists in and through the language we speak, the public symbols we acknowledge, the history and literature we were taught at school, the music we listen to, the currency we use, the sporting activities we enjoy, and the news bulletins on the television. These cultural artefacts enable us to recognise that our way of life has an objective external existence, and they constitute the social environment which we recognise as ours and in which we are 'at home'. The national culture is subject to change, and at any given time aspects will be subject to debate and criticism. Elements which were central may become marginal, and national rituals may change their meaning. The process of transformation and contestation is the process by which the nation is produced and reproduced. However, the nation also exists in the process by which individuals become aware of themselves as having a national identity. This is an aspect of our self-formation, and it is in virtue of the success of this process that we find ourselves at home in one social environment rather than another. We come to feel that our national identity is as natural and inescapable as our gender (another successful piece of *Bildung*). Our national culture provides a moment of self-recognition through which we both confirm our individual existence and become conscious of ourselves as having a collective existence.

The acquisition of language and other forms of communication is a crucial aspect of this. It is our native language which provides us with our primary mode of access to the objective world; and it also provides the means by which we are able to recognise others who share that mode of access. Though it is socially acquired, our language soon acquires a quasi-natural status. It constitutes the taken for granted framework through which we experience the world. It provides for a basic form of intersubjectivity: those who speak the same language are those with whom we can share our experiences, our emotions, our thoughts and our jokes. It also demarcates the realm of objectivity: users of the same language inhabit the same external world. And it is language which provides the crucial link between the individual and the wider public spheres of work and pleasure, the media, culture and tradition, and ultimately politics. Much of the strength of nationalism in the modern world flows from the appropriation of linguistic identity by the nation.[11] When this appropriation is successful, it becomes difficult to say or think who we are without identifying ourselves as members of a particular nation.

Of course, a shared culture also provides other forms of communication and means of recognition. The way we dress, the music we listen to, perhaps the religious symbols we acknowledge, and even the way we eat and drink, all provide forms in which we are able to communicate aspects of our lives to others – but not to all others – and to recognise those who share this privileged realm. In many circumstances, cultural differences of this kind (usually together with political differences) may be sufficient to form distinct identities despite the existence of a common language. Anglophone Canada and the United States are cases in point. In other cases, cultural identities may be formed which override linguistic difference. For example, Switzerland maintains a unitary sense of itself despite the fact that it is trilingual; bilingual Canada may or may not be able to sustain its national identity. These cases are sufficiently interesting to merit the fuller discussion they will receive later. For the time being, it is sufficient to note that differences in language are more usually conceived as – and thus tend to become – a source of disunity within a nation. While this potential disunity may be overcome by other features, e.g. a strong tradition of civic life, federal political institutions, the existence of a common enemy, etc., in the more usual case, the cultural unity of the nation is constructed on the basis of a common language.

The concept of culture is a relatively new one, dating back no further than the late eighteenth and early nineteenth centuries.[12] Indeed, it is significant that it first came into use in the period which also saw the birth of nationalism as self-conscious political project. The concept was part of the Romantic reaction to Enlightenment values, when it was especially contrasted with the concept of *civilisation* and, in Germany at least, conceived to be a superior value.[13] The concept of civilisation – also an eighteenth-century invention[14] – stood for a way of life which was the universal goal of historical development. Though its proponents believed that this way of life had in the first instance been achieved in England and/or France, it was in principle available to all countries which followed the same historical path. Culture, on the other hand, was rooted in specific ways of life, particular traditions and histories. It allowed for dimensions of feeling, poetry, mythology and oral tradition which were marginalised by the rationalistic, sterile and relatively superficial values of civilisation. It was also essentially plural: the culture of one nation was its own, and not a better or worse variant of another. The development of this concept was a crucial component in the emergence of nationalist consciousness. It permitted each nation to claim for itself a value which was in principle *not* available to others.

The nation is not the only form of culture, nor is national identity the only form of identity. The modern world provides many different cultural forms and associated identities which cut across, complement or conflict with the nation and its identity. Nonetheless, the nation has asserted its priority over other cultural forms, most obviously in its claim to a political embodiment. It is the nation – not religion, political principle, local community, or social class – which demands its own state. And it could not sustain this claim to priority unless national identity was experienced as more fundamental than others. At least part of the reason for this is that the nation has appropriated to itself the basic means of self-expression and communication. The very means by which individuals form a conception of who they are defines them as members of a specific nation. We shall return to this issue later.

As I have already mentioned, national identities are subject to change and political contestation. For example, religion (Protestantism, the English Church) was a central feature of eighteenth-century English national identity, and race became important in the imperial identity of the nineteenth century ('white men's burdens'); neither have been as significant in the twentieth. Often differences which are contained within one national identity are the differentiating mark between others. For example, difference of religious background (Catholic and Protestant, Islamic and Orthodox) are sufficient to establish what are taken to be national differences in Northern Ireland and former Yugoslavia; these differences are irrelevant or, at worst, minor irritants in Australia or New Zealand. And there may also be major differences in the ways in which different elements in the population conceive of the nation. What is important is not so much that everyone imagines the same nation, but that they imagine that they imagine the same nation.[15]

This diversity amongst and within national cultures means that there can be no simple account of the various elements which define national identity. The claim of each nation to have its own unique identity is not just illusion: each nation has its own story to tell. This has led many, especially empirically minded historians, to despair of finding a general characterisation of the nation. Hugh Seton Watson, for example, finds himself 'driven to the conclusion that no "scientific definition" of a nation can be devised'.[16] But the pessimism is premature. Though there is an enormous diversity amongst national self-conceptions, there are significant common elements.

Every nation, for example, claims its own homeland, one which is described in the national literature, depicted in its art, and celebrated in its music.[17] The homeland is not the mute object defined by physical geography (though geographers have their role to play in the national imagining[18]); it is endowed with a personality and a moral character which complements and sustains the personality and moral character of those who inhabit it (or, in some familiar cases, ought to inhabit it). The homeland is the ground in a near literal sense of national identity. It is significant that the land is conceived as a common possession, something all members of the nation share. However, the concept of possession is a symbolic one, and though it can be given a socialist meaning, it is compatible with a regime of private property. It is noteworthy that Woodie Guthrie's socialist anthem

> This land is your land, this land is my land,
> From California to the New York Island,
> From the redwood forests to the Gulf Stream waters,
> This land belongs to you and me.

has without evident strain become appropriated to a conservative nationalist agenda. But if the land belongs to all, those who work the land – the peasants and farmers – are often assigned a special role in the national iconography (and often have a special claim on the nation's assets). However, the task of extracting the land's moral resources and appropriating them for the nation has been carried out, not by its farmers, but by poets, writers and artists.

A second common factor is history: every nation has its own story of triumphs and tragedies, victories and betrayals. These may be to do with the struggle to gain possession of that land which rightfully belongs to the nation, or to keep it from those who would usurp it. Or it may be the struggle of the nation to acquire that political sovereignty and recognition from other nations which is its due. These stories will celebrate the achievements of those who performed heroic acts on behalf of the nation and of the nation which inspired these acts. No doubt the defeat and destruction of enemies will play a role in these stories; but a larger role is played by death and suffering. It is as if those who have sacrificed themselves on behalf of the nation have demonstrated in their lives – or their deaths – that its worth transcends other values. Hence, the significance of cenotaphs, tombs of the unknown soldier, memorial services, and the like.[19] If in recent years popular history – 'history from below' – has taken precedence over stories of statecraft and battle, such projects are more often than not part of a self-conscious attempt to redefine a national identity in terms of the activity of the common people, rather than of ruling élites. They continue to invoke the nation as a lived historical reality.

Nationalism is a populist doctrine; and the nation it invokes is a community in which all are equal. While nationalism has been compatible with enormous inequalities of political power, property and income, status and prestige; it posits an underlying equality between its members. The nation is, as Anderson puts it, 'always conceived as a deep, horizontal comradeship'.[20] Despite the differences in the understanding of and contributions to a nation's culture, it is regarded as the common heritage of all. Indeed, it is an index of the strength of a national culture that it has the scope and flexibility to speak to – and thus for – all members of the nation. The egalitarianism of nationalism seems to mark it as belonging – along with its sometime allies, sometime rivals, representative democracy, liberalism and socialism – squarely in the modern world. However, one should not read too much into this. Many religious conceptions, including Christianity, posit an equality of all believers before God, but at the same time sanction enormous inequalities of other kinds. In many respects, the nation is like the Christian God, in that all who accept its embrace are in this respect – though perhaps only in this respect – equal. Still, the egalitarianism of nationalism does provide an affinity with modern political doctrines. Nationalism fits well in a world in which the affairs of the State are conceived, not as the responsibility and privilege of an élite, but as the business of the mass of the population. Indeed, it is plausible to suggest that nationalism has provided the form in which the doctrine of popular sovereignty has been practised in the modern world.[21]

As I remarked earlier, one of the great strengths of Anderson's concept of an imagined community is that it recognises the element of creativity in the formation of the nation. This does not mean that it is somehow arbitrary. What we must seek to understand is why, at certain times in history, large numbers of people began to think of themselves as belonging to communities of this kind – as having a homeland (most of which they will never have seen), a history and a culture (of which they will largely be ignorant), and an identity in terms of which they are equal to their fellow countrymen and women (despite massive and obvious inequalities). We must seek to understand why it was that the idea of a national community came to play such a crucial role in political life, and the political project of uniting nation and State came to seem not merely possible, but inescapable. We have gone as far as is productive at this point in attempting to provide a preliminary characterisation of the concept of the nation. It is time to turn to the question of explanation.

The Gellner thesis: nationalism and industrialisation

The conventional wisdom amongst theorists is that nationalism is a creature of the modern world. Whether or not the conventional wisdom is correct – and I shall have something to say about this later in the chapter – there is little doubt that the modern world has been especially hospitable to nationalism. This suggests that we should be able to say what it is about the modern world which has given rise to and sustained nationalism. If modernity has encouraged the nationalist principle, we should be able to explain why.

The most elegant and powerful attempt to meet this challenge is that of Ernest Gellner.[22] His argument is a simple one: Both the principle of nationalism and the conception of the nation it invokes are unique to and pervasive in the modern world. Their explanation must therefore be sought in a fundamental feature of the modern world. For Gellner, that feature is *industrialisation*. His argument is intended to show that nationalism is the *inevitable* consequence of industrialisation.

According to Gellner, the basic form of society in the premodern world was *agrarian*. For most of world history, the bulk of the population has lived in small, largely self-contained and self-sufficient agricultural communities. Most people lived and died in the same geographical area, were illiterate, and had no experience of and very little access to information about a wider world. For them, culture was specific and local. People might even have had difficulties in making themselves understood by those living in a precisely similar situation one hundred kilometres away. Their religion might have located them with respect to a wider community of believers, but not one which coincided with political boundaries. They would have been subject to intermittent interference by various political masters, but whatever led them to submit to their rulers, it was unlikely to be the idea that they shared a common culture. Indeed, members of the literate élites would have felt that they had more in common with the élites of other countries than with the illiterate peasants over whom they ruled. In these circumstances, Gellner argues, the nationalist project of unifying polity and culture would not have made sense.

The crucial change took place with industrialisation. This imposed mobility of various kinds on those affected: geographic, as workers were forced to move from one area to another; occupational, as old trades became redundant and new ones were invented; and social, as fortunes were made and lost. The new technologies imposed a corresponding conception of rationality on society, so all came to share the same cognitive map on the world and the same instrumental attitude towards it. The State played a much greater role in social life in order to secure the conditions for economic development. Though industrial societies are characterised by a highly developed division of labour and occupational specialisation, this presupposed that all members of society were equipped with relevantly similar conceptual and technical skills. Literacy came to be a requirement of work, and inevitably the State assumed responsibility for providing the rudiments of literacy to all members of the population. If, in agricultural societies, the family and village provided all the training that most members of society needed, industrial society requires a specialised educational apparatus. This will impose common forms of writing and speech, and provide the foundation for a common culture. Possession of this common culture comes to be the *sine qua non* of participation in economic life:

> Culture is no longer merely the adornment, confirmation and legitimation of a social order...culture is now the necessary shared medium, the life-blood or perhaps rather the minimal shared atmosphere, within which alone the members of society can breathe and survive and produce.[23]

In industrial society, the project of uniting politics and culture becomes not merely possible, but unavoidable. 'This is what national-ism is about, and why we live in an age of nationalism.'[24]

There is, as Gellner recognises, a range of secondary cases. As a country or an area industrialises, a dominant economic/political group will attempt to impose its language and culture on others. Members of other cultural groups will have the choice of assimilating or resisting. While the path of resistance has been the more conspicuous one, assimilation has been, as Gellner points out, easily the most common option. Most potential nationalisms have surrendered without an appreciable struggle. But some will resist, and counter-nationalisms will be born. Where nationalism becomes the norm, then multicultural – now multinational – states and empires will become unstable. Acquisition of new territories will involve more than a change in political rulers; it will require the imposition of a new culture, and it will provoke resistance in the name of the now oppressed, but perhaps newly created, national sentiment of the people. Much of modern history has been taken up with the working out of these tensions.

Given its simplicity and scope, it is not surprising that Gellner's argument has difficulties. I will focus on three of these which are of particular importance.

The first and most obvious problem concerns the dating of nation-alism.[25] The Industrial Revolution began in England in the second half of the eighteenth century, and, though its impact was immediate, it remains the case that there were no industrial societies of the kind required by Gellner's model until well into the nineteenth century. His theory implies therefore that nationalism is an essentially nineteenth-century phenomenon. But almost all accounts of nationalism date it a good deal earlier than this. Until very recently, the conventional wisdom was that it emerged at the end of the eighteenth and the beginning of the nineteenth centuries.[26] If anything, very recent scholarship has tended to locate it even earlier.[27] But, in either case, industrialisation comes on the scene far too late to explain the origins of nationalism.

We need to tread carefully here. It is important to distinguish between the emergence of a *conception* of the nation as a culturally distinct and politically sovereign community and the actual *spread* of this idea through the relevant population. There is little doubt that the conception of the nation began to play a large role in the rhetoric of intellectuals, administrators and political leaders during the period of the French Revolution, Napoleonic Wars, and the German resistance. Nationalism as a self-conscious political programme was formulated at this time, and was then available to be taken up in the nineteenth century. But this tells us very little about the spread of nationalist sentiment in the community at large, and it may be that John Breuilly and Eric Hobsbawm are right to be sceptical about the extent to which ordinary people fell under the spell of nationalism.[28] Certainly Eugen Weber provides evidence to suggest that its spread amongst peasants was much narrower in late nineteenth-century France than is often assumed.[29] For most of the periods we are concerned with, the only evidence historians have to go on is the use of nationalist rhetoric and the appearance of nationalist ideas in the popular press, pamphlets, educational practices, literary works, etc., and it may well be that the impact of these was more limited than their proponents and later historians supposed.

On the other hand, once we have recognised the emergence of the concept of the nation at the end of the eighteenth century, we can trace its origins very much earlier than this. Linda Colley has provided a detailed and persuasive case for the development and spread of nationalist sentiment in Britain (including Scotland and Wales) in the eighteenth century.[30] Others have discerned elements of a nationalist rhetoric in the debates surrounding the Civil War and the Glorious Revolution in the seventeenth century.[31] But the theme of the special character and therefore of the special rights of the English was already present in Tudor England. Richard Helgerson has shown how an idea of England – its land, history, language, institutions, etc. – was created in a wide range of Elizabethan writings,[32] while Liah Greenfeld has argued that the idea that the English nation was the foundation of its political power was emerging as an element in the rhetoric of the Tudor monarchs. [33]

If the idea of England – and later Britain – as a primary object of political affiliation was in play for at least two centuries before the Industrial Revolution began to have an impact on the wider society, then we need to look elsewhere for its explanation.[34] While it is possible that industrialisation might play a role in the later spread of nationalist sentiments through the population, this possibility can be put to one side until we have arrived at a better account of the emergence of the concept of the nation as the primary object of political allegiance.

A second problem in Gellner's account arises from his failure to take sufficient note of the tension between nationalism and other characteristically modern modes of thought.[35] Gellner provides a typically lucid account of the 'spirit' of industrialisation. Following Max Weber, he emphasises the notion of *rationality*: the selection of efficient means to achieve one's goals (instrumental reason), and the adoption of principles of formal consistency in one's reasoning (reason as universality).[36] Modern rationality, Gellner argues, assumes that there is 'one coherent world' which is the final arbiter of truth and it investigates this world in causal and analytical terms. As he puts it in a striking passage, modern rationality imposes a 'universal conceptual currency' in which:

> all facts are located within a single continuous logical space...statements reporting them can be conjoined and generally related to each other, so that in principle one single language describes the world.[37]

What Gellner does not recognise is that the 'spirit of modernity' thus described *would have no place for nationalism*. For nationalism, there is no 'universal conceptual currency', nor is there a 'one coherent world'. Each nation is its own world, and each national language provides its own specific and unique mode of access to that world. Language is not merely a means by which we describe a world; it is a way in which we form and express our special place in the world. A particular language is formed through the poetry, novels and songs which have been expressed in it, and these cannot be translated without loss into another language. Not even in principle could there be 'one single language'. For those who find their identity in the nation, the nation is the whole which gives meaning to their lives, and it is for this reason that it so often inspires them to act in ways which are inconsistent with the demands of formal consistency or instrumental reasoning. For the nationalist, the nation is not a means, but a meaning. The task which Gellner does not confront is to show how the modern world generates and sustains meanings of this kind.[38]

A third and related set of problems for Gellner's account arises from its reductionism. For Gellner, industrialisation is the cause; nationalism the effect. We might equally well 'explain' other characteristically modern doctrines such as liberalism, socialism and religious fundamentalism as more or less remote effects of the same case. But these doctrines have arisen, not because a set of economic conditions have generated certain sets of ideas, but because men and women reflecting on the conditions of their life and the changes taking place have put forward ideas which we can now identify as liberal, socialist, fundamentalist or nationalist. Reflection does not take place in an intellectual void. Those who created these doctrines were influenced by the intellectual, religious, political and moral traditions which were available to them. Some theorists were more insightful, others more influential; and we should take this into account. But it is egregious to think we can read bodies of thought off some – allegedly neutral – account of technological changes.[39] At the very least, we need a conception of the political and cultural spheres which provided the context in which ideas were produced and disseminated. We almost certainly also need to make some reference to the ideas of specific nationalist thinkers. Indeed, despite his claim that 'we shall not learn too much about nationalism from the study of its own prophets',[40] Gellner himself makes use of concepts developed under the impetus of nationalism. I have already mentioned that the concept of culture was a product of that period of intellectual life in which nationalism itself came to self-consciousness. Herder, the 'prophet' of nationalism, played an important role in developing this concept (he seems to have been the first, for example, to have used the term in the plural[41]). Fichte and Herder emphasised the role of language in forming a conception of the nation, and they were amongst the first to realise that language was not merely a vehicle for the transmission of ideas, but was – more fundamentally – a constituent of identity. Gellner's own use of these ideas provides reason to think that we will not get very far in coming to terms with the explanation of nationalism, let alone understanding its intellectual and moral force if we are not prepared to learn what we can from the ideas and beliefs associated with it.

Explaining the nation

Can we do better than Gellner? I think we can, though we must be prepared to lower our sights a little. Gellner's own project was to provide an explanation of nationalism, i.e. to show that it is an *effect* of more fundamental social processes. My more modest aim is to render the emergence of nationalism *intelligible* in terms of other social changes which have taken place over the past four or five hundred years. I do not claim that the changes I discuss are more causally fundamental than nationalism, or even that we can identify them independently of it. My claim is rather that nationalism as a political project began to make sense because it was an attractive way, and for many the only way, in which people could come to terms with the changes which were taking place – changes which were instrumental in the making of what we can now identify as the modern world. The idea that a large and rather heterogeneous group of people were all – equally – members of the one nation began to make sense – perhaps for the first time in history. It provided a framework within which a large variety of different individual and collective projects could be worked out in ways which were both practical and meaningful.

My project then is to locate nationalism within the major economic, political and cultural changes which were characteristic of the development of Western modernity. Let us take these in order.

The economy

The initial economic change involved the spread of *market* relations. If the premodern market was an occasion for artisans, peasants and merchants to meet in order to exchange an occasional surplus, in the modern world it has become the constitutive framework within which almost all productive activity takes place. The development of trade and the reorganisation of production towards the market placed small, hitherto self-contained, agricultural communities in a larger framework well before the Industrial Revolution. The intensified division of labour and extended network of social interdependence, celebrated by Adam Smith and other eighteenth-century theorists, were two of its most obvious consequences. The development of improved transport, both for commodities and for people, was another. The market encouraged mobility, both geographic, as workers moved from one area and occupation to another, and social, as wealth was acquired and lost. Of course, the market was always international, and some of the key developments in early modern Europe involved long-distance trading relations. But despite its international ramifications, the most intensive development of market relations – especially of the labour market – took place within the borders of established states such as England and France.[42] Indeed, most of the changes which Gellner attributed to industrialisation can with much greater chronological plausibility be attributed to the market. When industrialisation did occur, it had dramatic effects on all aspects of social life. However, the break up of culturally fragmented and isolated rural communities was already well under way. Though early twentieth-century Marxists were wrong to think of the market as a sufficient explanation for nationalism, they were on the right track. It was the early spread of market relations which provided the social space within which nationalism was to develop.

The State

The second part of the story lies in the massively increased role of the State.[43] To some extent this involved an increase in the coercive power exercised by the State, the elimination of rival centres of power, and a more complete control over its territory. This was the period in which the State not only claimed the sole right to the legitimate use of coercion within a given territory, but in which it acquired the power to make this claim stick. The modern concept of sovereignty – developed by Hobbes, Bentham and Austin – according to which there must be one source of authority in a specific area, was no doubt always a myth rather than a reality. However, it corresponded precisely to the aspirations of the modern State; indeed, many states came close to achieving it. But the increase in State power also involved the development of new capacities and technologies. The State changed from being a body whose main function was to collect an occasional tribute from its subjects in order to engage in wars which were of little relevance to them, to an institution which played a necessary and continuing role in the reproduction of social life. From the sixteenth century onwards, the legal and administrative responsibilities of the State increased enormously, and it came increasingly to play a role in education, transport and even welfare. Increasingly, the State monitored and recorded the significant stages of individual life: birth, education certification, marriage, and finally death.[44] In order to carry out these expanded responsibilities, states had to expand their own administrative machinery, and service to the State became a full-time and socially ubiquitous occupation. The State played an immense role in securing the social, legal and political conditions necessary for the market to operate, a role which has been partially obscured by the rhetoric of *laissez-faire*. For much of the eighteenth century and later, states such as England and France conceived it as their responsibility – on mercantilist lines – to increase their country's wealth as against other states. Within its own territory, the State became a continuing presence in all aspects of everyday life, and men – and eventually women as well – acquired legal and political identities as a condition of participating in other aspects of social life. The concept of citizenship came to be conceived, not as the prerogative of a political élite, but as a right of all – or most – inhabitants of the country.

Culture

A third part of the explanation concerns the transformation of cultural life which took place in Western Europe and North America in the period of early modernity. This was of course only possible in conjunction with the economic and political changes I have sketched in (and probably vice versa). The explosion in the quantity and range of printed material which became available in the centuries after the invention of the printing press could not have occurred without the framework of a developing market economy.[45] The use of vernacular languages was in the interests both of publishers and writers, and it provided an incentive for the development of literatures within the bounds of those languages. National print languages came into existence, and those local dialects which did not acquire this status assumed a secondary rank. New literary forms developed: the novel, the broadsheet, the journal, the newspaper. All of these were exploited by writers eager to make a living, have an influence, or both. Given the proliferation of outlets and the relative ease with which a printing workshop could be set up, effective centralised control – even by the developing State apparatuses of the time – was impossible. First in England, North America and France, then in Germany and many other places as well, national cultures were created within the framework of the developing print languages. Through these cultures, people were able to form conceptions of who they were, of the country in which they lived, of the traditions to which they belonged, and of the vast community of those who shared their identity. In almost all cases, the emergence of a sense of national identity coincided with a flourishing of national culture. One of the great values of Benedict Anderson's evocative and sensitive account is that it brings out the depth and richness of the cultural resources which were created and appropriated by the nation.[46] What the new national cultures provided was a discursive realm – a gallery of representations, descriptions, stories – within which it was possible for men and women to discover who they were. If the market was eroding the largely self-contained communities within which men and women had hitherto led their lives, the emerging national cultures provided new and immensely richer sources of identity.

The cultural realm produced by the poets, novelists, writers and philosophers might have remained the property of an élite if it had not been associated with institutions and practices which extended its purchase. Growing literacy, especially in the urban centres, was a condition for this extension. Journals, broadsheets and eventually newspapers were amongst the institutions which created and disseminated the sense of nationhood. Schools and, for the privileged, universities came to play an increasing role; and novels and poetry had a large circulation and a larger audience. Churches, long accustomed to accommodating the State, reminded their flocks of the national content of their religion and the religious content of their nation. And we should not overlook the cultural content of a range of administrative, political and legal practices. The growth of 'policing' (in the broad sense of this term common in the eighteenth century), the local legal tribunals, and experience in the militia or the army reminded people, sometimes in a very forcible way, that their first loyalties lay with the nation.

In an important early work, Jürgen Habermas has described some of the key developments in England and France in terms of the emergence of the bourgeois 'public sphere'.[47] For Habermas, this consisted of institutions such as coffee shops, salons, reading groups, societies for the discussion of scientific and philosophical ideas, and journals of literary criticism and political discussion, all of which provided the social space for the discussion, circulation and evaluation of ideas, and especially political ideas. Certain conventions obtained within these institutions: all participants had access to the relevant information, all had the right to speak, and difference in social position, wealth or power did not count. In principle at least, the only power was that of argument. The public sphere had the potential to create an informed and rational public opinion to which the State might be answerable. Habermas does not, of course, ignore the fact that in practice the institutions of the public sphere did not live up to this ideal. Nevertheless, he argues that they provided a promise, which later bourgeois societies have notably failed to keep, of a freely formed public opinion which would inform both cultural and political life.

Habermas provides, however, a much too constricted account of the eighteenth-century public spheres, and as a consequence he misconstrues the potential that he ascribes to them. While the institutions he lists were important for the development of a literary culture, he ignores a range of more popular institutions and practices, which were just as significant for the dissemination and discussion of political and other matters. In the case of England, Habermas ignored the parish churches (especially important in rural England), as well as such popular meeting places as ale houses and fairs.[48] No doubt many of these institutions lacked the qualities of decorous, informed and rational discussion which Habermas attributes to the coffee shops and salons. But it may also be, as Stallybrass and White have argued, that the conception of rational discussion which was formed by frequenters of coffee shops and salons was constructed by the repudiation of the characteristics associated with more popular and less polished spheres.[49] What was excluded – the popular public spheres – was part of a process of opinion formation which is much more complex, conflictive and full blooded than the exiguous process of rational debate recognised by Habermas.[50]

Habermas's narrow conception of the public sphere is connected to his failure to recognise that it was largely *national* in scope and focus. The language in which ideas were expressed and circulated was the newly emerging national print language; the audience which was sought was those who could read that language; the State which participants sought to influence or reform was their own; and, above all, the culture which was created was a national culture. As it was conceived by Habermas, the aim of the public sphere was the formation of a rational public opinion; however, the effect of the actual public spheres was to generate a conception of the *nation*. If public opinion was intended to express the consensus of polished and articulate coffee drinkers and journal readers, the nation was to embody the inarticulate aspirations and feelings of a far broader range of the population. It may be true, as Habermas argues, that his favoured institutions provided a glimpse of a liberal practice of rationality and freedom of speech; but they also contributed to the creation of the national cultures which have always informed and often limited those practices.

For Habermas, the promise of the bourgeois public sphere was to create the rationally formed public opinion necessary for a meaningful practice of democracy. What these public spheres were to produce – the potential that was already present in the practices of discussion and opinion formation in the eighteenth century – was not this ideal, but another one: a conception of the *nation*. It was to be the nation to which the modern State would henceforth be answerable.

These factors provide the conditions for the emergence of the conception of a nation as a politically sovereign community. However, there were a host of other – more local – factors at work in the formation of a sense of national identity in particular cases. For example in England – arguably the first nation – Henry VIII's breach with the Papacy created the conditions which allowed Protestantism to play a key role in English national identity for the next 300 years. The unprecedented period of cultural activity in Elizabethan and Jacobean England contributed to the creation of a widely shared conception of what is was to be English, and it provided later generations (and especially the eighteenth century) with a myth of England in its prime ('merrie England'). The fact that absolutism failed in seventeenth-century England while it succeeded in France meant that the British monarchy was able to become part of the national agenda in the eighteenth century in a way in which the French monarchy did not. In the eighteenth century, English nationalism contributed to the cohesion of the body politic, while French nationalism undermined it. The division of French society into estates, and the burdens and political insignificance of the Third Estate, made it possible for an emerging conception of the French nation to be used *against* the First and Second Estates.[51] When French nationalism burst on to the world stage it did so in the explicit form of the democratic sovereignty of the people. Initially, perhaps, the concept of the people was constituted by a willed identification with the Revolution. For Tallien, 'Il n'y a pas d'étranger en France que les mauvais citoyens'.[52] But even by 1795 when Tallien made this claim, the *levée en masse*, the administrative centralisation and the educational reforms undertaken by the Revolution had put in place the institutional forms through which the 'people' were to become French, and 'les étrangers' – what one suspects they had always been – foreign.

The conventional wisdom is that it was during the Revolutionary and Napoleonic Wars that nationalism first entered the stage of world history in its own right. An idiosyncratically different view is proposed by Benedict Anderson who argues that it was the colonists of the Americas who developed a sense of national identity '*well before most of Europe*' (Anderson's emphasis).[53] Anderson argues that colonial administrators, politicians and intellectuals developed a sense of common identity *against* the culture of the metropolitan centres. However, the best candidate for a 'Creole nationalism' prior to 1789 was the American Revolution, and the evidence here is mixed. While there can be no doubt that some element of later American nationalism can be discerned in this period, there were other elements as well. Appeals to the traditional rights of Englishmen played a central role in the rhetoric of the colonists, and there were significant elements from the civic republican tradition as well.[54] It would seem more plausible to locate the emergence of an American nationalism in the subsequent period of political ferment and construction and the self-conscious nation building of the early nineteenth century. Fortunately the issue need not be pursued here. Anderson's own sensitive and evocative account of 'print capitalism' and the cultural changes for which it was responsible suggests that the conditions for the emergence of nationalism were in place in Western Europe well before either the French or American Revolutions. What was achieved in the Revolutionary and Napoleonic period – and perhaps in the American Revolution as well – was that the nationalism which was already an implicit presence in the political and cultural life of France and England came to be recognised for what it was.

Once nationalism was an explicit presence on the political landscape, it was available to be taken up by politicians and administrators, bureaucrats and intellectuals, reformers and revolutionaries. This was done with great enthusiasm in the nineteenth century – the great period of 'official nationalism' in Seton Watson's terminology.[55] Indeed, it may well be that John Breuilly is right to argue that it is only when national identity became an object of State policy that it became a mass possession.[56] The established states certainly had a head start. Mass educational systems were established and the children of peasants and labourers learned to read; in many countries, they spent important formative years in the army. The State itself began to define much more precisely the area of its rule, and, while it was eliminating internal barriers, it was also becoming much more effective in policing its external borders. As a consequence, movement became increasingly easy within the borders of a state, and increasingly difficult outside it. The spread of literacy meant there was an increased demand for printed material, and this created new forms of employment for journalists, school teachers, writers and other intellectual workers. The nation – its language, its territory and its history – was both the context and the product of their work. If the industrialisation of production and the continuing spread of market relations was eroding more traditional identities, the new form of national identity was available to take its place.

As nationalism became the self-conscious language of the State, it also became the language of political resistance. Struggles for secession, the expulsion of foreign rulers, or for political unification, all took place in the name of the nation. Often this agenda was imposed by élites who consciously modelled their political rhetoric on the established nationalisms of Western Europe and North America despite the fact that the economic, cultural and – especially – political conditions sustaining the earlier nationalisms were absent. Oppressed groups also had their 'official nationalists'. But very often, the nationalist impulse was also a reaction to cultural oppression and marginalisation. With the advent of the nation-state, political rule acquired a cultural dimension, and political domination meant cultural domination as well. Inevitably, political resistance also took a cultural form. In many cases the struggles towards national liberation were the crucible through which a national identity was forged: the sense of national identity emerged *against* the oppressor. However, all too often with these 'reactive nationalisms', the new postcolonial nations have had great difficulty in sustaining a sense of national identity after the struggle was over. The challenge confronting the new states has been, on the one hand, to displace the network of primary allegiances (to kin, tribe, locality, etc.) with an identification with the nation, and, on the other, to preserve existing cultural identities against further erosion. In the original nationalisms of Western Europe, the process of displacing existing identities had been carried out by the spread of market relations, which both destroyed the social bases of earlier forms of allegiance and forced large numbers of people to lead their lives in contexts in which earlier allegiances had little relevance. Construction of the new identity required the discovery or creation of linguistic and cultural resources which were sufficiently rich, complex and fulfilling to replace those which have been lost. The contradictory task of many postcolonial states has been to build and sustain a new national identity and at the same time affirm existing cultural identities.[57]

The failure of many official and reactive nationalisms should be an effective reminder that the ingredients of a lasting sense of national identity are not created by political fiat. In these circumstances, the reliance on the rhetoric and sometimes the actuality of conflict is not altogether surprising.

The modernity of nations

I mentioned earlier the conventional wisdom that nationalism is not merely characteristic of the modern world but unique to it. It is now time to say something about this claim.[58] But not too much. Once certain conceptual issues are sorted out, it becomes a largely historical question whether some premodern forms of political allegiance and commitment are to be counted as nationalist or not, and this is not the place to pursue an investigation of this kind.

Nationalism comes on the scene when the idea that a people is constituted as a political community through a shared cultural identity enters political discourse, and a large (enough) number of people come to believe that this identity takes priority over others. What crucially differentiates nationalism from other political discourses is the idea that it is the nation which is the ultimate object of political allegiance, and that one's fundamental political identity derives from membership of the nation. Now it is at least *conceivable* that nation-like groups have existed in history, without members making *political* claims on their behalf. It is possible, in other words, that nations pre-existed nationalism.[59] While this possibility cannot be ruled out, I think that we should be wary about drawing too sharp a distinction between a nation and its political manifestation. The concept of the nation is a hermeneutic one: a nation only exists in and through the consciousness of its members. If there were nations in the premodern world, then this will have been expressed in the ways in which people conceived of themselves and others, and the terms in which they explained and justified their behaviour. In order to establish the existence of nations, it will be necessary to show that there were significant cultural communities whose members conceived of themselves in terms of a common land and history and as fundamentally equal in respect of this conception, and who believed that this perspective marked a fundamental divide between themselves and others. It is certainly not impossible that communities of this kind existed; indeed, in a moment I will point to some likely candidates. However, the best reason we are likely to have to believe in their existence is when we find evidence of a struggle for an appropriate *political* recognition. This is not merely an epistemological issue. As David Miller has noted, a:

> distinguishing aspect of national identity is that it is an active identity. Nations are communities that do things together, take decisions, achieve results, and so forth.[60]

If a community's basic self-understanding involves a claim to a common life on a specific territory, it will almost inevitably seek political recognition of this claim. Without some evidence of *nationalist* aspirations, we are not likely to grant a community the status of *nation*. What this means is that in practice the distinction between cultural community and political expression – between nation and nationalism – is not a clear-cut one.

Be this as it may, the strongest candidates for premodern nations are also strong candidates for premodern nationalisms. Certainly, in the case of the Israel of the Torah[61] and perhaps also of the Athens depicted in Pericles' 'Funeral Oration', it appears that a common and unique culture carried with it the claim of political sovereignty. An argument that Israel and Athens were nations would be, at least in part, based on the evidence of a political agenda. Other plausible cases arise where the ruling classes of a state which has been incorporated into a larger empire attempt to mobilise resistance from peasants they are no longer in a position to coerce. In the case, for example, of the prolonged Vietnamese resistance to Chinese imperialism, it may be that the existence of a common enemy stimulated a sense of common identity which was strong enough to override pre-existing cultural differences.[62] While this case and others like it would need to be demonstrated through an examination of the terms in which the resistance was carried out, it would prejudge the issue to insist from the beginning that there could be no cases of nationalism prior to the modern world.

Still, there is an important truth behind the conventional wisdom. Nationalism did not appear in the modern world *ex nihilo*. It developed because the modern world has provided internal economic, political and cultural conditions which have created and sustained the nationalist enterprise. It is very hard to see how comparable conditions could have existed in earlier periods. It seems highly unlikely, for example, that there could have been a sufficient degree of cultural communication and mobility to make plausible the imagining of an identity common to all classes and strata of the population, especially one which took priority over other identities. If, as Gellner argued,[63] the normal condition of premodern societies was one in which political authority was legitimised by the cultural difference of the ruling élite, then the development of a shared cultural identity will be – to say the least – unusual.

Of course it is also true that nationalism in the modern world has always been *international*, i.e. it has worked through a framework of real or imagined oppositions to other nations. Even in the 'primary' nationalisms of England and France (and perhaps also Spain and the Netherlands), this oppositional relation supplemented the internal conditions. In other cases, where the internal conditions were absent or undeveloped, a sense of national identity has been sustained almost entirely by an opposition to and the exclusion of some alien other. If there were premodern nationalisms, it seems likely that they would have been reactive nationalisms of this kind. Since the conditions which have sustained nationalism in the modern world were absent and the conditions of premodern life were largely antithetical to the unification of culture and State, it is probable that these nationalisms would have little survival value when the struggle was over. This is an empirical question. It is possible that other social conditions existed to generate nationalism, and that it was a more resilient phenomenon than I have suggested. It is even possible that the recognition of premodern nationalisms will lead us to expand our understanding of the concept. However, in the absence of any decisive evidence one way or the other, the question remains a highly speculative one.

All in all, there is little reason to hold dogmatically to the conventional view that nationalism came into existence for the very first time in the modern world. At the very least, the possibility of premodern nationalism should not be ruled out a priori. There is however a more modest version of the conventional wisdom available: that it was developments in the early modern world which marked the beginning of the *age of nationalism*. There may have been instances of nationalism in early periods, but they remained relatively isolated episodes, sustaining a revolt or legitimising a new regime, but these did not initiate a world historic project. It was not until the modern world that nationalism began to play a dominant role in world history, with almost all major political projects being carried out within its overriding logic. This weaker version of the conventional wisdom may seem so obvious as to be uninteresting; but it does have the virtue of being true.

Culture, will and ethnicity

> A nation...presupposes a past; it is summarised, however, in the present by a tangible fact, namely, consent, the clearly expressed desire to continue a common life. A nation's existence is, if you will pardon the metaphor, a daily plebiscite, just as an individual's existence is a perpetual affirmation of life.
>
> (Ernest Renan)[64]

The account that I have given of the nation is a 'culturalist' one: it is sameness of culture, and especially of language, which constitutes a nation. As such it seems to conflict with the fact that many putative nations are in fact culturally, and even linguistically, diverse. To take an extreme case discussed by Harry Beran, the three million or so inhabitants of Papua New Guinea 'speak seven hundred different languages, and differ in culture more than the nations of Europe'.[65] Or, to take an example that I have already mentioned, the population of Switzerland falls into three major language groups, and the cultural differences between them are at least as great as between each group and its near neighbours across the state border. Examples like this, which could easily be multiplied, suggest that a more empirically adequate account of the nation would not emphasise sameness of culture, but the existence of a common *will*: a nation is a group which – for whatever reason – *wants* to be treated as politically sovereign. Ernest Renan's famous address 'What is a nation?' is often taken to exemplify this position. For Renan, the important thing about the nation is 'consent, the clearly expressed desire to continue a common life'. The will to be a nation is expressed in the everyday life of its members; it is for this reason that the existence of the nation is a 'daily plebiscite'.[66]

However, this contrast is based on a misunderstanding of the relationship between *will* and *culture*. As the great theorist of the general will, Jean Jacques Rousseau, recognised, a political will must be embodied, not merely in the laws and institutions, but also in the educational practices, the rituals of public life, the festivals, and even the modes of dress of the citizens. The will to form a state must find expression in the cultural life of the country if it is to be maintained through later generations. It is the culture of the nation which forms the will of its members.[67] As I suggested above, there is no doubt that many new states are formed out of the experience of oppression and the political activism of educated or military élites, often on the basis of the administrative legacy of colonialism, where there is no common language or culture. These are nations by courtesy, potential nations which have to become such if they are to maintain their status. If they are to succeed in this task, they must put in place the elements of a common culture so that the political will which founded the State finds its place in the everyday consciousness of its members. The problems confronting postcolonial states are different in degree but not in kind from that of other states: how the political will of one generation is to be transmitted to the next. If, as Renan argued, the existence of the nation is a 'daily plebiscite', then it is the national culture which secures the votes. The will to form a community is essential to nationhood; it is *for this very reason* that national identity must be expressed in culture.

It is important, however, not to overemphasise the degree of cultural homogeneity required by the nation-state. There were, for example, enormous regional and class differences in seventeenth- and eighteenth-century England, and still more in the Great Britain which was formed after the Act of Union of 1707. But these did not stand in the way of an emerging English identity, nor even – as Linda Colley has shown – of an emerging British identity. The differences were not denied, but were conceived of as contained within, even as contributing to an overarching identity. For the formation of an identity which contains difference, it is necessary that there be (or be thought to be) common elements which are sufficiently central to people's lives to override difference. In the case of eighteenth-century England/Britain, a major common element was Protestantism. The expulsion of James II constituted England as a Protestant nation, and this was an important unifying element when England and Scotland came together as Great Britain. Protestantism was a signifier of Britishness, and those who were Catholic were for that reason not full members of the British nation. But the Protestant identity allowed for an enormous diversity, between regions, between social classes, and so on. These differences did not diminish the capacity to be British (unless, of course, they were associated with Catholicism or some other proscribed form of difference). Indeed, the emerging national literature celebrated the various differences as part of the mosaic of English – later British – social life.[68] It is probable, as Colley has argued, that the adherence to Protestantism could count as a unifying factor just so long as this was defined in opposition to Catholicism, and this was associated with the external social, political and military threat posed by France.[69]

The British case is unusual not because it contains considerable diversity: this is true of *all* national identities.[70] It is unusual because it contains *national* diversity. Scotland and Wales might well have been – and indeed, might well become – politically sovereign nations in their own right. But it is at least somewhat paradoxical that a sense of national identity developed under English tutelage. In the case of Scotland, for example, there were legal, political and education traditions reaching back well before the Act of Union. However, the sense of Scotland as a cultural whole, and not divided into a backward and barbaric highlands and more civilised – and English-oriented – lowland region, probably did not develop until the nineteenth century when the Waverley novels, Scottish regiments, kilts and tartans helped engender a sense of Scottish distinctiveness, though a distinctiveness that was contained within a more comprehensive British identity.[71] It was, perhaps, one of the great achievements of English imperialism to have created a concept of Britishness which allowed for diversity but sustained English hegemony.[72] But Britain is not unique in containing national diversity. Switzerland, Canada and perhaps the United States are all multinational nations. Each has a dominant national culture, comprising a history, traditions and sense of place, through which public affairs are conducted; but each contains territorially located cultural minorities which could well make the claim to be independent nations in their own right. That some multinational nations, e.g. Yugoslavia and the Soviet Union, have broken up, and others such as Canada are under threat, does not mean that there are none.

Of course there are significant limits to the kinds of diversity which are compatible with national identity, and, in some cases, difference counts as deviance. The dominant national culture may contain diversity, but it still provides norms by which other cultures and sub-cultures are assessed and found wanting. Gypsies and Jews, for example, have been marginalised and excluded in almost all nations. It is a moot point – to be discussed in Chapter 4 below – whether a national identity can sustain an explicit and public policy of multicul-turalism. But many discussions of the relationship between multicul-turalism and national identity are flawed from the beginning by a failure to recognise the extent to which existing national identities allow for diversity. Typically, theorists will recognise the diversity in their own domestic culture, but regard it *for this reason* as different from other nations. For example, Michael Walzer powerfully celebrates the various different ways in which it is possible to be American. However, he downplays the extent to which these differences are contained within a normative public culture (formed through the primacy of the English language, the political and cultural history, the constitution and associated political institutions, Hollywood, popular music, etc.), and he also fails to recognise the extent to which other nations contain similar diversity. As a conse-quence, he radically overestimates the singularity of the American case. A national union of culturally diverse elements is the normal condition for most nations.[73]

There is a widespread assumption that the concept of *ethnicity* is central to the understanding of the nation. For William H. McNeill, for example, a nation simply *is* an ethnic community and nationalism is the principle that 'rightful sovereignty' rests with 'those who shared a common ethnic heritage'.[74] McNeill argues that the few hundred years of recent history in which this principle has played a central role represent an inevitably unsuccessful – and fortunately transient – attempt to deviate from a historical norm of polyethnicity. For Walker Connor, a nation is a 'self-aware ethnic group', and he castigates those who would use the term differently.[75] A more complex, although also less clear, view is that of Anthony D. Smith, who argues that modern nations have an 'ethnic core', in the sense that they are historically derivative of premodern communities which identify themselves on ethnic lines.[76] Indeed, it is because, he suggests, the modern nation is able to call upon these more fundamental ethnic ties that it is able to attract the allegiance of so many.[77]

The major problem in coming to terms with these positions is the elusiveness of the concept of ethnicity. Presumably, what makes a community an ethnic group, rather than a community of some other kind, has to do with the centrality of descent in the group's self-understanding. But what is to count as descent? If it is understood in a narrowly procreative sense, an ethnic group will be something like an extended family or kinship group, and membership of it will be determined by birth (one is literally born into the group) or by rules governing entry (e.g. through marriage, degree of kin relationship, adoption, etc.). Except in certain defined circumstances (e.g. perhaps marrying into another ethnic group), we will bear the identity we were born with throughout our lives. We will not normally acquire a new ethnic identity (except by marriage, adoption or other rituals by which one acquires a kin status) however much we imbibe the relevant culture.

On this narrow, but moderately clear, account, there is no plausibility in the identification of the modern nation with an ethnic community. Almost all nations are ethnically diverse and recognised to be such. Daniel Defoe provides a succinct and witty demolition of the view that lineage was essential to the self-understanding of early eighteenth-century England:

> Thus from a Mixture of all kinds began,
> That Het'rogeneous Thing, *An Englishman*:
> In eager Rapes, and furious Lust begot,
> Betwixt a Painted *Britton* and a *Scot*:
> Whose gend'ring Offspring quickly learnt to bow,
> And yoke their Heifers to the *Roman* Plough:
> From whence a Mongrel half-bred Race there came,
> With neither Name nor nation, Speech or Fame.
> In whose hot Veins now Mixtures quickly ran,
> Infus'd betwixt a *Saxon* and a *Dane*.
> While their Rank Daughters, to their Parents just,
> Receiv'd all Nations with Promiscuous Lust.
> This Nauseous Brood directly did contain
> The well-extracted Blood of *Englishmen*[78]

Polyethnicity was even more obviously true of the British nation formed by the inclusion of Scotland, as well as countries of immigration such as nineteenth-century America and twentieth-century Australia. It is important, of course, to recognise that there have been limits to the ethnic diversity of these nations: Black Americans were long written out of the American nation and Aboriginal Australians out of Australia, as were the French Canadians marginalised in the Canada of William McNeill's childhood. There are many cases in which some ethnic or quasi-ethnic groups – e.g. the Normans in England, the English in Great Britain, the WASPs in the United States – played a dominant role in setting the cultural tone of a nation and in defining who was to be excluded. But this does not make the nation itself an ethnic community.

It is possible to construe the notion of descent in a broader way, and the concept of ethnicity will become correspondingly more inclusive. Anthony Smith takes this route: Ethnic communities are, he writes, 'constituted, not by lines of physical descent, but by the sense of continuity, shared memory and collective destiny'.[79] This allows Smith to find an ethnic continuity between modern and classical Greeks, despite the massive demographic shifts that have taken place in the intervening two and a half thousand years. The problem with this is that it collapses the concept of ethnicity into that of culture. *Every* significant cultural group or tradition is characterised by a 'sense of continuity, shared memory and collective destiny'. Since even the most apparently polyethnic of nations, for example, the United States and Australia, define themselves in terms of origins, stories of founding fathers, and the like, Smith's thesis that nations have an ethnic core becomes true by definition. But this is not very useful. If the concept of descent is defined as broadly as this, we would also have to count the orthodox psychoanalytic establishment, the Boy Scouts, and the Roman Catholic Church as ethnic communities. And this is stretching the notion of ethnicity beyond reasonable limits.

All in all, it is preferable to retain a relatively narrow and precise conception of ethnicity. Even with this, the distinction between an ethnic and a non-ethnic group will often be blurred and uncertain. Cultural conceptions of transmission often make use of concepts of 'family', 'blood', 'kin' and the like, and it may not be clear – even to members of the cultural group – just how seriously these metaphors should be taken. Different ethnic groups will define the circumstances in which an identity is lost or gained with different degrees of stringency. There may indeed be controversy within the community on precisely this question. However, the fact that the distinction between ethnic and non-ethnic communities is an uncertain and shifting one is hardly surprising. It is precisely what one would expect when one recognises that ethnicity is not different from, but a distinct kind of, cultural identity.

Perhaps the most serious problem with accounts which seek to explain or understand the phenomenon of nationalism in terms of the concept of ethnicity is that they fail to recognise the implications of the fact that ethnicity is not a naturally given ('objective') fact about the human condition, but something which is culturally constructed and mediated in innumerably different ways. No doubt conceptions of ethnic descent do form part of the self-understanding of many groups. But not all groups understand themselves in ethnic terms, and those that do understand their ethnicity in very different ways. What is needed is an explanation of why ethnicity becomes important in certain circumstances and why it takes the particular forms that it does. To use the concept of ethnicity as a *datum* in the explanation of nationalism ignores the fact that it is as much in need of explanation as nationalism itself.

The claim that nations *are* ethnic communities should be distinguished from the more interesting and somewhat more plausible thesis that there is an important *distinction* between two forms of nationalism – a fundamentally benign 'civic' or 'territorial' nationalism, characteristic of Western countries such as Britain, the United States and perhaps France, and a more problematic 'ethnic' nationalism characteristic of less enlightened Eastern countries. This view was first proposed by Hans Kohn and has become the received wisdom amongst the majority of commentators on nationalism.[80] Given the pliability of the notion of ethnicity, one has to tread very carefully. The clearest examples of ethnic nations are those in which certain ethnic requirements are written into the conception of citizenship. Germany, for example, offers citizenship to ethnic Germans, even those whose families have lived outside Germany for centuries, while it refuses citizenship to the German born children of Turkish or Maltese workers who may have lived and worked in Germany for many years. France on the other hand offers citizenship to all who are born on its soil.[81] In other cases, where the issue is a matter of culture and tradition rather than law, it will not be so clear-cut whether a nation's self-understanding involves some notion of common ethnicity. To complicate matters further, there is often a genuine ambiguity in the way in which a tradition is to be interpreted. If a national culture embodies the idea that present members of the nation inherit the achievements of their predecessors and are expected to build on those achievements, it may simply not be clear whether the relationship is one of biological or cultural descent. Often there will be conflict within the nation on precisely this issue.

For these reasons, we should be wary of supposing that there is a clear distinction between ethnic and non-ethnic nations. When Hans Kohn initially proposed the distinction between 'civic' and 'ethnic' nations he explained it in terms of different patterns of historical development. He argued that Western nations, such as England, France and the United States, developed within the boundaries of existing states (hence, they are 'territorial' nations), and their national identities were formed in terms of the particular political traditions of the State. Happily, these Western nations were also forward looking, and influenced by Enlightenment ideals of liberty and reason, so 'civic' or 'territorial' nationalism was hospitable to liberalism and representative democracy. On the other hand, the less fortunate Eastern nations, such as those of Germany and Russia, were formed in opposition to existing political structures; hence, their identities were formed in terms of cultural or ethnic patterns, not political ones, and they emphasised natural and organic forms of belonging rather than political ones. Because of their political and cultural inferiority to the advanced Western countries, these nations tended to avoid the unpleasant empirical truths of their own history and rely on mythical conceptions of their past.[82]

There is clearly something in the circumstances in which different nationalisms developed. But we should not try to press it too far. Indeed, it is not hard to find in Kohn's account the mean-spirited opposition to what is other that it tries to locate elsewhere. There were, as we have seen, significant differences between the development of British and French nationalisms. British political institutions and histories (the Crown, the Glorious Revolution, etc.) were embodied in eighteenth-century British identity; in France, the nation was employed as a political principle against the political status quo. Yet, despite this, France is, alongside Britain, a paradigm 'territorial' or 'civic' nation. So too is America, despite the fact that its history is markedly different again. It is also important to remember – indeed, these days it is impossible to forget – that from the perspective of those who were excluded – Jews, Blacks, Gypsies – the most civic of nations always had an 'ethnic' side to them.

Nor should we underestimate the way in which national identities change. Sometimes new ethnic identities are created: for example, in the nineteenth century, while the Protestant content of British national identity became less central, the imperialist burden of superior races to educate and civilise the world became a significant part of British national imagining. Imaginary genealogies were taken seriously (for example, the stories of King Arthur), and being British was conceived as a near *racial* identity. If, as Hobsbawm has pointed out,[83] the nineteenth century was a time of 'inventing' traditions, it was also a time of 'inventing' ethnicities. However, ethnicity has become much less central to British national identity in the twentieth century (although disputes about levels of West Indian and Asian immigration showed that the issue was not dead). And there are many other examples of a similar shift. In the past fifty years, the conception of Australia as a British (i.e. 'Anglo-Celtic' – yet another invented ethnic category) nation was expanded to include, first, immigrants from other European countries, then immigrants from Asia, and finally the indigenous inhabitants of the country. In Quebec, the grounds for being authentically Québécois have changed in recent years from being ethnically French to a preparedness to assimilate to Québécois culture (by learning the language, history, etc.).[84]

The point is that the content of various nationalisms is not determined by history, but by ongoing political struggles and debates. These contribute, not merely to the nation's sense of its present and its future, but also to the ways in which it interprets its past. Every national identity is subject to change. Instead of trying to discover a clear distinction between civic and ethnic nationalisms, we should recognise that the temptation to conceive of a deep cultural identity as founded, not in the contingencies of social life, but in the unalterable, natural determinants of one's existence, is present in all nationalisms. A national identity is always a form of difference and thus a form of exclusion. Others who do not share an identity are not entitled to participate in a certain form of communal life. However, the exclusion need not be an absolute one: a nation may be open to new members. Of course, acquiring a national identity is always difficult: it involves acquiring a new culture, usually a new language, and a new perspective on the world. In the case of most immigrants, the process is never complete. However, most nations provide entry for some who are prepared to undertake this project of remaking themselves. Undoubtedly, Benedict Anderson's claim that 'even the most insular nations accept the principle of *naturalisation* (wonderful word!), no matter how difficult in practice they make it'[85] is too optimistic. There are nations such as Germany who do not accept this principle, while almost all others make it much more difficult for some aliens to become citizens than others. Anderson does not sufficiently recognise that the temptation towards a form of closure which cannot be overcome by 'naturalisation' because it is rooted in ineluctable facts about ethnic (or racial) origin is present in all nationalisms. Instead of seeing the susceptibility to this temptation as one rooted in different histories (especially in the complacent assumption that it is rooted in the difference between 'our' history and 'theirs'), we should investigate the social and political circumstances in which these forms of closure come onto the political agenda. Ultimately, the difference between 'ethnic' and 'civic' nations is not a matter of history or geography, but of morality and politics.

2 National and other identities

And so it comes about that we begin to conceptualize matters of identity at the very time in history when they become a problem.

(Erik H. Erikson)[1]

The term '*identity*' figures in the title of this book and plays a large role in its argument. I have already used it freely in the preceding chapter. It is time to give an account of it.

While the term is inescapable in recent discussions of culture, politics and social issues, its currency is of relatively recent origin and dates back no further than the 1950s.[2] The responsibility for the vogue in 'identity' talk can probably be assigned to the psychoanalyst Erik H. Erikson,[3] who introduced the term as part of his attempt to apply psychoanalytic categories to social and historical issues. For Erikson, the concept of identity referred to the point at which the demands of the developing individual – the adolescent – were met or failed to be met by the forms of social life in which he or she lived. It was Erikson's influential thesis that modern American society failed to provide the secure sense of adult identity which was necessary for young people to resolve the various conflicts of childhood and adolescence, and this led to what he called an 'identity crisis' in which they more or less literally did not know who they were.

It is unlikely that many who use the term these days would wish to be committed too far in the direction of Erikson's particular brand of psychoanalytic theory. However, his use of the term to propose a nexus between social life and self-conception was seminal. If there is a defensible core underlying the variety of ways in which the term has been used since Erikson, it is the idea that we come to understand who we are through the resources provided for us by the forms of social life within which we exist. More explicitly: we have an *identity* because we *identify* with figures or representations which are made available to us. The concept of identity implies that there is a constitutive linkage between forms of *subjectivity*, i.e. the ways in which we conceive of ourselves, and forms of social *objectivity*, the patterns of social life within which we exist.

My guess is that in the long run some form of psychoanalytic theory will be necessary to explain this relationship between self and society.[4] My main project in this chapter is, however, the more preliminary one of explaining and justifying the use I have made – and will make – of the concept of identity. For this exercise, it is important to avoid offering too many hostages to the outcome of current debates within and about psychoanalytic theory. Instead, I will use some of the resources available within philosophy to explore the concept. This may seem an unpromising route. Most contemporary philosophers strive to maintain a professional innocence of what is going on in allied social disciplines, and philosophy has not suffered the proliferation of identity talk characteristic of other disciplines. Many philosophers assume that the only identity worth discussing is that of the *person*, and they trace the lineage of this concept over two centuries before Erikson to John Locke, if not before. For these philosophers, personhood is a form of identity which is *independent* of the forms of social life within which we exist. It may be that other identities – and most would consider this term to be a loose and inaccurate one – refer to social aspects of our existence; however, the concept of a personhood captures the underlying unity: the self conceived independently of the social contingencies within which it is entangled.[5]

It will emerge that there are philosophical traditions which reject the assumed primacy of personhood. However, it will be useful to examine the concept of a person as it has been conceived by mainstream contemporary philosophy. My aim is to show that the concept of a person is not metaphysically privileged, but is as much a socially formed identity as any other. By bringing out the inadequacy of the philosophical assumption that there is an identity – a form of the self – which is in some sense asocial, it will be possible to reach a better understanding of the thesis that *all* identities are constituted in and through particular forms of social life.

Discussion of the concept of a person will also enable me to pursue a second major concern of this chapter: to bring out the *moral* dimension of the relationship between self and society. In so far as our identities are formed through specific conceptions of social life, we find ourselves subject to the commitments and constraints, standards of behaviour and criteria of success provided by these conceptions. We do not choose these; nevertheless, we find them difficult, and sometimes impossible, to eschew. This is to say that we are – always, already – inscribed within particular forms of the moral life. An identity is a form of inscription: as such, it embodies a specific evaluative point of view. All identities involve values and commitments, and the acquisition of an identity means coming to accept these values and commitments. This, I will suggest, is as true of the aseptic concept of personhood favoured by philosophers as it is of the concept of national identity discussed in this book.

For many philosophers there is a gap between the facts of social existence and the demands of morality, and moral philosophy is the project of finding a rational basis for the moral principles we need to guide our lives. However, in our everyday existence, we have a different problem. Moral claims are inescapable aspects of our experience, and the problem we face is that they are often at variance with one another. Our moral life consists less in the search for moral principles than in the attempt to reconcile those we already have. Our task is to find some order in the moral conflict which is such a familiar part of our experience. I will suggest that this experience of moral conflict and its resolution provides a better passage to moral knowledge – a better way of moving from the 'is' of social existence to the 'ought to be' of morality – than the search by philosophers for fundamental principles. Undoubtedly, philosophers are right to conceive of morality in terms of principle; but we will only understand the demands of principle if we are prepared to explore the moral resources of the socially formed identities which form our conception of what and who we are.

Persons

> the simple abstraction 'person' has something contemptuous about it, even as an expression.
>
> (Hegel)

I have suggested that it was probably John Locke who is responsible for the philosopher's obsession with personal identity. However, the term already had a considerable history before Locke's famous discussion in *An Essay concerning Human Understanding*. It is likely that the original sense – stretching back to the Etruscan origins of Roman civilisation – involved the notion of a mask, and, by extension, a role or representation: one adopted a *persona* in order to claim the right to participate in certain rituals or privileged activities. A later association was with jurisprudence: to be a person in Roman law was to be a full subject of the law, with the appropriate range of legal rights and duties. The anthropologist Marcel Mauss argued that this legal sense was derived from the original notion of a mask.[6] One's *persona* was the mask or representation which secured recognition of one's right to participate in the rituals of Roman public law. It was the signifier of a certain legal status, one which was not available to slaves or, though Mauss does not mention this, to women.

The original Roman notion of person as mask seems never to have passed into English.[7] However, the notion of person as role or character in a theatrical sense, was present in seventeenth-century English (it survives in the phrase '*dramatis personae*'). A legal sense was also well established in which the term signified a mode of agency: one's person was the public position or office which gave one the right to act in certain ways. Thomas Hobbes was able to combine these two senses through a doctrine of representation: the person as public role gained authority to act from the claim to represent the individual(s) impersonated:

> a *person*, is the same that an *actor* is, both on the stage and in common conversation; and to *personate*, is to *act*, or to *represent* himself, or another; and he that acteth another, is said to bear his person, or act in his name.[8]

It is significant that Hobbes here allows that a person might 'represent himself'. This notion of a person – in Hobbes's terminology, a 'natural person' – marks an important transition. The term 'person' was coming to signify, not just the public role in virtue of which an agent had the right to perform certain activities, but also the inner being of the agent who occupied the role. If the notion of a position or office still carried something of the original distinction between the mask and its wearer, this passage indicates that a new sense of 'person' was emerging which erased that distinction. A person in this sense was not the representation but what was represented, not a social role but an intrinsic nature.

However, it was not Hobbes but Locke who entrenched this shift in philosophy. Indeed, he did this so successfully as almost to obliterate the traces of the earlier distinction. Locke recognised – as most of his successors did not – that 'person' was a legal concept: '*Person* is a Forensick Term appropriating Actions and their Merit.'[9] But Locke was not concerned to inquire into the legal practice by which 'Actions and their merit' were assigned, but to investigate the conditions under which this practice might be justified. His discussion of personal identity was designed to uncover the relationship between an individual existing at one time and another individual existing at an earlier time, so that the latter could be held legally – and thus morally – accountable for the doings of the former:

> In this *Personal Identity* is founded all the Right and Justice of Reward and Punishment.[10]

Locke's persons were primarily legal subjects ('subject to Law' is Locke's phrase); however, the concept he was articulating (one might almost say, inventing) was not that of a legal role which we might occupy under certain circumstances. For Locke, it was a way of picking out what each of us essentially is: a 'self'. In other words, Locke equates the subject of legal responsibility with what is crucial to our existence. What is at issue in the identity of the person is survival of the self. What this move precludes is the possibility that being a person is only *one* of the forms taken by the self, and that there are *other* modes of identity, *other* ways of saying 'I'.

Locke distinguishes the identity of the person in this now privileged sense from that of the *human* – the 'man in a physical sense' or the 'natural man'. A 'natural man' is a complex form of organic life, and its identity – like that of all living things – consists in continuity of life and bodily organisation.[11] But the 'natural man' is not as such a person. It counts as a person – or a 'moral man' – in having the characteristics in virtue of which it is subject to law and morality, i.e. being self-conscious, rational and a language-user. Not all humans are persons in this sense, and it is at least conceptually possible that some non-human animals might be counted as persons:

> whether a Child or a Changeling be a *Man* in a physical Sense, may amongst the Naturalists be as disputable as it will, it concerns not at all the *moral Man*, as I may call him…*a corporeal rational Being*. For were there a Monkey, or any other creature to be found, that had the use of Reason, to such a degree, as to be able to understand general Signs, and to deduce Consequences about general *Ideas*, he would no doubt be subject to Law, and in that Sense, be a *Man*, how much soever he differ'd in Shape from others of that Name.[12]

Locke's reasoning here is that while 'the use of Reason', the ability 'to understand general Signs' and so on are characteristic of human beings, they are not universal. The term 'Person' (or 'moral Man') designates only those who have this distinction. But, he suggests, precisely these characteristics might inhere in other, non-human forms of life (in the passage above it is monkeys; elsewhere he tells a story of a language-using parrot); in which case these too must be counted as persons. In principle *anything* which has these characteristics would be a person.

Having abstracted the person from the human, Locke's task is to provide an account of identity for this abstraction; that is, of the conditions under which a present person may be identified with some past person and held responsible for what that person did or failed to do. His reasoning here has a deceptive simplicity. A man – or presumably a being of another kind – becomes a person in virtue of a certain kind of consciousness: it is consciousness 'that makes everyone to be, what he calls *self* '. But if one's identity at a time is constituted by consciousness of self at that time, then it is tempting to think that one's identity over a period of time is constituted by one's consciousness ranging over that period. That is to say, the fact that I am able to bring past actions and thoughts to present consciousness establishes that I was the person who did or thought those things in the past: 'And as far as this consciousness can be extended backwards to any past Action or Thought, so far reaches the Identity of that *Person*; it is the same *self* now it was then.'[13]

There are two problems in this account which are relevant to my concerns in this chapter. In the first place, there is an unclarity about the nature of the relationship between the person/self and consciousness. If this is taken to mean that in (self-)consciousness, the self becomes aware of something which exists independently of consciousness, this implies that the nature of this independent existence is not determined by consciousness, and we need a further account of the nature of that independent existence.[14] If, on the other hand, we conceive of the self as an intentional object, literally constituted by consciousness, we must ask: *whose* consciousness? Unless we posit the existence of a further subject of consciousness, we must suppose that the person is the creation of its own mental activity. While this may not be strictly incoherent, it needs a much fuller account than anything provided by Locke.[15]

The second problem concerns the relationship with the past which establishes personal identity. Often, as in the passage quoted above, Locke seems to claim that it is the fact of my being able to recollect a past experience ('memory') which constitutes my identity with the subject of that experience. However, as David Behan has suggested,[16] a close reading reveals that the kind of consciousness which is relevant to the identity of the person is not the mere retention of some past experience in memory, but the agent's current *appropriation* of that memory. It is the existence of a certain kind of *concern* for the past agent, a sympathetic apprehension of his or her happiness and misery, and an appropriation of those past memories as *mine* which constitutes my identity with the person involved. Thus, Locke writes:

> For if we take wholly away all Consciousness of our Actions and Sensations, especially of Pleasure and Pain, *and the concernment that accompanies it*, it will be hard to know wherein to place personal Identity.[17]

And again:

> For as to this point of being the same *self*, it matters not whether this present *self* be made up of the same or other Substances, I being as much concern'd, and as justly accountable for any Action was done a thousand Years since, *appropriated to me now by this self-consciousness*, as I am, for what I did the last moment.[18]

On Behan's reading of Locke, I am responsible for actions I did in the past, not merely because I can remember them, but because in remembering them I identify myself with the person who performed them. It is because past actions are 'appropriated to me now by this self-consciousness' that present feelings of pride, shame, guilt, remorse, pleasure, obligation are usually present and appropriate. It is because I identify with a certain past that others are justified in holding me now responsible for that past.

This account of personal identity raises many questions. Why do we have appropriative consciousness? Why does the past remain a presence in our lives? Is our appropriative consciousness of the past a mere sign of personal identity or does it, in some way not explained by Locke, constitute it? I will return to these questions shortly.

A hundred years later, Immanuel Kant provided a strikingly similar account of persons. Once again, the issue of morality was central. Persons are those beings 'whose acts are subject to imputation', beings who are the moral 'origin' of their acts, and hence are legally and morally responsible for what they do.[19] The conditions of moral responsibility require, Kant argued, that persons be conceived not as creatures of nature, but of reason. This was in part because our human propensities – of which Kant took a rather dim view – were too unreliable to ground the moral law, and in part because the reach of morality extended well beyond the realm of humanity: whatever being has the reason to comprehend the moral law – and this includes angels and devils – is *ipso facto* subject to it. That we are subject to the demands of morality, i.e. are persons, is not due to our human nature, but to the property that we share with other moral agents – reason itself. If we were merely natural creatures – human animals – we would only have 'relative value': 'Man in the system of nature...is a being of slight importance'; however:

> man regarded as a *person* – that is, as the subject of morally practical reason – is exalted above any price; for as such...he is not to be valued as a mere means to the ends of others or even to his own ends, but as an end in himself.[20]

To be a person in the full Kantian sense is to be a bearer of rights; it is also, in virtue of one's reason, to be capable of recognising other persons as equal bearers of rights, and of modifying one's behaviour accordingly. For Kant, my moral personality is a universal: it is what I share with other persons, not what distinguishes me from them. To be a person is to transcend the particularities of one's merely empirical, merely human existence.

In neither Locke nor Kant is the concept of a person that of a spiritual substance distinct from the human body. In one sense, personhood is an attribute which certain privileged humans possess. But for Locke and Kant, personhood is not merely an attribute; it is the subject. Personhood is a form of identity which defines what we are: it is our essential being; humanity a mere contingency.

This account of persons is alive and well in contemporary philosophy. Indeed, it is the current orthodoxy on the topic. In what is perhaps the most influential article on persons in recent years, Harry Frankfurt writes:

> Our concept of ourselves as persons is not to be understood...as a concept of attributes that are necessarily species-specific. It is conceptually possible that members of novel or even of familiar non-human species should be persons; and it is also conceptually possible that some members of the human species are not persons.[21]

For Frankfurt, as for many other contemporary philosophers,[22] a person is to be understood in terms of those characteristics which *differentiate* persons from other things. While these philosophers acknowledge that all the persons we know are human beings, they argue that the characteristics which make us interested in persons – their moral accountability, rationality, free will, or whatever – are not universal in humans, so that to be a person is not *just* to be human. And they also argue that we can imagine these characteristics embodied in other forms of life (or even of non-life), so that being human is not *essential* to being a person. To be a person is to be understood in terms of characteristics which both differentiate us from and are independent of our human nature. We are then invited to *identify* ourselves with these characteristics.

Something has gone badly wrong here. Assume for a moment that it is legitimate to treat the differentiating characteristics in abstraction from the other attributes of a human being – our rationality or moral responsibility, for example, in abstraction from our organic nature. It is a *further* question to ascertain the importance of these *differentia* in our life. Why, for example, must I identify myself with my rationality, moral agency, or whatever? Why should these characteristics be taken to define what I am? It may be that we can define a concept of personhood in abstraction from the human; but this does not establish that this concept picks out what we essentially are, and still less does it provide us with a reason to adopt this identity.

But it is a prior mistake to think that we can understand the *differentia* of personhood in isolation from the specific form of organic life which is human existence. Locke, Kant and others may be right to assume that there are features of the moral life of some human beings which may be used to demarcate a special category of agents, namely persons. But this does not justify the assumption that their chosen *differentia* can be understood in abstraction from the quite specific form of life on which they arose; that is, quite independently of the fact that they belong to human beings, and that they have developed out of human life. The assumption that they can be is usually buttressed by the unsupported and unworked through suggestion that we can envisage precisely these features existing in quite a distinct form of life (or, in certain cases, non-life). This fantasy has encouraged philosophers to conceive of our desires, hopes and aspirations, fears and anxieties, our intellectual, moral and spiritual life as if these could be understood in abstraction from the specific form of organic life from which these have developed. It is this distinction which allows contemporary analytical philosophers and other devotees of science fiction to indulge the fantasy or the nightmare that automata might some day be counted as persons.

It is hard to overestimate the calamitous consequences of the construction of an identity which is differentiated in so absolute a manner from the human. In one move, it dissociates us from some of the most morally significant aspects of our existence. It draws attention away from the fundamental fact that in order to live we must enter into physical interaction with our physical environment. The significance in our lives of bodily integrity, of protection from certain kinds of intrusion and of physical intimacy, becomes mysterious. It only allows an indirect recognition of the way in which the narratives of our lives are structured around the facts of birth, immaturity and dependence, growth and development, and finally decay and dissolution. Human existence has involved a continuous transformation of its biological beginnings; but we never transcend them. We are not *just* humans; but we will not get very far in understanding what it is that we are if we forget that we are still human. A morality based on a conception of existence abstracted from the human is going to have little to say about sexuality and procreation, life and death, and almost everything else that is significant in our existence.[23]

A better account of persons was provided by Hegel. For Hegel, personhood was a form of identity created and sustained by certain forms of social life. On Hegel's view, Locke and Kant were right to see a connection between the concept of a person and the practices of law and morality. However, they got the connection the wrong way round. The concept of a person is not the *foundation* of the various moral and legal practices of promise making, contracts, punishment, guilt, and so on; it is rather their *effect*. It is not because we are persons that we may participate in these practices; we are persons because we participate in them. The concept of a person is an artefact of those systems of law and associated morality – such as those of the Roman imperium and the modern State – which recognise the equal rights of all who are subject to them and which provide the framework within which right-bearing individuals can own property and enter into contracts. The identity imposed by these legal systems is that of a subject of rights, and it abstracts from all those characteristics which differentiate one subject from another. Morality and law have an essentially performative character: when we are recognised by them, we are deemed to be persons. In a certain sense, personhood is an intentional identity, i.e. it is in part constituted by consciousness. But the intentionality is not that of an individual: it is a *social intentionality*. Locke's difficulties with the relationship between the person/self and consciousness are resolved when we recognise that the persons are constituted as such, not primarily by their own self-awareness, but through the forms of awareness embodied in a range of legal and moral institutions and practices: individuals *count as* persons in so far as they participate (or are deemed to participate) in those practices. Of course, an appropriate form of self-awareness is also an outcome of this process of identity formation: individuals *become* persons in so far as their own self-awareness is formed through these practices. Becoming a person is a form of acculturation – of *Bildung*, in the sense outlined in Chapter 1. It is one way (though as we shall see, not the only way) in which the human individual becomes a *self*.

Hegel's own attitude to this identity is a nuanced one. On the one hand, personhood is a considerable attainment, indeed 'the highest achievement of a human being'.[24] Only humans can live the 'contradiction' between the utter determinateness of particular existence and the conception of the self as an abstract subject of rights. But this abstraction is not a foundational, still less a final, state of human existence. Indeed, in the very paragraph in which Hegel identifies personhood as 'the highest achievement of a human being', he goes on to say that 'in spite of this, the simple abstraction "person" has something contemptuous about it, even as an expression'.[25] Hegel's point here is that the term 'person' is absolutely non-specific. Though it is a 'commandment of right' that one '*be a person and respect others as persons*',[26] this prescription abstracts from the very specificities which give one a special claim on the regard of others. To treat someone merely as a person implies that his or her particular life has no significance of its own. 'Person' is a lowest common denominator; hence, a term of contempt.

We are all persons. For this very reason, the application of the term to me says nothing which it does not say to every other person. My uniqueness must gain recognition elsewhere. Because it identifies me in universal terms, it is not an identity which can provide significance for me. What is more, personhood detaches us from the lived experience of bodily difference and particularity, and abstracts us from the narrative resources – birth, growth and development, sexuality, procreation, friendship, decay, death – which we require to make sense of our lives. It is through these resources that we are able to form conceptions of ourselves which do justice to our existence as individuals and which at the same time provide us with a location within a larger framework. Personhood does not provide a story at all, let alone a story which is ours.[27]

The mistake of the tradition initiated by Locke and Kant is to conceive the conception of self generated by the law and legalistic morality as the only or primary one which is available to us. It is no accident that Locke and Kant, the two major philosophical protagonists in the story of persons, occupy such a prominent place in the liberal pantheon. While this conception is not unique to liberalism, it is especially characteristic of it. Personhood is the appropriate form of identity in a liberal moral, legal and political order. But the law and its attendant morality constitute only one of the frameworks of meaning within which we live our lives, and personhood is only one of the identities available to us. We *are* persons; but we are not *just* persons. As we participate in other forms of social life we acquire other identities. For example, we are parents; or we are citizens; or we may have a particular religious identity; and we have a national identity. None of these identities is reducible to personhood, nor are their attendant moralities reducible to liberalism.

What is the raw material for this story of the social constitution of identities? There is a temptation here to discover a further self, a foundational presocial self which assumes or has imposed on it certain forms of representation – a real *I* behind the various social *mes*. But there is no reason to succumb to this temptation. The raw material is nothing but the human animal – Locke's 'man in a physical sense' and Kant's 'man in the system of nature' – which becomes a self on entry into social life.

But this raises another issue. How does the human animal become a person? If personhood is a form of identity appropriate for those moral systems which recognise each individual as a bearer of rights, it demands of each individual the recognition of the rights of others. Persons must also be able to act with the knowledge that their future selves will take responsibility for what they do and recognise that they bear the responsibility for what their past selves have done. What are the costs and what are the rewards for this process of moral education (or *Bildung*)?

These are the questions posed by Nietzsche in the Second Essay in *On the Genealogy of Morals*:

> To breed an animal *with the right to make promises* – is not this the paradoxical task that nature has set itself in the case of man?[28]

If we are to possess the right to make promises, we must be able to act with the knowledge that some future self will take responsibility for that act. Unless some future I feels bound by what I do now, I will not be able to *commit* myself to do something in the future. That we have this capacity is such a familiar fact of everyday life that we are inclined to take it for granted. But Nietzsche was right to see a problem here. For it is plausible to argue – either on evolutionary grounds or from considerations of practical rationality – that the human animal will maximise its chances of doing well in the world if it has the capacity to learn from the past, but not be bound by it. At any given time, we would look upon the past, including our own past, as providing information relevant to the carrying out of our current projects, but we would not think of it as binding us to act in one way or the other. But if we were like this, we would not be able to commit our future selves to the performance of our promises. So the task which 'nature' has to perform, and must have performed if social life was to become possible, was to 'breed' an animal with the 'right to make promises', an animal which knows that the moral determinants of what it *now* does must include what it *has* done, and that what it now does will be a determinant of what it *will* do in the future. For these beings, every present will be resonant with a past and a future. But how did we become such beings?

The answer to these questions, Nietzsche suggests, lies in the acquisition by the human animal of a certain kind of memory:

> This involves no mere passive inability to rid oneself of an impression, no mere indigestion through a once-pledged word with which one cannot 'have done', but an active *desire* not to rid oneself, a desire for the continuance of something desired once, a real *memory of the will*.[29]

We learn to remember what we have done, not merely in the sense that certain acts remain present to consciousness, but because we *identify* ourselves with the self that performed those acts. We *appropriate* the past as our past. We were that self which promised, its will is our will, and the suffering it would endure with the failure of its projects is our suffering. What is this capacity, this 'instinct', which underlies the right to make promises?

The answer is beyond doubt: this sovereign man calls it his *conscience*.[30] A conscience does not merely provide the human animal with knowledge of right and wrong; it is also the source of the unique pleasure which arises from the knowledge that one has acted rightly and – as the 'bad conscience' – of the pain of guilt which is induced by the knowledge that one has not done as one ought.

How does 'nature' inculcate this kind of memory? The infliction of pain is part of the story:

> If something is to stay in the memory, it must be burned in: only that which never ceases to *hurt* stays in the memory.[31]

But pain by itself is not enough. If it were, then the mechanism of punishments would be sufficient to induce the requisite memory. But often punishment does not make criminals feel guilt at what they have done; it only 'makes men hard and cold...[and] strengthens the power of resistance'.[32] Nor is guilt merely a matter of internalising the infliction of pain. This would simply produce new forms of cunning; we would learn to evade the prohibitions in much the way we avoid eating on a sore tooth.

The relevant model here is not punishment but initiation. Rites of passage involve the infliction of pain, not just because 'pain is the most powerful aid to mnemonics',[33] but because pain is the price which the neophyte must pay for entry into a new form of life. The initiate must not only remember and internalise the administration of pain, but come to identify with those who inflicted it. The human animal is ready for social life when it takes the prohibitions and restrictions into itself as its own, and is ready to punish infringements, even – or especially – its own. It comes to conceive of itself as a moral agent, the possessor of a conscience, the ability to tell right from wrong, and, perhaps above all else, to feel pleasure and pain at what it did in the past and in anticipation of what it will do in the future. It has acquired the 'right to make promises'.

For Kant, we are moral agents because we have a nature which we share with angels and other rational beings. For Nietzsche, this misrecognition is the result of a process through which we have come to identify ourselves with something other than our merely human, animal natures. This identification has become a source of pride to us: what is important about us is not what we share with the animals, even human animals, but that which differentiates us. Social life requires that we repress our natural instincts, so these become the occasion of guilt and the object of repression. It is the internalised reactive force of these natural desires which are denied their direct expression, not the austere authority of the moral law, which generates the power of the bad conscience – the ever present pain of guilt:

> Those fearful bulwarks with which the political organization protected itself against the old instincts...brought about that all

those instincts of wild, free, prowling man turned backward *against man himself*. Hostility, cruelty, joy in persecuting, in attacking, in change, in destruction – all this turned against the possessors of such instincts: *that* is the origin of the 'bad conscience'.[34]

Paradoxically, one of the rewards of the moral life is that it offers gratification of the very desires – cruelty, hostility and the like – which it is the task of morality to contain.[35] As we come to identify ourselves with something other than our human nature, what we were becomes an object of repression. But we can never repudiate it completely, so it remains a source of guilt and denial. The price we pay for our entry into the moral life is alienation from our human embodied existence.

It is illuminating to contrast Nietzsche's account of appropriative consciousness – memory – with Locke's. Its role in Nietzsche's story is not to provide an empirical basis for the personal identity required by morality and the law. Rather, it is the task of morality and the law to inculcate the requisite memory: 'a memory had to be *made*'.[36] We must be taught to overcome our more primitive inclinations to put the past aside, and learn to retain it in our present awareness; we must learn to identify our present selves with that past. The moral self which ponders how it must act is constituted, not by its present desires, but by a certain conception of its life. It knows that it has existed in the past and will exist in the future. Memory and anticipation are not merely epistemologically uncertain modes of access to that past and that future; they enter into the very identity of the self.

Personhood is not, as philosophers have supposed, a foundational identity. It is one of the forms of identity – a way of saying 'I' – which is available to the human animal. It arises in those contexts which treat the human animal in abstraction from many of its human properties. A legal context seems to have been the first of these, and it remains important. Closely related are those moral contexts in which morality is conceived on a legalistic model. Those subject to the law and morality come to be conceived of, and to conceive themselves, as persons. But if we are *deemed* persons in those contexts, we only *become* persons when we acquire the appropriate form of consciousness; that is, we think of ourselves as bound by our past and able to bind our future. Personhood, like every other identity, involves a certain kind of memory. But this memory is not a natural attribute of the human animal (though it is not unnatural either): it had to be made.

There are other contexts which invite or demand a similar kind of abstraction. Cognitive scientists, for example, are more impressed with our capacity to do maths and logic than the fact that we can dance or make love, so they construct a concept of a person on the basis of this preferred attribute. In itself this move is harmless enough, and may even be useful in certain contexts. But we should be wary of assuming that this concept signifies what we most essentially are, or even that we can in the final analysis understand our cognitive abilities in abstraction from the fact that they are exercised by socialised human beings with a range of other capacities and attributes as well. That the temptation to make these assumptions is one to which philosophers are especially prone is, perhaps, not too surprising given our professional concerns and cloistered ways of life – though we should not overlook Nietzsche's charge that the tradition of Western philosophy is largely motivated by fear and repudiation of the body. However, the temptation is not confined to philosophers. Its prevalence suggests that an alienation from our human, animal and bodily existence is widespread in the modern world. The reification of the concept of a person is as much a symptom of this alienation as it is the consequence of a series of philosophical mistakes stretching back at least to Locke some 300 years ago.

Nothing in this section has been intended to show that we should reject the concept of a person. On the contrary. That we are persons is a significant identity in the modern world, and it inscribes us in an important form of the moral life. My argument has been that we should reject the idea that personhood is a metaphysically privileged form of identity and the associated assumption that this form of morality – liberalism – is the only one available to us.

Self-interpreting animals

If human beings are, in Charles Taylor's phrase, 'self-interpreting animals',[37] Nietzsche serves to remind us that however creative, exotic and even perverse our self-interpretations, we remain animals, albeit animals of an interesting and complex kind. Physical vulnerability and eventual death are inescapable features of our animal condition. Like all animals, our life has a beginning and an end. Between these points there is a pattern of immaturity, development, maturity and decay which is unique to humans, and certain central and pervasive features of our life flow from this. If as persons we *exist*, as humans we *live*; and the manner of our living is rooted in the kind of animal we are. For a long early period we are physically dependent on the availability of others who are prepared to secure the conditions of our continued life. While this dependence becomes less in later years, it never disappears entirely. We may be able to interfere with the details of the characteristic pattern of physical development, maturity and decay, and sometimes in quite radical ways, but there is little that we are yet able to do about the general framework. When we do develop the capacity to change it in fundamental respects, this will have profound effects on our conceptions of ourselves. What we should learn from Nietzsche is that those interpretations of human existence which ignore or marginalise the fact that we are animals are for this very reason *mis*interpretations and do not provide the resources to understand human life. However, we must also resist – as Nietzsche himself was never able fully to resist – the temptation to think that being a human animal constitutes a more fundamental and healthy form of existence than those provided by social life. That we are human is an inescapable fact about our lives; but it is not as such an identity. It is only through social life that we become, not merely human, but human *selves*.

We are not *just* animals. We are animals who interpret ourselves. I take Taylor's dictum to mean, not merely that we have opinions about ourselves, but that we are animals who become *selves* through interpretation. Our selves – the selves that we are – *are* interpretations. It is through self-interpretation that we become conscious of ourselves as subjects of experience and action. We come to understand ourselves in certain ways, and these modes of self-understanding constitute the identities in terms of which we confront and act on the world. Of course, the forms in which we interpret ourselves are not created by ourselves *de novo*. They are, at least in the first instance, provided by the forms of social life into which we are inducted. The prevailing language and culture not only provide the conceptual resources through which we become aware of the world and of others in the world, but the resources through which we become aware of ourselves as part of that world.

We need be clear about the nature of the relationship between self and society which is involved here. Consider, for a moment, the notion of a *social object*. A piece of paper is a bank note, a physical movement an insult, a complex set of dispositions and practices is a university, in part because enough people understand them that way. In social life, we exist in a world of already interpreted objects, objects whose identity is constituted, at least in part, by these interpretations. This does not mean that a social object – an insult, a banknote, a university – is just what we think it is. These objects are constituted by interpretation, but they may also be misinterpreted, and they may well have features of which people are unaware. There is no doubt that social objects have all the ontological depth that we might demand of inhabitants of the real world, and that they are proper subjects of scientific investigation and explanation (in some suitably generous sense of these terms). However, we will not come to understand these objects unless we work through the understanding of those whose interpretations make them the objects they are.

On the understanding of identity proposed here, *we* are also social objects: that is, we are constituted as selves by the ways in which we are interpreted. If, as human animals, our life is *causally* dependent upon the activities of others, as human selves it is *conceptually* dependent upon the interpretations of others. We are the selves that we are through the forms – the conceptual resources and the social practices – within which we exist.

An identity is not just a form in which we and others are aware of ourselves; it is also a form in which we experience the world and act on it. We are not just social *objects*; we are also social *subjects*. There are two interrelated aspects of this. First, an identity provides its bearer with a mode of cognitive access to the world. Because we have a certain identity, we understand (or misunderstand) the world in certain ways. It provides a perspective on the world: a point from which and a framework within which we know the world. Second, an identity is also a mode of agency. It provides us, not only with a conception of how we should act in certain circumstances, but also with a motivation to do so. It both tells us what to do and prompts us to do it. It is important to recognise that these two aspects – understanding and agency, cognition and conation – go together. I have a certain understanding of the world and this understanding moves me to act in a certain way. The link between understanding and agency is formed by identity. It is because I have a certain conception of myself – in a sense, I am that conception – that the world is relevant to me in certain ways. In Taylor's language, the world has a certain 'import' for me: it will call upon me to act in one way or another.

Consider Taylor's example of coming across a man who is injured and in need of help. This situation requires us, or those of us with the appropriate identity, to render assistance. For Taylor: 'The situation bears this import for me, in virtue of the kind of being I am; and this is a logical truth, internal to the meaning of import.'[38]

Taylor's point is not that we will necessarily respond to this import. We may have conflicting demands on us, and we may offer a redescription of the situation so that it has a different import ('The man is not hurt very badly; he probably deserved it; someone better able to help will arrive soon; etc.'). It is rather that given a certain conception of our identity and a corresponding understanding of the world, we cannot but recognise that we are called upon to help. The very fact that I may attempt to evade the obligation by offering a redescription of it concedes the motivational force of the initial description.

This account may seem to go against the model of agency which dominates most contemporary discussion, so it is important to spell out what is involved. According to the dominant model – loosely derived from David Hume – beliefs do not as such have a motivational force. They acquire this force, i.e. they count as *reasons* to act in one way rather than another, when they specify conditions which are relevant to the satisfaction of independently existing desires. That I see a man who is in need of help that I am easily able to give, will move me to act just so long as I have a relevant desire, e.g. the desire to help others, perhaps the desire to win praise or appear in a good light, or something of the sort. Behind every intentional act is a desire, and this desire provides the motivational force – the energy – needed to generate the action. However, when the Humean model is interpreted narrowly, it has little plausibility. We are all too familiar with cases where we have reason to act – indeed, when we do act – against what we would antecedently have identified as our desires. A more plausible interpretation – and one more in keeping with Hume's own account – is that of Bernard Williams, which interprets the notion of desire broadly so as to include all the elements in an agent's 'subjective motivational set', including 'such things as dispositions of evaluation, patterns of emotional reaction, personal loyalties, and various projects...embodying commitments of the agent'.[39] On this more inclusive reading, there is no incompatibility between the two accounts: the beliefs which move us to act are precisely those which activate the values, emotions, loyalties and commitments comprised by our identity.

There is another respect, also suggested by Williams, in which the Humean model of agency must be interpreted broadly. There are many ways in which a belief may be relevant to the satisfaction of our desires (commitments, values, etc.), and these are not all reducible to the relationship of causal means to a predetermined end.[40] It is often the case that when we understand a situation in a certain way, this understanding constitutes a reason to act in one way rather than another. The connection between the way in which we understand a situation and our motivation is a *conceptual* one. An identity not only involves a certain conception of ourselves, but it also provides a certain preliminary articulation of the world. When a situation calls upon us to act in a certain way, it is because it appears to us, not merely as a causal means for the satisfaction of our desires, but as having a meaning which speaks to our meanings. Consider, for example, our conception of ourselves as persons. As such, we think of ourselves as the bearer of certain rights and duties; and we also recognise that we exist in relationship to other bearers of rights and duties. In other words, the conception of ourselves as persons provides a preliminary articulation of the world in which we exist. In certain circumstances, we will discover that other persons have rights against us, and that we therefore have duties towards them. In the simplest – Lockean – case, we recall that we have made a promise, and this memory provides us with a reason to fulfil the promise, because, as persons, we appropriate that past promise as our present responsibility. In other words, the world as we conceive it has that particular 'import' for us: it calls upon us to do our duty. Of course, we may evade that call, perhaps by offering a redescription of the situation, or by claiming that other demands take priority, or simply through weakness. But these strategies fall within a perspective of the world formed by our identity as persons.

Of course we are not just persons. We have other identities, and these also make demands upon us. Most of us, for example, are also members of families, and our family identity provides us with a different perspective on the world and inscribes us within a different moral agenda. As family members, we find ourselves involved with particular others who have certain expectations of us and of whom we have expectations. Sometimes, we have a special responsibility to these others or they to us, responsibilities which are different in kind to those of personhood: we may, for example, have specific responsibilities of love, care and nurture which would be out of place in the realm of formal rights and duties characteristic of the relations between persons.[41] As persons we are inclined to think of our obligations as self-incurred: we enter a contract (or do something which has contractual implications) and we incur an obligation to carry out our end of the bargain.[42] As family members, on the other hand, we inherit (sometimes literally) responsibilities which we as individuals have done nothing to incur. We find ourselves involved – almost against our will – when a close member of our family does something of which we are ashamed or stands in need of particular help. These two moral identities – personhood and family membership – place us in different relationships to the world and, indeed, in different worlds.

In this case, the borders between the two worlds are policed by the operation of the public/private distinction. But the border is poorly defined, the guards are often inattentive, and border crossings are legion. When the demands of the two identities conflict, we find ourselves caught between different visions of the world and our place in it. And there are other identities without even this semblance of a border. Much of our moral life consists of our dealing with conflicts of this kind, and seeking resolutions to what are unsettling and in extreme cases untenable positions of this kind.

Probably all identities involve values, standards and norms. Each of them imposes certain codes of conducts on us and carries criteria of success and failure. Which means that we are – always, already – inscribed into forms of the moral life. There may be extreme cases of *anomie* where an individual finds him or herself without values, trying vainly to move from a conception of how things are to a conception of how they ought to be. But this situation is not, as one might expect from the philosophical attention paid to it this century, the normal human condition; it is one of rare social or individual pathology – perhaps like that of Meursault in Albert Camus's *L'Étranger* – worthy of a case history or a novel. Much more common is the *conflict* of values, where we find ourselves, not without conceptions of how we should act, but with too many: we are called upon to act in contrary ways. This is the stuff of human life and, in extreme cases, of tragedy.

Every identity carries a conception of its past and its future. The self which acts is always a temporally extended self. It exists, not merely at the moment of action, but through time. As I suggested earlier, memory and anticipation are not merely modes of cognitive access to what we did in the past and will do in the future, but are the very forms through which our identity is constructed. As in memory and anticipation we identify with past and future selves and appropriate their action as ours, so we *make* ourselves one with those past and future selves. Different identities convey different pasts and futures, and they locate us differently in these pasts and futures. As persons, for example, we identify with specific past selves whose actions we are now responsible for, and we project future selves who will bear the responsibility for what we now do. As members of a family, on the other hand, our appropriative memories extend further. We find ourselves with a past which encompasses more than our own individual doings, perhaps as a source of pride, perhaps of shame; and we appropriate a future which extends beyond our own lives. There is nothing mysterious in this. Memories are embodied in institutions and in practices as well as in brain traces. As we live within various institutions and participate in the associated practices, we acquire the appropriate memories. This is not because we have a spiritual access to a past life, but because the environment within which we work out our lives is partly formed through residues of the past. Every present time – every *now* – is in part constituted by a past.

Beneath the various identities which are available to us is the inescapable fact that we are human beings, i.e. we live a particular form of animal life. While this is not itself an identity, it places certain constraints on the kinds of identity available to us. An identity is a form of selfhood: a way of being and saying 'I', and it is difficult, perhaps ultimately impossible, to envisage a self – an 'I' – which endures beyond our own specifically individualised parcel of organic life. When my human life comes to an end, so do I. This does not mean that I cannot appropriate events in the distant past or enjoy the future results of projects which I am not engaged in. But I do this, not as an 'I', but as part of a 'we'. I imagine a community – for example, the family – which is in part defined by these memories and anticipations, which includes me as a member, and where membership contributes to my sense of self. For my identity as a family member, the 'we' – the community – is a condition of existence of the 'I' – the self, and it is through this 'we' that I am able to identify with events in the past and the future. It is perhaps only through the concept of a constitutive community – an 'imagined community' in Benedict Anderson's sense – that we can transcend the limits of our individual lives. The collective 'we' does not eliminate the 'I'; on the contrary, it is its condition of existence. But the 'I' remains a very human and vulnerable one, and will not survive its human extinction. If this were not so, the extreme demands these communities sometimes make of their members would hardly count as *sacrifices*. And the communities themselves are very much concerned with the individual lives of their members. As Hegel saw, much of the business of the family is the concern with the physical vulnerability and mortality of its members.[43]

The concept of identity presupposes the existence of a constitutive linkage between conceptions of the self and forms of social existence. In this sense, *all* identities are social. However, some identities conceal this linkage. As we have seen, the concept of a person presupposes a range of legal/moral practices, but it does not explicitly refer to these. Rather, it focusses on a set of relations which seem only to involve individual persons. There is no 'imagined community' to inform the consciousness of all of us who are persons. Our identity as persons does not require that we be aware of the network of social relation which make this identity possible. It is a form of self-identity which defines an 'I', but not a 'we'. Perhaps it is this feature of personhood which underlies the philosophical temptation to conceive of this identity as asocial, and more fundamental than other explicitly social identities. But it is a mistake to succumb to this temptation: the concept of a person is as much an effect of social institutions and practices as any other.

In the case of identities which are more explicitly social, the individual who bears the identity will be conscious of the significance of certain others to his or her sense of self, and bearers of that identity will find and secure their sense of self through activities directed towards those others. My identity as a parent, for example, is confirmed by actions directed towards the care of my children. Where the identity invokes the idea of a community – the 'imagined community' which informs the activities of its members – bearers of the identity will find and secure their sense of self through activities directed towards that community. For example, one's sense of oneself as a member of a church or a nation – one's religious or national identity – will be confirmed as one acts in ways which are directed towards the preservation of the church or the nation. In these cases, there is no gulf between self and the community: one's self-interest will be furthered as one acts in the interests of the group to which one belongs.

In social life, we occupy many different positions and roles, each of which makes demands of us and which invoke specific expectations. Often we internalise these demands and expectations so they become second nature to us. But not every position or role counts as an identity. The concept of identity comes into play when a self-understanding is pervasive, important and relatively inescapable. An identity is something which we carry with us into a range of different social situations, even when it is not formally in play. It is present, perhaps in the background, but informing our perception of the world and ready to make demands of us. It has a certain centrality to our lives, and its perceptions and demands are not ones we can lightly put aside. They are, in a rather non-Kantian sense, categorical: not merely a means to contingently acquired ends, but a pervasive presence in our lives. Though we may fail to act as an identity requires, this failure will remain with us. This is one of the reasons why conflict between the demands of different identities so often has a tragic dimension. It is not merely that one cannot act as an identity requires; but that one cannot escape the guilt that failure brings with it.

There is a range of borderline cases. We all know of people who have assimilated a role so completely that this has become part of their identity: academics, business people or politicians whose lives are completely dominated by their occupation. We also know of people who adopt as a role what is for others an identity: for example, the busy professional who plays at parenthood. But we should not exaggerate the indeterminacy or the scope of subjective decision. What creates and sustains an identity is not usually the choice of the individual, but the cultural circumstances within which individuals live their lives. It is through interaction with others, the need to be understood and to understand, to act together with others, and to be recognised and confirmed in our lives through our relations with others that our identities are formed.

The fact that we have – in a sense, we are – many selves will often be a problem for us, as each presents different conceptions of the world and makes different demands on us. It may be that finding coherence between these identities is an inescapable project for us. A singular identity is never a given but a project: how to form a unity of the various different and dissonant elements which each of us is. I will return to this question later.

National identity

> To be an African is not a choice, it is a condition...To be [an African] is not through lack of being integrated in Europe...neither is it from regret of the crimes perpetrated by 'my people'...No, it is simply the only opening I have for making use of all my senses and capabilities...The [African] earth was the first to speak. I have been pronounced once and for all.
>
> (Breyten Breytenbach)[44]

For the past two centuries or more, a good deal of rhetoric and a not inconsiderable amount of blood have been expended to demonstrate that our national identity is the primary form of identity available to us, that it underlies and informs all our other identities, and that in case of conflict it should take priority over them. Many people have been prepared to sacrifice, not only themselves but those dear to them, and have put the claims of the nation ahead of the demands of religion, political commitment and morality. We now need to ask: What is it about national identity which has rendered these claims and sacrifices so terribly plausible?

The beginnings of an answer to this question were provided by one of the very first theorists of nationalism, Johann Gottlieb Herder.[45]

Herder argued that a nation is constituted through its language and culture. He emphasised the significance of the practices, customs and rituals of everyday life, and of the stories, folk beliefs and myths in terms of which people make sense of their lives – indeed, he can claim to be one of the first theorists of what we now call 'popular culture'. The most fundamental constituent of a culture was the language in which these stories, beliefs and myths find expression. Language and culture were not, Herder argued, merely aspects of the social environment within which people made their lives; they were constitutive of their very identity. For Herder – as for Charles Taylor who explicitly follows Herder in this respect – human identity exists only in a framework of interpretation. The basic framework is provided by the language and cultural symbols in terms of which we become aware of ourselves and of others. Though our native language is not part of our natural equipment, it becomes a second nature. It provides the taken for granted and inescapable framework within which we think, experience, imagine and dream. It provides us with a primary form of self- and other-consciousness. It is most intimately involved in the ways in which we perceive the world, the forms in which we think, and even in the manner in which we experience our feelings and emotions. But as it enters into our most intimate sense of self, at the same time it defines a special relationship with those other selves who share the same world, think in the same way, and experience the same emotions.

Cultural identity does not always take the form of national identity. As I suggested in Chapter 1, it is plausible to think that, for most of human history, the cultural and linguistic horizons of the vast majority of people were limited to the small rural communities in which they lived. Those who ruled over them did not think of themselves as sharing a common culture with their subjects, and certainly did not claim political legitimacy on this basis. Part of the secret of national identity lies in the emergence of vernacular print languages, their spread through large numbers of the population, and their coming to play a privileged role in public and private life. As these languages formed the identities of those who lived in a particular region, they provided the foundation for a shared sense of belonging to the same community. But a common language is not the whole story. On its own, this would only create an extended network of mutual recognition. The users of a specific language might well recognise other users of that language; but they need not form the concept of a *community* of which they are all members. In this respect they might be like participants who will recognise other participants (potential buyers and sellers), but need not form the concept of a market to which all buyers and sellers belong. Or, to take an example nearer at hand, they might be like persons who recognise other persons (i.e. other bearers of rights and duties), but who do not form the concept of a moral community to which they all belong. So the other aspect of the story of national identity was the mobilisation of linguistic and other cultural resources to create a representation of the *nation* to which those who shared a language and a culture belonged. A nation – like all 'imagined communities' – is not merely an extended web of relationships between those who share a certain identity; it also involves a conception of the community to which the members of the nation belong.[46]

A major source of the strength of national identity has been in its inescapability. For much of the modern world, the nation has appropriated to itself the linguistic and cultural means necessary for the articulation of the sense of self of its members. The fusion of language, culture and polity defined by the nation has so entered our conception of ourselves that it becomes difficult to address the question of who we are except in terms which presuppose that we already have a national identity. As we come to have a sense of who we were, we form a conception of ourselves as belonging to a particular nation. As we speak, we find ourselves spoken for. We are, in Breytenbach's words, 'pronounced, once and for all'. The strength and inescapability of the feelings and commitments associated with national identity has tempted some theorists to see them as evidence of deep and primordial attachments.[47] There is no need to take this route. The language and cultural symbols through which we now understand who we are may be relatively recent phenomena, but for most of us they have come to provide an inescapable structure of experience.

Another aspect of the strength of a national identity lies in the richness of the cultural resources which are employed in forming the conception of national community. This identity provides us with a land in which we are at home, a history which is ours, and a privileged access to a vast heritage of culture and creativity. It not only provides us with the means to understand this heritage; it also assures us that it is *ours*. If on occasion the nation may require that we endure losses and hardships on its behalf, it also makes available a fund of meanings, pleasures and rewards beyond anything that we are likely to find in our individual lives. Where it asks us to make sacrifices, even to the extent of giving up our lives for the sake of the nation, the voluntary act of renunciation exemplifies an identity which transcends the limitations of our own particular and limited concerns. Paradoxically, the greater the sacrifice, the more significant the values embodied in the nation. By its capacity to demand sacrifices, the nation provides its members with a share in a life which transcends their own.[48]

Like other identities, a national identity provides us with a specific *moral* agenda. Indeed, it has been suspicion about the content of this agenda which has led many to be wary of the claims of nationalism. Our national identity, for example, is often used as an argument for the existence of special obligations. It is suggested that I have a responsibility to my compatriots that I do not have to other – perhaps equally deserving – foreigners. That one's fellow nationals are morally privileged in this way has seemed to many as one of the most problematic features of nationalism.[49] What moral reason do I, as a member of a relatively affluent country, have to give preference to someone merely because he or she happens to be a fellow citizen, when there are many who are vastly more in need of assistance? There is a genuine issue here. Too often, national identity has served as a reason to ignore morally more urgent demands outside the borders of one's own nation. Still, we need to recognise that the nation is not the only moral community which privileges mutual responsibilities between members over those from outside the group. To be a member of a family, a group of friends, or even a university, for example, means that one has greater responsibilities to some than one has to others. To enter into certain kinds of human relationship simply *is* to acknowledge that the concerns of those who are also involved in those relationships will, in certain respects, take priority over the concerns of others. These relations are, in part, constituted by a framework of special responsibilities. They could not exist except on this basis.[50] The point is not to object to preferential treatment *per se*. We should rather ask whether the relationship and communities which require preferential treatment are inescapable or desirable features of human life, and whether they contribute to larger human goals. No doubt the extent of the preferential treatment licensed by the nation – and by the family for that matter – should be limited by considerations of equality and justice. But that preferences should be limited does not mean that they should not exist.[51] Indeed, as David Miller has argued, there is good reason to suppose that the nation has provided its members with a stronger motivation to extend their concerns to the needs of a larger community than has the appeal to universal principle.[52]

It is also important to recognise that the existence of special obligations between members of a nation does not exhaust the moral content of national identity. The moral agenda defined by the nation is more complex than this. For example, if I have special responsibilities *to* my co-nationals, e.g. to provide assistance when they need it, to provide for their welfare through the taxation system, etc., it is also the case that I have a special involvement in what they do.[53] This aspect of the moral agenda of national identity is most apparent in those cases where we take pride in the achievements of our co-nationals, for example, in the sporting triumphs of athletes or the discoveries of scientists. This is not a pride in what I as an individual achieved, nor even in what I imagine myself to have achieved. The emotion of pride attests to the belief that I share an identity with the athlete or scientist, and their achievement belongs to all who share that identity. On the other hand, we sometimes find ourselves implicated in the failings of our compatriots. This involvement may be minimal: I feel a twinge of embarrassment at the boorish behaviour of Australian tourists overseas. But it may involve much more than this: I may well feel some responsibility to make amends for what has been done by compatriots, especially if it is done in the name of the nation to which I belong. As with the case of pride, the embarrassment or feeling of responsibility attests to a shared identity.[54]

The moral agenda of national identity overlaps with that of persons, but is not identical with it. As a person, I feel pride or guilt at what I as an individual have done or failed to do. If what I have done is especially meritorious, I may deserve to be rewarded; if it is especially bad, I may deserve to be punished. In each case, the moral responsibility is sheeted home to me as an individual.[55] Guilt, and the sense of pride in which it is the contrary of guilt, belongs within an individualist model agenda. On the other hand, when I am embarrassed at the behaviour of my fellow nationals, the emotion I feel is that of *shame*. Guilt would only be appropriate if I felt that I was somehow responsible for their poor behaviour (perhaps I gave them too much to drink). And when I am proud of my compatriots' achievements, it is not the pride of individual responsibility, but of collective identity. It is not I who should be punished or rewarded; but the individuals concerned.[56]

It is useful to contrast the moral world of persons with that of national identity in terms of their different relations to the past. Part of the process of my becoming a person is learning to take responsibility for my past and carry out the commitments incurred in the past. Acquiring the 'right to make promises' is a crucial part of the moral education of persons. When I discover that I have done things in the past which I have forgotten or repressed, I must recognise that I now must take responsibility for them. Unless special circumstances obtain, the credit or blame which was mine remains. Acquiring a national identity also involves learning to take responsibility for past events. As I become conscious of myself as a member of a nation, I become aware of a certain past – the history of my nation – and I learn to appropriate it as a past which is mine – though one I share with many others. This may be a source of pleasure and pride, or perhaps of shame; in either case, it is a past in which I am morally implicated. I may have been brought up with the idea that my nation had a heroic imperial past; but I am then told that it was one of exploitation and oppression. I may resist this account. But if I am persuaded to accept it, I must also accept that this national repressed past is one for which I must now take some responsibility. What was a source of pride is now a source of shame.

It is this moral involvement in the past which fuels the controversies about the meaning of national histories, for example, of the involvement of the United States in slavery, of postcolonial countries in the expropriation and genocide of their indigenous peoples, of Germany in the Holocaust, and so on, which have been familiar items in recent public debate. These are not matters of mere scholarly interest; they concern the self-conception of the nation, and often define its present responsibilities. It has been suggested by many, even by such sympathetic interpreters of nationalism as Ernest Renan and David Miller, that there is an inevitable element of myth in the stories which nations tell themselves.[57] No doubt this is true. But it should not be exaggerated. Celebratory national histories are subject to public debate and criticism; and it is not inevitable that the forces of historical self-justification and glorification will win out. The long and painful debates about national histories, in the United States, Germany, Canada and Australia, would be pointless unless there was some commitment to establishing the truth about the national past.

If the moral agenda associated with national identity includes an involvement with the national past, it may well carry with it a responsibility to make reparation for what was done in the past.[58] To many this has seemed unjust. Why should people living now be held to share responsibility for acts which were performed (in some cases) many years before they were born? While this is not the place to explore this issue in depth (I will say something more about it in the next section), it is important to distinguish the different ways in which the issue of 'collective responsibility' arises in the moral world of persons and in other spheres. As persons, we can only be held responsible for the consequences of acts which we as individuals have performed. We have a general responsibility to respect the rights of other persons, but, after that, our responsibilities are up to us. But of course we are not just persons, and this is not the only moral world we inhabit. As I have already noted, as members of a family, we may find that we have responsibilities – and also sources of pleasure and pride – which are not consequent upon anything that we as an individual have done. As a member of a nation we are in a similar position. Our national identity carries with it a moral involvement in our nation's past and its future, an involvement which may bring with it special sources of joy and happiness, but also special responsibilities to compensate, make reparation, or to remember.

In certain circumstances, governments inherit the obligation to make reparation for what was done in the past. For example, the postwar Federal Republic of Germany acknowledged its responsibility to make reparations for crimes committed against Jews by its predecessor. There is an institutional imperative here. There must be a mechanism which establishes a continuity of commitment between one government and its successor. However, underlying this mechanism, even in the case of institutional continuity but especially where one form of State power replaces another (as in the German case), is the idea that it is the nation which inherits the responsibilities – as well as the glories – of its past.

For most of us, our national identity was not chosen, but determined by the contingencies of birth and upbringing. It is this very contingency which makes this identity seem morally suspect. How can something so arbitrary, over which I have had such little control, determine a significant part of my moral agenda? Part of the answer lies in the fact that these contingencies have become pervasive and inescapable features of our lives. They come to us in the language we speak, the culture we identify with, and the political responsibilities we may evade but which we cannot escape. If, from a more global perspective, they are local and particular, they have come to form an essential part of identity. As such, they bring with them commitments and responsibilities which we may evade, but we cannot deny.[59] The contours of national identity are often most apparent to the expatriate, most poignantly perhaps to the political exile. That the experience of exile is one of loss, even of tragedy; and the fact that the political allegiances of so many exiles still lie with the destiny of their nation attests to the centrality of national identity in our lives. Even those, who think of themselves in transnational or cosmopolitan terms, still find themselves morally implicated by what has been done in the name of their nation, as Australians are implicated in the expropriation and genocide of the Aboriginal population, Americans in slavery, Germans in the Holocaust, English in Ireland, and so on. The moral reach of national identity remains present, even in the thoughts and emotions of those who would reject the claims of nationalism.

National identity and moral philosophy

National identity is only one of the identities available to us. The fact that it has often asserted a priority over other identities gives us no reason to believe that it *ought* to have priority. Indeed, there has seemed to many good reason to argue that it ought not. As I have already mentioned, liberals are often sceptical about the particularism of nationalism: the fact that it stands in the way of more universalistic commitments. These worries deepen when we take into account the evils that have been enacted in the name of the nation. All too often, nationalism has been associated with the denigration of and contempt for people of other nations. The rhetoric of nationalism has mobilised millions of men – and sometimes women – to kill or be killed on behalf of their nation. There is no end to the stories of human barbarity and suffering inflicted by otherwise decent people for no better reason than that it was demanded of them by their nation. Confronted with the horrors of modern nationalism, it is all too tempting to deny it any moral credibility whatsoever. That we have a certain national identity may be an inescapable fact of modern life; but it seems that we should not lend this fact any moral legitimacy by deducing values from it.

The specific problems concerning national identity only give an especially dramatic form to the problems of allowing moral force to *any* identity. After all, an identity is only the subjective mode of existence of a set of social practices and institutions, and the values and norms associated with that identity are those required by those practices and institutions. The fact that these have entered into the way in which we experience ourselves and the world gives them a presence that is hard to escape; in the final analysis they represent what exists, not what *ought* to exist. Surely what is needed, it might be argued, is a moral standpoint from which we can evaluate existing practices and institutions, and the identities they inform. The attempt to establish a standpoint of this kind has been almost definitive of the project of modern moral philosophy. It was most clearly formulated by Kant, but it also underlies the enterprise of classical utilitarianism.

In one way or another, moral philosophers have sought to leave behind the realm of the merely social and contingent in order to discover values and norms by which they might assess the social and contingent. It has been the project of moral philosophy to establish an 'ought to be' of morality with which to evaluate the 'is' of everyday moral consciousness.

This is not the place to mount a sustained critique of this project. Nor would I want to reject it altogether. Indeed, as I will suggest shortly, this tradition of moral inquiry has much to contribute to ordinary moral understanding. However, there are large problems in the way of this project. There is no agreement on the epistemology underlying it. We simply do not know how to go about discovering and validating a set of moral principles which might be used to assess existing moral practices. We might compare the situation in moral philosophy with that of the natural sciences, where there is, if not agreement, at least convergence both on the procedures needed to establish principles which are worthy of assent by informed members of the relevant community and on the kinds of criticism which might appropriately be levelled at these procedures. It is an index of the epistemological force of these procedures that, when there is an apparent conflict between our common-sense knowledge of the natural world and the deliverances of science, we are usually prepared to forego common sense and to prefer the latter, especially where we also have an account of why common sense lets us down. Nothing like this obtains in moral philosophy, nor is it likely to.[60] There is no convergence on procedures and appropriate forms of criticism and very few of us would be prepared to allow the conclusions of the seminar room and the treatise to override the firm convictions of everyday life.

Even if philosophers were to discover moral principles by which they might evaluate existing social practices and their associated forms of identity, it is not clear what *motivational* purchase these principles would have on us. The principles would of necessity be highly general and abstract – they would enjoin us to seek the greatest happiness of the greatest number, to act on universalisable principles, and the like. However, the motives we have tend to be local and specific. It is difficult to see how the principles sought by moral philosophers would have a significant presence in our everyday moral deliberations, especially if they were at variance with our ordinary moral practices. If the ultimate point of acquiring moral knowledge is to inform our practice, then it must have some purchase on our motives, at least in the sense that it provides for us reasons to act in one way rather than another. Whatever the final content of morality, its message must be addressed to those who are supposed to be subject to it.[61]

Perhaps the basic problem with the project of moral philosophy lies in its ambivalent relation to the moral knowledge that we already have. Officially, the search for moral principles aims to replace the – presumably inadequate – moral knowledge that we exercise in ordinary life. However, when it comes to the point few but the most confident of moral theorists have been prepared to assert the priority of theory over practice, and most have tried to render the deliverances of theory compatible with our antecedent moral convictions. A more consistent procedure would be to take these moral convictions seriously from the beginning. After all, we do not undertake the task of deciding how we should act from a moral void. As I have already pointed out, we are already within morality. A better way to conceive of the enterprise of moral philosophy is not that it should aim to *replace* our existing moral knowledge, but that it should make it *better*.

But how to go about this? Clearly, we should begin by attempting to discover what our moral knowledge is. We need to reflect on our everyday moral judgements – in a cool hour, as it were – in order to discern the principles and values they express. We should attempt to make it more systematic, to resolve inconsistencies, and so on. We do not need to have immediate recourse to highly abstract and speculative moral theory in order to find criteria by which to improve the moral knowledge that we already have. What we do need is the capacity to reflect on this knowledge in order to establish its general organising principles and deal with tensions and inconsistencies within it. The tools necessary to take the first step in moral reflection are those provided by the precepts of common-sense reason. Of course, we need to go further than this. We must be prepared to learn from the arguments of moral philosophers. Not only is the tradition of moral philosophy a rich source of moral insights, but the enterprise of moral theory – the attempt to systematise morality by reference to a set of very general principles – will suggest ways in which our ordinary moral knowledge might be improved. We have, for example, to consider our normal moral preference for those who are close to us in the light of the demands of impartiality conveyed by, say, utilitarian and Kantian approaches to morality. This may lead us to reject the requirements of universalistic theory, or perhaps to work out complexities in their application, or to change our everyday conception of what morality requires, or at least to understand its limitations.

This procedure will be familiar to students of John Rawls's conception of 'reflective equilibrium' as he presented it in *A Theory of Justice*.[62] On the account Rawls provided there, the aim of moral philosophy is to bring the results of philosophical investigation into line with our considered moral judgements. This does not mean that our everyday moral judgements – our 'moral intuitions' – are the final arbiters of philosophical acceptability. It may be that on reflection we are prepared to change our moral intuitions when confronted with a sufficiently attractive moral theory. However, the other alternative is also possible: we may change the theory in order to make it acceptable to our moral intuition. Or it may be that we will do both. The task of moral philosophy is the never completed search for a reflective equilibrium between the deliverances of philosophy and those of everyday morality.

This account has the great merit of taking ordinary moral knowledge seriously, but not too seriously. It provides it with a voice in the debate, but not the last word. However, it retains too great an attachment to the project of moral philosophy. As presented in *A Theory of Justice* , the quest for reflective equilibrium is the search for a consensus between two voices, that of moral intuition on the one side, and moral philosophy on the other. This gives moral philosophy far too big a say in the debate. Although it is one of the voices which should engage with ordinary moral knowledge, it is not the only one. There are other voices which deserve to be heard. In later accounts, Rawls explicitly recognises this and presents a broader conception of reflective equilibrium.[63] The consensus sought now involves three participants: moral intuition, moral philosophy, and a set of relevant background theories. The final category is a rather heterogeneous one, but includes those empirical theories which bear on the content and place of morality, for example, accounts of human psychology, social and political theory, accounts of the role of morality in society, and so on.

This triadic model is certainly an improvement. However, it will be misleading if it tempts us to underestimate the variety of forms of knowledge which might be subsumed under 'relevant background theory'. Two of these are especially important, though they receive very little attention in Rawls. One of these is knowledge of moral practices other than our own. Sometimes we will acquire this knowledge through the work of anthropologists and historians; but on other – and more unsettling – occasions it will be through acquaintance with the lives of our neighbours. The knowledge that our taken for granted morality is not the only one should make an important contribution to the assessment of our own. However, in order properly to hear the voice of different moral practices we must be prepared to treat them, as we treat our own moral practices, as forms of moral *knowledge*. We must recognise that a conception of morality is an attempt to answer certain basic moral questions. What is the good life for human beings? What forms of social relationship are conducive to the good life? What forms of human conduct should be absolutely prohibited? Different conceptions of morality – those of other cultures or of our own culture at other times – provide different answers to these questions. Sometimes these are merely different: they indicate alternative ways in which people might choose to live (just as the life of philosophy is an alternative to that of a musician, neither better nor worse). Sometimes they are competing, as a belief in hierarchy competes with the principle of equality, and we need to consider which is *better*. This is not an easy task. It would be impossible, if we were not able to conceive of the moralities which contained these principles as providing competing answers to the same fundamental questions.

Being forced to recognise the very specific and limited nature of some of the moral knowledge which we claim as our own is a first step towards a more adequate form of that knowledge. It also requires another form of investigation. We need to inquire into the social and historical conditions for particular forms of moral knowledge. It is after all an anthropological truism that the kinds of moral practices appropriate to a small hunter–gatherer society are likely to be quite different to those appropriate to a mass society based on industrial production and the market. To take an example which will be of concern in the next chapter, it is likely that a certain conception of individual freedom is characteristic of and perhaps unique to Western modernity. This suggests that we should be prepared to investigate what it is about the modern world which has encouraged or made possible this particular emphasis and what it is about other societies which has encouraged different emphases. This investigation may reinforce the belief in the centrality of individual freedom; but it may also suggest limitations. This suggests that different moralities may be good – or bad – answers to certain questions *under certain historical and social conditions*. Of course it may then be possible to argue that these conditions themselves ought to be changed, but this in turn requires that we consider whether these changes are possible or desirable.[64]

I have argued in Chapter 1 that we have reason to suppose that nationalism is characteristic of, even if not quite unique to, modern societies. The methodological principle underlying this argument was that we will be in a better position to appreciate both the moral strengths and limitations of nationalism when we have identified the features of the modern world which have made this particular conception of commitment attractive and plausible. That certain forms of moral knowledge have specific historical conditions does not of itself invalidate them; it does however provide the basis for understanding them a good deal better. We will only be in a position to pass judgement on the claims that a national identity makes on us when we are able to comprehend its role in modern social and political life. Until we are able seriously to consider alternatives, then the fact that its demands may conflict with those of other moral principles presents us with a moral problem to resolve; it does not provide a reason for rejecting the conception altogether.

On this account, the search for reflective equilibrium must encompass a broader range of issues than Rawls, at least explicitly, allows himself. Still, it is important to retain one of Rawls's central ideas: that the notion of a 'reflective equilibrium' serves as a heuristic ideal, rather than something we will ever reach.[65] We have no better reason to expect that we will arrive at a final resting point to knowledge than in any other scientific or cultural inquiry. There is no end to the kinds of knowledge which bear on the issue of how we might best live together with other humans, and thus no end to the possibility of debate and revision of our moral ideals.

The great advantage of this procedure is that it should keep us in contact with the motivation already associated with our existing moral knowledge. As I suggested earlier in this chapter, our self-interpretations – our identities – provide us with moral perspectives on the world. These perspectives will provide interpretations of the world which call upon us to act in appropriate ways because they have a meaning – an 'import' – which speaks to us. The task of improving our moral knowledge does not require that we ignore our existing motivation; it is rather that we attempt to render it more coherent. Our moral knowledge is not merely an interpretation of the world; it also expresses the way in which we interpret ourselves. But these ways are plural, and sometimes they conflict. Indeed, the moral conflicts with which we are most familiar are not those between ourselves and others, but occur within ourselves, as different interpretations of the world – different identities – struggle with each other. The notion of reflective equilibrium suggests that it is when we are able adequately to resolve these conflicts that we move towards a more coherent body of moral knowledge. A latent tension, uncertainty or ambiguity has become explicit and has been removed, clarified, or reinterpreted.

There is no reason to resist the thought that this is a movement towards moral truth. But it is also a movement towards a more unified sense of self. The ever receding moment at which we achieve reflective equilibrium is also the moment at which we finally acquire a coherent sense of who we are – we 'become what we are' in Nietzsche's phrase.[66] Moral inquiry is the search for reflective equilibrium; as such, it is the search for a final answer to the question 'How should I live?' It is also, I suggest, coextensive with the search for a final answer to the question 'Who am I?'

It is at the level of reflection on our moral knowledge that we can properly come to terms with the place of freedom in our moral lives. Let us consider, to take an especially pertinent example, the issue of collective responsibility: the idea that we may, as members of a family, a nation or some other community, find ourselves morally implicated by the actions of others. To many, the suggestion that we may share some responsibility for actions we have not performed – and even, in some cases, would not have performed – has seemed to offend against a strong intuition that we are morally responsible for what we ourselves do and not, except in clearly defined and limited circumstances, for what others do. This intuition finds expression in the doctrine of 'voluntarism' (I borrow the terminology from Samuel Scheffler): 'all genuine special responsibilities must be based on consent or on some other voluntary act'.[67] Prima facie, this doctrine is not especially plausible. Our everyday moral practices define a realm of responsibility which extends well beyond the reach of what we have freely chosen to do. We expect children to have a special concern for the well-being of their parents, citizens for their country, and so on, and these responsibilities do not on the face of it stem from a voluntary act. Of course, the voluntarist may choose to deny the existence of these special responsibilities; or to argue that contrary to appearances they do stem from a voluntary act (e.g. the acceptance of benefits); or make use of some combination of these strategies. While these strategies do not seem very promising, there is no doubt that the intuition behind the voluntarist position is an attractive one, and that an adequate account of moral obligation must do justice to it. So let us try another tack.

Even the most committed voluntarist will accept that there are *some* responsibilities which are not based on consent or some analogous voluntary act. The doctrine of voluntarism is limited to *special* responsibilities, i.e. responsibilities which some of us have to particular others. There are, however, *general* responsibilities – the 'natural duties' – which *all* of us have to *all* others. These include the obligation to respect the rights of others, to keep our promises, and so on. These cannot be conceived of as voluntarily entered into.[68] It would be immoral to suppose that I only have an obligation not to harm others if I have agreed to it; it is incoherent to think that every obligation, including the obligation to keep my promises, stems from a promise. These duties must, therefore, receive a different justification. They provide the moral framework within which we exercise our freedom of choice; they are not themselves the product of this same freedom. Most of us would also recognise that it is an important part of our moral education that we come to recognise that our freedom of choice should be limited by these duties: that we accept the obligation to keep our promises, not to harm others, and so on. This does not mean, however, that freedom has no place here. We exercise our freedom, not as a condition of incurring these obligations, but when we reflect on this framework, come to understand the conditions under which it arose, consider the possibility of alternative frameworks, and so on. In the process of philosophical reflection, we evaluate the ways in which we are inscribed into certain moral agendas and the moral agendas themselves. This process of reflection – the search for reflective equilibrium – may or may not leave the agendas unchanged. What is important in this context is that it is an exercise in freedom, but a different kind of freedom to that which the framework of natural duties makes possible.

The special responsibilities which we have for the actions of those who are members of certain moral communities are subject to the same process of reflection and criticism. It is rare that we acquire these responsibilities, for example, those to family members or to compatriots, by specific acts of choice. For most of us, they are the results of the contingencies of birth and culture. This does not mean, however, that they are not subject to evaluation and change as the result of philosophical reflection. We exercise our freedom, not in incurring these responsibilities, but in reflecting on them. To the extent they survive this process of reflection, i.e. they are acceptable in reflective equilibrium, then we have reason to accept these obligations.[69] In this respect, they are in exactly the same position as our natural duties. The mistake of voluntarism is not in the emphasis on freedom. If we are to have reason to accept our responsibilities, they must survive the test of freedom. But this does not mean they must be preceded by an act of choice. Indeed, it may well be a condition of the moral framework constituted by these responsibilities that it not be conceived of as subject to choice. We shall return to this issue in the next chapter.

In so far as our national identity has asserted a certain precedence over other identities, it has claimed to be at least part of the final answer to the question of how we might live. But rarely if ever has it claimed to be a complete answer. Our national identity provides us with a place in the world and a perspective on it. It will be a presence in many, and perhaps all of our dealings with the world, and, on occasion, it will make certain demands on us. Its claim to priority consists in the fact that these demands will claim precedence over values and commitments. However, there are many areas of life about which our national identity is silent. It has little to say about how we should conduct ourselves with our friends and lovers, colleagues and bosses, and so on. Unlike religion, nationalism rarely claims to be a comprehensive moral doctrine. It provides the space, therefore, for other identities, and there is always potential conflict between them. One of those identities, that of personhood, is the basic form of identity required by a liberal programme, and as such has been the favoured candidate for moral supremacy proposed by many philosophers. My argument in this chapter has been that there is no special reason why it should be given that priority. We shall see, in the next chapter, there is some reason to suppose that it should not be.

3 Three concepts of freedom
Liberalism, republicanism and nationalism

I have already touched on the central place that freedom occupies amongst the values of the modern world. Indeed, it may well be *the* central value of modernity. Every significant political ideology professes to speak in the name of freedom, and, while the accounts they provide of freedom differ, each claims to have captured its essence and that the pretensions of its competitors are bogus.

In this chapter, I wish to evaluate these claims with respect to three major political doctrines at work in the modern world. The central concern of *liberalism* is with the freedom of individuals to make up their own minds how they are to live. For reasons which are historically – if not philosophically – inescapable, liberals have considered that the main threat to freedom has come from the actions of others, and especially of the minions of the State; so the liberal affirmation of freedom of choice has been combined with the idea that freedom is best secured when the individual is protected from others. Freedom is conceived '*negatively*' as the *absence* of certain kinds of interference. This understanding of freedom contrasts with a strong *republican* tradition in which the various responsibilities associated with citizenship, and in particular the responsibility to sustain the political community, are conceived of as modes of free activity. While there are various ways in which this more '*positive*' conception of freedom may be interpreted, I will suggest that the most attractive account involves the idea that political activity is a form of *self-formation*: in political activity, citizens form themselves, and, at the same time, form the State to which they are subject. The *nationalist* understanding of freedom often makes use of the rhetoric of republicanism, and is in some respects quite close to it. However, the dominant (and most defensible) nationalist conception of freedom involves living in a social and political world which expresses and sustain one's national identity. Freedom is a matter of being 'at home' in the world. Citizens do not form the State through their own activity; rather, they find themselves in it. It is a form of representation – cultural *mimesis* – not of political activity, which constitutes the relationship between the individual and the State.

As will emerge, there are various relationships of interdependence between these conceptions. I will suggest that the negative freedom valued by liberals presupposes a characteristically republican conception of positive freedom. However, I will also suggest that the traditional republican understanding of political community is no longer viable (it is a moot point whether it ever was), and that the freedom valued by the republican must take a nationalist form. In brief, the argument of this chapter is that a responsible liberal will be a republican, but that a modern republican should be a nationalist. No doubt there are also tensions between the various conceptions of freedom; however, there is no reason to assume that any one of them can claim to be the sole legitimate conception. Debates about freedom are not advanced by the assumption that there is one and only one genuine conception, and the rest are fraudulent.

My major concern here, as elsewhere in this book, is with the modern world. However, it will be useful to begin with a conception of political life and the place of freedom within it as these may have existed in the ancient world. This will serve to provide a contrast with the conceptions of political life and freedom which are available in the modern world. Making the social preconditions of this model explicit may also serve as a partial antidote for the nostalgia for antiquity which continues to play such a prominent role in much contemporary political philosophy.

Freedom and citizenship in the classical world

Once upon a time, perhaps in the Greek city state and the early Roman Republic of philosophical imagination, freedom was identical with citizenship. But what sense of freedom and what of citizenship were required to sustain this equation? Can it be recreated in the very different conditions of the modern world? And if so, at what cost?

To be a citizen in what I will call the 'classical' sense was to be free, and this privileged status was contrasted with the unfreedom of those, such as slaves, who lacked it.[1] It required that the citizen participate in those activities – perhaps including contribution to law making, administration, cultural and religious activities, military service, and the like – which were conceived of as necessary to sustain the *polis* to which he belonged.[2] No doubt the citizen was free of the constraints which defined the lives of his slaves (and, for that matter, his wife), but it was the activities which he was expected to undertake, not the absence of constraints, which constituted his freedom.

There are two ways in which we can make sense of this identification of freedom with certain privileged activities. The first is through the idea that these activities express a man's essential nature. If, as Aristotle had it, 'man is by nature a political animal',[3] then he realises his nature by being a citizen and by involving himself in the activities appropriate to citizenship. For Aristotle, man is oriented towards a good appropriate to his nature, and fulfilling the responsibilities of citizenship will be a means towards that good and partially constitutive of it. In acting as a citizen, the individual will contribute to the well-being of the State, and his own happiness will consist at least in part in making that contribution. His life will then express what he essentially is, and this congruence between activity and essence is freedom. The second way of making sense of the identification of freedom with citizenship is also to be found in Aristotle, though it is perhaps only in retrospect distinguishable from the first. The life of politics involved participation in law making, the direction of State policy and the selection of public officials. The citizen was one who was not ruled by anyone else (he was not a slave or a woman), but was involved in the process of ruling himself. In so far as this required that he also be ruled by others, these others were essentially like himself. To be ruled by them was not different in kind to being ruled by one's own (better) self. Politics was self-rule, and self-rule was a good appropriate to humans. So freedom was not simply the realisation of a pre-existing essence; it was also the exercise of political sovereignty. And, for Aristotle at least, this exercise was the appropriate expression of man's political nature.

The conception of politics involved here was a broad one. Though it was structured around affairs which are political in a narrow sense – contestations for power, defence of the State against internal and external enemies, distribution of those benefits which are at the disposal of the State – it also encompassed religious, social and cultural activities. The life of politics which was required of citizens was a rich and no doubt a rewarding one.

According to Michael Walzer, as the Roman Republic extended its dominion and began to grant citizenship to culturally and ethnically distinct peoples, a new understanding of citizenship developed.[4] By the first century AD, citizenship had come to mean a claim to be treated with respect, not to be hindered as one went about one's business, to have certain legal privileges, and to be protected in these claims by the

Roman state. It no longer involved the responsibility to contribute to its political life. This more passive or, as I will call it, 'formal' sense of citizenship re-emerged in the absolutist states of early modern Europe, and has since come to constitute the dominant legal understanding of citizenship in the modern world. By the eighteenth century people were beginning to conceive of their well-being in terms of the pursuit of wealth and of domestic happiness. Citizenship provided the framework of rights which enabled the individual to pursue these goals. If the classical conception presupposed that the business of politics was central to human life, the formal conception assumed that the life of the citizen was centred elsewhere. In these circumstances, the responsibilities which were associated with belonging to a particular political community came to be thought of as duties, perhaps important, but external to the main business of life. At the same time, the practice of politics came to be more narrowly conceived, more or less exclusively concerned with power, authority, defence, administration and the like. Social, cultural and religious life took place elsewhere.

Corresponding to the formal conception of citizenship has been the emergence of a new understanding of freedom. For the modern world, freedom is not a matter of expressing a pre-given essence, nor does it consist in the exercise of one's political responsibilities. Freedom is the capacity to choose between a range of alternatives; it is the right of individuals to make up their own minds about what to believe, how to act, and how to live their lives. The free individual is one whose actions correspond to his or her choices. According to Hegel:

> The right of the subject's *particularity* to find satisfaction, or – to put it differently – the right of *subjective freedom*, is the pivotal and focal point in the difference between *antiquity* and the *modern* age.[5]

If, on the classical conception, the free activity of the citizen expressed a nature which he had in common with other citizens, the modern sphere of freedom enables each individual to express what is specific and even unique.

It is this new understanding of freedom which is celebrated in Benjamin Constant's famous address, 'The liberty of the ancients compared with that of the moderns'. For the ancients, Constant argued, liberty was bought at the price of an enormous amount of surveillance and control over the details of their day to day existence, including their opinions, their religious beliefs, their occupations, and even their family lives. For moderns, on the other hand, it is precisely these areas which are of primary concern. Freedom is the right to make up one's own mind about religion and other matters, to travel freely, to choose one's own occupation, to own property, and so on. If ancient liberty was the 'active and constant participation in public power', modern liberty consists in 'peaceful enjoyment and private independence'.[6] While modern citizens might claim certain political rights – perhaps to vote in occasional elections, to petition the authorities, and so on – the freedom they cherish is that of being left alone to lead their own lives in their own way. The exercise of political rights is at best a means towards that end.

The classical identification of freedom with citizenship has had its adherents in the modern world. Both Constant and Walzer cite Rousseau and the Jacobins in the French Revolution as advocates of this identification, and both argue that the attempt to recreate classical citizenship with its attendant concept of liberty in the changed circumstances of the modern world can only lead to disaster. The classical notion of citizenship was appropriate only to small-scale societies, in which it is plausible to think of politics as the business of all citizens, whose contributions all make a noticeable impact on the deliberations of the group as a whole. Formal citizenship is more appropriate to a large-scale anonymous society, where politics is the specialised business of a relatively small number of people in the community. Constant argued that modern commercial societies both require and generate a spirit of independence, which will only be thwarted by direct Government interference. In a commercial society, in which each occupation demands its own specialised training and knowledge, it is natural to suppose that the business of government should be left to the experts, and the role of the citizen become the more passive one of keeping to the rules of political life.

If these considerations suggest that the classical identification of freedom with citizenship is unavailable in the modern world, there are also reasons to think that it is undesirable. However it is understood, politics is a time-consuming activity. As Constant emphasised, citizens were only free to devote their best energies to the life of the *polis* on condition that non-citizens were able to take care of more mundane activities. Though many citizens were forced to undertake manual labour, this was a matter of shame. As Perry Anderson has pointed out,[7] the idea of labour was tainted by the fact that it was performed by slaves. It is noteworthy that the way of life which Aristotle and other philosophers thought appropriate to the citizen of the Greek city state did not include manual labour.[8] In practice, political life in classical Athens was dominated by the wealthier slave-owning citizens, who had the free time to devote to it. A similar pattern of exclusion arises with domestic labour and the having and raising of children. Just because the essence of the Aristotelian citizen was to spend his life in the public sphere, private domestic activities were marginalised. Women were counted as citizens for the purposes of reproduction, but were not expected to participate in political life. This meant that central human activities – productive labour and family life – were excluded from the form of life which realised the nature of the ideal citizen. This pattern of exclusion meant that the classical concept of citizenship could not be universalised. The way of life of the citizen was available to some only on condition that it was not available to all. The freedom of the citizens was dependent on the unfreedom of slaves and women.

By the eighteenth century it had become much less fashionable to define the human essence in terms of political activities. Labour was no longer conceived as a more or less unfortunate necessity, but close to the core of a fully human existence. Many – Marx in some moods, for example – were tempted to define the human essence in terms of productive activity. Others – including Kant and Hegel, and Marx in other moods – were more inclined to see human nature in terms of the capacity for freedom. Both moves were in keeping with modern social developments; and neither were compatible with the classical justification of citizenship. By contrast, the more formal conception of citizenship seems to require no special assumptions about the nature of a full human life. To be a citizen is to be free to pursue any of a wide range of activities. It does not therefore require any special pattern of exclusions. All it demands is that those who live their lives within and through certain political structures be ascribed certain rights and duties. While this conception of citizenship began its history as the prerogative of a minority within the relevant political community, it was extended, and continues to be so. Prima facie, there is nothing in the formal conception of citizenship which precludes it from becoming universal.

From negative to positive freedom

Isaiah Berlin's 'Two concepts of liberty' is a canonical text of contemporary liberalism.[9] The distinction which gives the essay its title – between 'negative' and 'positive' conceptions of liberty – was used by Berlin and countless followers to draw a line between the liberal tradition and its enemies (who are sometimes enemies within its own ranks). I will argue here that the distinction will not bear the weight that is put on it. This is not merely because it is – as Berlin himself recognises – a blurred and shifting one, but because a serious concern with liberty in the negative sense must carry with it an engagement with liberty in its positive sense as well.[10]

At the heart of Berlin's account of negative freedom is the idea that our freedom is defined by the range of choices which are available to us and is diminished when the range is limited as a consequence of human interference. Negative freedom is 'the absence of obstacles to possible choices and activities'.[11] Freedom in this negative sense is closely related, as Berlin acknowledges, to Constant's notion of 'modern' liberty, and also, as he does not, to Hegel's idea of 'subjective freedom': it is the right of 'particularity to find satisfaction'. This conception of freedom is, Berlin, Constant and Hegel all agree, especially characteristic of, and perhaps even unique to, the modern world.

The conceptual centre of the contrasting notion of positive freedom is the idea of self-mastery. Berlin introduces positive freedom as 'the freedom which consists of being one's own master',[12] and he displays the different forms of positive freedom as variant interpretations of the notion of 'self'. A problem with this characterisation is that there is a perfectly good sense of self-mastery in which it is not distinct from, but is presupposed by, Berlin's favoured conception of negative freedom. In a minimal sense, self-mastery may be understood as the capacity to impose some order on one's desires so that one is able to act in a reasonably coherent way. A condition of this kind would not be necessary if humans were relatively simple creatures with only a few needs, living in an environment which did not provide too great a diversity of ways in which these needs might be satisfied. Freedom – if such beings were to have a use for the concept – might consist in not being constrained from acting to satisfy the strongest desire of the moment. But human existence is not like this. We have an enormous variety of different desires and the social world we inhabit provides a vast number of different routes towards their gratification. We must learn to impose some order of priority on our desires, appreciate the difference between those which are long term and those which are transient, and not simply be at the mercy of the strongest desire of the moment. If we were not able to have some degree of rational agency, we could not be said to be free, nor would freedom be a value worth aspiring to. No doubt spelling out the conditions of rational agency will not be easy; but this provides no reason to suppose that they are not necessary for freedom of the most negative kind. It is not easy to conceive of someone valuing negative freedom who did not also value self-mastery in this minimal sense. Of course it may be, as Berlin argues, that the term 'self-mastery' – 'with its suggestion of a man divided against himself'[13] – lends itself to manipulation, and this may provide a reason to avoid it. But the *concept* – and most contemporary philosophers speak of 'autonomy' here – is crucial to any understanding of freedom.

If there is an acceptable understanding of self-mastery in which it is a necessary condition of negative freedom, the fragile unity of Berlin's conception of positive freedom shatters. The one term covers a variety of different conceptions. This in itself may not matter too much, for there is little doubt which is the most important of these. The conception of positive freedom which Berlin is most concerned to reject is that which identifies freedom with a prescribed range of actions. Freedom in this sense involves acting in a certain prescribed way. This notion of positive freedom is, as Charles Taylor puts it, an 'exercise' concept; the contrasting notion of negative freedom is an 'opportunity' concept.[14] In the central cases discussed by Berlin, the claim that certain actions constitute freedom is justified by the argument that these actions express the 'real nature' or the 'true self' of the individual. (This provides one of the links with the notion of 'self-mastery'.) A further step is taken when the 'real nature' or 'true self' is endowed with certain social characteristics, and the way is then open for the equation of the life of the citizen, including the various services to the State that it involves, with freedom. Berlin argues that it is this identification, or 'monstrous impersonation', which has licensed oppression in the name of freedom. It leads directly to the disastrous Rousseauian paradox that men may need to be forced to be free.

We should certainly share Berlin's worries about the possible misuse of the concept of freedom. But the roots of Rousseau's paradox lie much deeper than he is prepared to allow. Rousseau's own version of the argument is worth considering:

> [W]hoever refuses to obey the general will shall be constrained to do so by the whole body; which means nothing else but that he shall be forced to be free; for such is the condition which, uniting every Citizen to his Homeland, guarantees him from all personal dependence, a condition that ensures the control and working of the political machine, and alone renders legitimate civil engagements, which, without it, would be absurd and tyrannical, and subject to the most enormous abuse.[15]

The fact that we are subject to the State – that our individual wills are subject to the 'general will' – is not a matter of choice. If we live in a certain territory we are, *eo ipso*, under the authority of the laws and edicts of the local state; and, if we move, it will be to exchange that authority, not to escape it. If negative freedom is freedom of choice, then our subjection to the State does not fall within the sphere of negative freedom. Rousseau's argument is that we will not enjoy personal independence, the freedom to enter into engagements with others, and so on, unless we live our lives in the context of State authority. In other words, subjection to the State is a necessary condition for freedom of choice. That is why we must be (and Rousseau uses the phrase with deliberate irony) 'forced to be free'.

It is important to recognise that this argument does not depend upon an appeal to a positive conception of freedom. Indeed, Quentin Skinner has recently argued that the conclusion can be derived from Berlin's favoured conception of negative liberty.[16] Skinner bases his argument on a reading of Machiavelli and the republican tradition he inaugurated. He argues that Machiavelli rejected the idea that there are certain ways of life which are constitutive of freedom, and adopted an exemplary negative conception of freedom: being able to choose from a variety of goals. Machiavelli did not assume that there is a socially committed true self underlying the selfishness, ambition and laziness which are all too manifest in political and social life. He argued, however, that freedom in the negative sense is only possible within a certain form of political life, essentially that of the citizen of a self-governing republic. Of course, citizens are subject to the rule of law, and this means that certain activities are not available to them. But the rule of law also makes possible a range of choices which would not otherwise be available. The freedoms which are diminished by the law are insignificant when compared with those which are enabled. Law, on this account, is not the enemy of freedom, as Berlin (following Hobbes and Bentham) was to argue; it is its condition. So even with a negative conception of freedom, it makes sense to argue that we may need to be forced to be free.

Philip Pettit has presented a stronger version of this argument. According to Pettit, the conception of freedom central to the republican tradition is not merely freedom from interference, but *independence*, i.e. freedom from *domination* by others.[17] For example, it may well be that a slave whose master is too beneficent or lazy to interfere with his activities will suffer no more *actual* interference than a citizen. In this situation each will enjoy the same degree of negative freedom as the other. However, Pettit argues that citizens enjoy a freedom denied to slaves: their lives are not dependent upon the will of another. Or, to take an example which was of concern to John Stuart Mill, a nineteenth-century husband might well not have made use of the legal powers assigned to him; nevertheless, his wife's freedom was dependent upon his good will. In order to capture the sense in which the slave and the wife lacked freedom, Pettit suggests that it involves the absence of domination. Freedom in this sense is achieved when one is not dependent on, or in other ways subject to, the arbitrary will of another.

Pettit claims that freedom as non-domination is a third conception, intermediate between negative and positive freedom. However, it is considerably closer in spirit to the negative than the positive conception.[18] Both negative freedom and freedom as non-domination are defined as the *absence* of freedom-diminishing conditions – coercion and domination respectively; both are 'opportunity' rather than 'exercise' concepts – they do not suggest that a certain privileged activity is constitutive of freedom. If the conception of freedom as non-domination goes beyond the strict conception of negative freedom,[19] it does so without defining freedom in terms of a certain preferred activity, and does not therefore fall prey to the dangers which Berlin discovered in positive freedom. In so far as certain coercive laws 'constitute' (Pettit's phrase) our freedom, there is a sense in which we might be forced to be free. However, the freedom thus constituted does not *consist* in obeying the law; it is rather the arena of choice which is made possible by that obedience.[20] Pettit's account is important in that it focusses attention on the political, legal and perhaps social conditions which are necessary for freedom to exist. If freedom is independence, it requires a rule of law which guarantees a range of individual rights; it requires an effective administration; and it requires that the administration be subject to criticisms and punishment where necessary.[21] We will return to these matters shortly.

We have no choice but to be subject to the coercive power of the law and the State; if these are necessary for freedom, then we are – in this sense – 'forced to be free'. However, it is important to spell out very carefully what this involves. For a start, it is worth emphasising that very few theorists would accept this formula as it stands. Rousseau's use of the phrase is clearly intended to be ironic. Almost all theorists of positive freedom recognise that choosing to act in the required way is necessary for freedom.[22] This is not merely a conceptual point. For the self-governing republic which Machiavelli envisaged, it is not sufficient that citizens keep to the law just because they are likely to be punished for breaking it. They must do so willingly. Machiavelli recognised that the law will not be an effective guardian of liberty unless it receives support in the public spirit – the *virtue* – of the citizens. They must be prepared to keep the law even when their natural selfishness prompts a breach. They must also be aware of those whose ambitions would threaten the stability of the republic and be able to organise to counter those ambitions. In times of internal and external threat, they must be ready to fight in defence of the republic. Virtue requires, in other words, an informed capacity to subordinate self-interest to the well-being of the republic of which one is a citizen. But how was the citizen to acquire this capacity? Machiavelli himself placed some hope in education, a little more on the ability of rulers to manipulate the religious fears of their subjects, to inspire awe, or simply to provide an example; but most of all, he relied on the coercive power of law. Just as 'hunger and poverty make men industrious...the laws make them good'.[23] But since the laws presuppose the goodness of the citizens (at least of most of them), it is hard to see this as anything but a restatement of the problem.

Machiavelli's problem is not his alone. The practice of citizenship is, let us assume with Skinner, a condition of individuals having the negative freedom to choose between ways of life, and, also, now agreeing with Pettit, a condition of freedom from domination. But if citizenship presupposes the coercive power of the law to rule certain choices out of court, it also requires virtue: that citizens willingly do what is necessary to sustain the law. The two conditions are interdependent. Just as an effective body of law requires virtuous citizens, so also virtuous citizens require the assurance that their public-spirited behaviour is not wasted. Since both conditions are required to secure the free choice of the individual, neither can be left to the vagaries of its exercise. In an ideal republic, there would be a high probability that breaches of the law would be punished, and for that reason it would be in the self-interest of citizens to keep to the law. But it must also be the case that most citizens do so willingly, *and in that sense do freely* what they are unfree not to do, i.e. where there are constraints on their acting otherwise. For two reasons: First, the coercive power of law is effective only where it has to be employed in a minority of cases. Second, the virtuous activity of the citizen requires understanding, political sensitivity and skill. These can be encouraged, but cannot be compelled. While the coercive power of law would provide the context within which virtuous activity takes place, it would not determine the precise content of that activity. Nevertheless, citizens would accept the coercive power of the law, and willingly do what is necessary to sustain it; in so doing they would secure the conditions of their own freedom to choose between ways of life.

These considerations suggest that it would be a mistake to draw too sharp a line between the classical and formal conceptions of citizenship discussed in the previous section. To be a citizen, on any understanding of that term, is to be something more than a *person*. It is to be located with respect to a certain political structure, and not just a body of law, and while it means that one is entitled to make certain claims on that structure, it also implies that one has certain responsibilities to maintain and defend it. Payment of taxes, jury service, and even military service are associated with most concepts of citizenship, even the most formal. In so far as the laws protecting the rights of citizens may be well or poorly made, and well or poorly administered, a good number of citizens must be prepared to keep an eye on these matters. In times of crisis, the State will demand much more by way of sacrifice, up to and including life itself. In certain situations, the citizen must take an active part in politics if only to preserve the rights which formal citizenship is supposed to provide. As Walzer acknowledges, the 'passive enjoyment of citizenship requires, at least intermittently, the activist politics of citizens'.[24] Even Constant, who is hailed by Berlin as an exemplary exponent of negative liberty, finds a place for a more positive, politicised conception of freedom. Unless citizens are prepared to exercise their 'right to share in political power' with diligence and understanding, he argues, the framework of private independence will be in danger.[25] The demands made by the State on the everyday life of modern citizens are much less than those on their ancient counterparts. However, unless modern citizens are prepared to make a contribution to political life – to acknowledge the authority of the State, to live in such way as to sustain the political community, and occasionally to involve themselves in political debate – then the rights which they enjoy will be lost.

But if the citizen is one whose identity and major concerns lie elsewhere, what will provide the reason for him or her to act as citizenship requires? It may be that the chief business of the modern citizen is the pursuit of private goods; but can we make sense of the existence of civic obligations without assuming that there is something in his or her nature which transcends the private and takes priority over it? If proponents of the classical equation between citizenship and freedom could rely on the ultimate concomitance of individual nature and social service, this option is not available to the proponent of negative freedom and freedom as non-domination. The demands on the modern citizen are a good deal less onerous than those on the classical citizen. But in the context of modern social and political life they will also be a good deal more difficult to justify.

Quentin Skinner suggests that a republican conception of citizenship may be justified instrumentally, without going beyond the liberal, negative conception of freedom. Individuals ought to act as citizens because by doing so they further their own interest in having as much negative liberty as possible. According to Skinner, 'Corruption', i.e. giving preference to one's selfish interests over the requirements of the community 'is simply a failure of rationality, an inability to recognise that one's own liberty depends on committing oneself to a life of virtue and public service'.[26]

This is, sadly, too good to be true. Such reasoning may have been plausible in the tiny Florentine republic where the actions of one individual might contribute significantly to broader political ends, but, in large modern societies, no individual who is tempted towards corruption need be deterred by the thought that his or her failure in civic duty will shake the political edifice. What is necessary to sustain the sphere of negative freedom is that enough citizens, enough of the time, keep to the laws and live a life of virtue, and this will always give the individual the option of free riding. This is not due to a lack of foresight, nor even to the especially selfish nature of the individual's goals. It is the direct consequence of the instrumental reasoning recommended by Skinner. If individuals are solely concerned to maximise their own negative liberty, they will select courses of action which they have reason to expect will generate that result. There is no reason to expect that this will always, or indeed often, require virtuous behaviour.

Skinner runs together two distinct means/end considerations. The first is that active citizenship – at least by enough people, enough of the time – is a necessary means to the goal of negative freedom (from interference, from domination). This shows that a concern with liberal freedoms should lead to a recognition of the importance of republican values as a means – probably a necessary means – of securing them. In other words, there are good instrumental reasons why liberals should become republicans. However, this argument does not show that the citizens themselves should conceive of citizenship in an instrumental way. On the contrary. Though citizens should know that the health of the body politic is a condition of their liberal freedoms and also that this depends upon the virtuous activity of themselves and their fellows, they must *not* conceive of their own activity purely as a means to those ends. If they do, they will find many cases where their own contribution to the desired goals will be marginal, and they will choose to free ride on the contributions of others. But if all – or most – reason in this way, the political edifice – and the freedoms it sustains – will collapse. In other words, citizens must not behave virtuously merely in order to sustain their own freedom (or, for that matter, the freedom of others). They must conceive of the responsibilities which are associated with citizenship as *constituents of their freedom*, not merely as means for it.[27]

The virtuous citizen is one who will comply with the law even when it is possible to break it. Where most citizens are virtuous, however, the law will be effectively administered, and, most of the time, breaches will be punished. In this circumstance, virtuous citizens will do freely what they have no option not to do. While they will exercise choice in *how* they keep the law, keeping the law is not itself a matter of choice. The practice of citizenship may be a precondition of individuals having the freedom to choose between alternatives, but it does not itself fall within the freedom of choice it makes possible. At this point, we move decisively from the sphere of negative freedom – including Pettit's conception of freedom from domination – into the realm of positive freedom. The freedom we are concerned with here is *not* an opportunity concept: it is not the freedom to do or abstain from performing certain actions. It is an exercise concept, and it is realised in carrying out the responsibilities of citizenship.

However, this does not mean that we should take the dictum that we must be 'forced to be free' literally. Even where the responsibilities of citizenship are legal requirements, they retain something of the liberal emphasis on free choice. Virtuous citizens will choose to obey the law, even when they are compelled to do so. And it is important that they do so freely. The *way* in which they will obey the law requires knowledge, care and judgement, all of which involve the exercise of choice. And virtuous citizens will also perform a range of actions which are not legally required of them. They will take an intelligent interest in political debates, be prepared to criticise and mobilise resistance to political decisions they believe to be wrong, but also be prepared to accept the moral authority of the democratically elected Government. These are all conditions of the political health of a society and should be accepted as aspects of the responsibilities of citizens.

The move from negative to positive freedom is not, as Berlin rightly saw, merely a matter of finding different words to say much the same thing. It marks a profound shift of emphasis. For the liberal, the idea of negative freedom is that of a sphere in which individuals have the right to act more or less as they please without interference from other individuals or institutions. What the liberal seeks from society is the assurance that there are certain boundaries which will not be crossed. It is for this reason that the language of *rights* has become such an inescapable part of liberal discourse. For the republican – who may also be a liberal – a healthy political life requires a level of participation by the citizens. To some extent this participation may be secured by law: Individuals are required to pay taxes, do jury duty, etc. But it also requires a high – though perhaps not universal – level of commitment on the part of citizens. So the republican will be seeking, not merely the security of each person to do or abstain, but the commitment of every citizen to play a role in sustaining the form of political life to which he or she belongs. The language of negative freedom goes with the liberal quest for security; that of positive freedom with the republican commitment to participation.

This does not mean that republicans need be opposed to the freedoms valued by liberals (though they will be wary of the language of rights in which these are characteristically expressed). It means that they will recognise that a society which embodies liberal freedoms must rest on another basis. In every social order there must be a sphere of necessity, an arena of social behaviour which is not subject to the same freedom that is allowed elsewhere. Freedom presupposes necessity.

This argument has certain parallels with one advanced by Karl Marx regarding human labour. Marx argued that in every form of social life – even communism – there was a sphere of 'natural necessity' in which men and women must work on the natural world in order to produce and reproduce the conditions of human life. With the improvement of technology, the time spent on necessary labour would be shortened, but it would never be eliminated. In his early writings, Marx conceived labour to be the paradigmatic expression of the human essence and thus of human freedom.[28] The role of labour was precisely parallel to the classical republican account of political activity. In his later writings, however, Marx retreated from this position. While he emphasised the need to introduce as much freedom as possible into the realm of production, e.g. by bringing it under the collective control of the associated workers, by the use of labour-saving technology, etc., it 'always remains a realm of necessity':

> The true realm of freedom, the development of human powers as an end in itself, begins beyond it, though it can only flourish with this realm of necessity as its basis.[29]

For the later Marx, 'true' freedom presupposes the existence of genuine alternatives. In this, he is surprisingly close to the liberal conception of negative freedom. But he realised, as liberals rarely do, that this freedom will only be available when the material conditions of social reproduction are satisfied and thus that this sphere of human activity cannot be subject to the same freedom which is possible elsewhere. Marx's argument is parallel to the present argument about political necessity. Just as it is the task of the associated workers to reproduce the material life of society, so it is the task of the associated citizens to reproduce its political life.

The classical conception of citizenship located necessity in the nature of the individual, and identified freedom with the working out of that necessity. But modernity has taken a different path, and has emphasised the role of choice and the existence of alternatives in its account of freedom. It is just because of the modern emphasis on subjective freedom that the recognition of the necessity which lies at the heart of every social order has presented a special challenge to modern philosophy. If freedom of choice requires the commitment of the citizen, may it not erode that commitment? Can something of the ancient equation of citizenship and freedom be reinstated given the changed understanding of these concepts in the modern world?

Hegel: the making of the modern citizen

> When a father asked him for advice about the best way of educating his son in ethical matters, a Pythagorean replied: 'Make him the *citizen of a state with good laws.*'
>
> (Hegel)[30]

> Freedom is only present when there is no other that is not myself.
>
> (Hegel)[31]

It was probably Hegel who recognised more clearly than other philosophers the political conditions which had to be in place if the modern principle of subjective freedom was to be realised, and he came as close as any to providing a resolution of the tension between subjective freedom and the commitments necessary to sustain these political conditions.[32] While Hegel was not free of nostalgia for Greek antiquity, he was aware that the social conditions which sustained the classical conception of political life were irrevocably past, and that the injustices they involved were repugnant to modern morality. It is 'subjective freedom' which: 'constitutes the principle and determines the peculiar form of freedom in *our* world...[and which] forms the absolute basis of our political and religious life'.[33]

What modern civil society – and Hegel uses this term to comprise the market and its associated institutions – breeds is the *bourgeois*, someone whose life is governed by instrumental reasoning directed towards largely self-interested goals. Subjective freedom is the principle of civil society, and is valued by the *bourgeois* precisely because it allows for satisfaction of specific needs and the pursuit of particular goals. The *bourgeois* is not, as such, a citizen, and the qualities required of the *bourgeois* are not those of the citizen. Citizenship involves the everyday restraint on the pursuit of one's private goals and a latent readiness to make large sacrifices when the State demands them. Citizens must even be prepared to give their lives for their State, and there is no way that this can be rationalised as a means of securing private ends – even that of maximising negative liberty.[34]

The problem of citizenship cannot be solved so long as one remains within the perspective of the *bourgeois* who – like Machiavelli, Skinner and perhaps even Pettit – can only conceive of the requirements of citizenship instrumentally. These demands of citizenship cannot be justified in terms of goals that the *bourgeois* already has, nor through the exercise of the conception of rationality with which he is equipped. For the problem to be solved, modern social life must provide the *bourgeois* with a *path* by which he might move from an instrumental concern with his own private ends, through an understanding of the social and political preconditions for that way of life, and finally to an identification of his own well-being with the maintenance of those conditions. Social life must be educational, and, like any educational process, civil society must encourage the individual to develop a different self-understanding and new goals.[35] The German term *'Bildung'* is appropriate here, for what is involved is a process of self-formation, not merely the acquisition of new knowledge. The *bourgeois* will not cease to be a *bourgeois*; but he will acquire a new conception of himself, that of citizenship. This new identity means that he will take the responsibilities of civic life, not as means towards private ends, nor as duties which he is compelled to perform; but as constituents of his own way of life.[36] As I noted earlier, there is a hint of this in Machiavelli, but when it came to the point he relied on the coercive not the educational role of law. The educational aspect was, however, implicit in the eighteenth-century republican tradition, especially in the role assigned to civil society to 'civilise' (or 'polish') its members. It is this aspect of the republican tradition which is carried on by Hegel in his emphasis on those aspects of civil society which will raise the individual from a concern with his own particular ends towards 'the *form of universality*' and encourage him to 'seek and find...subsistence in this form'.[37]

The educational process carries with it a new understanding of freedom. The principle of subjective freedom is preserved, but only when it is properly understood. If it is assumed to be a self-sufficient principle, Hegel argues that the negative freedom to choose between alternatives is indistinguishable from arbitrariness, and, what is more, an arbitrariness which conceals the domination of given drives and inclinations.[38] For subjective freedom, it is necessary that individual choice be co-ordinated by principles of reason, and for Hegel the requisite principles are those which are embodied in the legal and political institutions of a rationally organised State. For the *bourgeois*, these institutions are constraints, to be accepted out of duty or compulsion; he may recognise their necessity, but they remain essentially external to his own goals and desires. The merely negative freedom which he cherishes must inevitably be limited by what is other. But when the *bourgeois* acquires the perspective of the citizen, he comes to conceive these demands, not as constraints but as conditions of existence of activities, pleasures, forms of knowledge, and meanings which would not otherwise be available to him. When he recognises that these laws are the very conditions of his subjective freedom, he affirms these, and, in so doing, he wills nothing else but freedom itself. Then, and perhaps only then, does the will have its own freedom as its object; and only then is it truly free.[39]

The relationship between the *bourgeois* and the citizen is analogous to the relationship between the novice and the practitioner of a craft, such as dancing, music, playing chess, or even speaking a language. What the novice must learn is that certain rules are not merely restrictions on his or her actions, but conditions of a new form of activity, which provides satisfactions and meanings which would not otherwise be possible. The self-aware citizen, as the self-aware practitioner, must *will* the conditions, which make a range of activities possible. The principles of this activity will then be no longer experienced as external constraints or even as duties, but as the objective correlates of the citizen's own will and identity.

> [T]he ethical substance and its laws and powers...are not something *alien* to the subject. On the contrary, the subject bears *spiritual witness* to them as *its own essence*, in which it has its *self-awareness*, and lives as in its element which is not distinct from

itself – a relationship which is immediate and closer to identity than even [a relationship of] *faith* or *trust*.[40]

If citizenship limits the freedom of choice of the modern individual, the limitation is a self-limitation. What the citizen has no choice but to do, he has no desire nor reason not to do. Merely subjective freedom gives way to what for Hegel was a more fundamental freedom: the freedom of those whose conditions of existence are as they would have them be. For Hegel's citizens, there is a correlation between their reason, their will and the civic order; they inhabit a political world in which they are at home.

Despite Hegel's claim to have recognised the modern principle of subjective freedom, the *Bildung* he projects remains within the sphere of necessity. The curriculum and its goal pre-exist the formation of the citizen, and he has no choice but to submit to it. What differentiates the *Bildung* of the modern citizen from that of his classical predecessor is the availability of an external perspective from which to evaluate and ultimately affirm the life of citizenship. In the classical world, the alternative to citizenship was life outside the *polis*, and this was not a moral option.[41] But Christianity – especially the Protestant Reformation – and life in civil society itself, provide the modern individual with forms of identity which provide a recognisably moral standpoint from which the existence of alternative ways of life might be evaluated. However, the moment of reflection in which the citizen affirms the life of citizenship should not be conceived on a contractual model. It does not involve adopting the perspective of a presocial individual who evaluates the life of citizenship on the basis of given interests. This procedure – characteristic of the social contracts of Hobbes and Locke – does not allow for the fact that the goals of the citizen are not comprehensible to the presocial individual any more than the goals of an accomplished musician are comprehensible to the novice. And though Hegel's account recognises the moral status of the individual – the *person* – it treats this as an aspect of social life, and not its moral centre. Hegel's reflective moment takes place 'after the event'; it consists of working through the various alternative modes of life which are available in the modern world, identifying their characteristic problems, and recognising that citizenship provides the resolution of these.[42] If the starting point of the process of reflection is life in the modern State, its goal is the reaffirmation of that life, or, at least, of a rational reconstruction of it. Hegel's argument in *The Philosophy of Right* is intended to provide this moment of reflection.

This procedure is essentially that of reflective equilibrium, as it was discussed in the last chapter. Hegel's starting point is the moral knowledge which is already embodied in existing institutions and practices. For this knowledge to approach the status of truth, we must be prepared to reflect on its origins, the role of the institutions and practices in social life, possible alternatives to them, and the place of this knowledge within a more encompassing moral theory. Reflection is inevitably informed by its starting point, so there is a certain circularity to the enterprise. But this is inevitable. All that we can do is make the circle of reflection as wide and encompassing as possible. Within that circle, we must reflect on the possibility of different knowledges and different starting points; and that reflection must inform our attitude to our own knowledge and origin. But we can only begin from where we are.

It is however highly dubious whether Hegel's account does pass the test of critical reflection. There is little reason to believe that modern civil society does provide the *Bildung* he envisaged. Later history has not provided much support for his claim that the experience of work, the administration of justice, the provision of State services ('police'), the bureaucracy, and the formation of interest groups ('corporations'), would encourage people to identify themselves as citizens. Indeed, it is more plausible to suggest that the institutions required for an education in citizenship are those civic organisations which resist the force of the market, not those closely allied to it.[43] What is more, Hegel does not provide an account of what is available to the citizen which is not available to the canny *bourgeois*. On the classical account, the life of the committed citizen provides access to a whole range of social and cultural activities which would not otherwise be available. But there seems little in the political commitments required in modern life which will play this role, nor does Hegel spend much time trying to establish that there is. He does not establish that a free riding *bourgeois* would not have access to exactly the same social goods. At this point Hegel's argument should be read, not as an elucidation of the rational core of the modern State, but as a challenge: if there is to be a practice of citizenship, then social life must provide the individual with a path from the calculative rationality and self-interest characteristic of much economic life to an identification of the self in terms of civic responsibilities; and this identification must provide the individual with a fulfilment and a meaning which is not otherwise available.

Hegel's account of political commitment builds on important themes from the republican tradition. However, there is one which he all but ignores: the idea that citizens participate in the governance of their republic, and thus play a role in forming the political order to which they are subject. The exercise of positive freedom does not merely sustain a particular form of political life; it also contributes to the process by which one is ruled.[44] Part of the reason for Hegel's omission of this theme was his belief that this conception of politics was only plausible for the ruling class of relatively small states and not for the modern world. He does allow for certain representative institutions, the 'Estates', in which 'the subjective moment of universal freedom...comes *into existence in relation to the state*'[45]; but these are allowed only a limited and largely advisory role. No doubt Hegel was being realistic in limiting the role of democratic institutions in his rational reconstruction of the State. The sheer size of modern society and the complexity of tasks of the modern State place severe limits on the possibility of a democratic practice. Indeed, it has been a similar scepticism about democracy which has encouraged liberals to develop a notion of freedom intended to protect the individual from the State, rather than one which encourages participation in it. Though Hegel rejects the liberal notion of freedom, he was just as concerned as liberals to formulate a conception of freedom which does not involve the individual playing a part in the exercise of State power.

The absence of a notion of citizenship as the exercise of political sovereignty does create an enormous problem for the Hegelian schema. If, as he recognises, 'the right of the subject's particularity to find satisfaction' is central to modernity, then this right must have some embodiment in a political sphere with which the subject can identify. Yet, for Hegel, this right is only properly recognised in civil society; it exists in a severely circumscribed form within the political order itself.[46] For Hegel, citizens identify with the State because it manifests a form of reason which they have come to recognise as their own, not because it is responsive to their particular needs, desires and aspirations. No doubt, as a realistic appraisal suggests, such responsiveness will always be limited and partial. However, as earlier republicans had insisted – and modern history has demonstrated – unless it is present in some form and to some extent, the individual's subjective freedom will be vulnerable to the exercise of arbitrary and unwelcome State power. Further, and more directly pertinent to Hegel's own argument, unless the citizen is given more reason to recognise his own particular aspirations in the practices of the State, its very universality means that it will be conceived as external and alien to him. In these circumstances, the individual will find fulfilment in the sphere of particularity, and the *bourgeois* will take precedence over the citizen.

The underlying logic of this situation may be described in terms of different senses – or aspects – of freedom. The liberal is concerned with negative freedom; however, this presupposes positive freedom as commitment to the practice of citizenship. Since some aspects of this practice will be prescribed by law, this freedom does not fall within the sphere of (negative) freedom of choice; but since it does require commitment and judgement, it must be freely given. On the classical model, the practice of citizenship falls within a further sense of positive freedom: the citizens participate in the process of determining the conditions in which they live. Hegel – in this respect at one with liberals[47] – rejected this idea as impractical for modern political life. However, without this, there is little to justify Hegel's claim that modern individuals will commit themselves to a practice of citizenship. But, unless there is some reason to suppose that individuals will find in citizenship the condition for the realisation of their own aspirations and goals, there is no reason to suppose that the practice of citizenship is a form of freedom.

Citizenship and national identity

Hegel was well aware of the emergence of political, cultural and intellectual nationalism in the early nineteenth century and he was contemptuous of it. For Hegel, nationalism substituted emotion for reason, and particularity for the universal.[48] But there is little doubt that the doctrine of national identity was to have much greater presence in later history than Hegel's own project of rational reconciliation. If we are to accept the judgement of the past 200 years of world history – and Hegel could hardly object to the choice of tribunal – then it is not the rational identification of the individual with the political structure but national identity which has provided the moral resources for modern citizenship.

There is a *Bildung* involved in the formation of national identity. However, it is not the narrative towards mature citizenship described by Hegel. It begins in the family. As Hegel's compatriot, Johann Gottlieb Herder, recognised, we begin to acquire our national identity literally on our mother's knee. We discover our nation – as we discover ourselves – in the bed-time stories we are told, the songs which put us to sleep, the games we play as children, the heroes we are taught to admire and the enemies we come to fear and detest. Our national identity comes to us in the language in which we learn to articulate our most primitive demands. As we learn to speak, we find ourselves already spoken for. If, in our later life, the market and its associated institutions contribute to our sense of national identity, this is not because of their character as rational economic activity, but because the transactions are performed in the language, the cultural forms and modes of interaction characteristic of the nation. Even the currency in which we are paid for our endeavours will bear its imprint. But the rewards which accrue to our national belonging are not, or not merely, financial. We are provided with access to a store of cultural achievement, a history of triumph and tragedy, and a land, all of which go well beyond the possibilities of our individual or local aspirations but which are nevertheless defined as ours. Our national identity – any identity, for that matter – would not be able to demand sacrifices of us if it did not also provide us with pleasures and satisfactions.

National identity is never fully available to the rational reflection and reappropriation which was such a central part of Hegel's presentation of life in the modern State. In part this is because the conceptions of reason which are available to us are as much cultural products as the language we speak. Reason may be universal in aspiration, but the forms in which it actually exists are almost as diverse as their host cultures. It does not provide an external vantage point from which claims of a specific national culture may be assessed. And if it did, it would *for that reason* be inadequate to the task. The resources which are necessary to understand national identity are those provided by the language, history, literature, music and other cultural traditions which form the national narrative. If reflection attempts to occupy a place outside the nation's narrative, it will deny itself the resources fully to understand it. Esperanto – or French – is not the language in which to appreciate the plays of Shakespeare nor the poetry of Pushkin. A good deal of the strength of a culture is only fully available to those who are within it. This is not only because those whose culture it is are more likely to have the resources to understand. In principle, these resources are available to the anthropologically inclined outsider. It is also because it is *their* culture. As Yael Tamir has emphasised, my nation – like my family – has a particular claim on me, not merely because it is different from others, nor because it can from some vantage point be judged to be superior to others. Its claim lies in the fact that it is mine.[49] For me to step outside that web of relationships in order to discover its sufficient reason would be to repudiate the very particularity which constitutes its moral force.

This does not mean that national identity is unreflective. All national cultures provide resources for internal criticism and are open to external influence. Every national culture is subject to development and change. Reflection is not the prerogative of the philosopher, nor is it only a matter of reason; it is part of the day to day business of politics and culture. Philosophy should seek both to understand what is at stake in these debates and also to contribute to them. But the very universality which is the ambition and the occasional achievement of philosophy places certain barriers in the way of both these projects. In searching for a form of reason adequate to evaluate the claims of a national culture, philosophical reflection risks overlooking the call of particularity. We must also recognise that other cultural forms – including literature, art, sport and music – have a role to play in contributing to the process by which a nation reflects on what it has been and what it ought to be. The role of reason is not, as Hegel imagined, to comprehend the whole; but to understand what it can, and also to understand the limits of that understanding. Philosophy too should recognise its own limitations. There is a certain hubris in the pretensions of philosophy to occupy a privileged position in the debates about national belonging.

It is difficult to trace the genealogy of national identity in seventeenth- and eighteenth-century political thought, not least because, as we have seen in Chapter 1, the new identity was being formulated in the language of the old. Rousseau and his Jacobin followers employed the rhetoric of citizenship in their attempts to conceive and construct a political community. Both Walzer and Constant treat this as an unsuccessful attempt to revive classical conceptions in the changed conditions of modern life. Perhaps this corresponds to Rousseau's own conception of his project. But, on a close reading, it is clear that, combined with a republican discourse about the nature of the State, political obligation and the like, Rousseau was employing another rhetoric about identity, culture, land, history and belonging. Rousseau is as much part of the story of modern nationalism as he is a late episode in classical republicanism.[50] Herder, on the other hand, is recognised to be a nationalist (though he had some very uncharacteristic ideas about political sovereignty); what is not so often noted is that he was also a republican.[51] The entanglement of citizenship with what we can now recognise as national identity is symptomatic of later developments. For modern citizenship has always relied for its moral force on its association with national identity, and national identity has always aspired to citizenship. The French Revolutionary appeal to citizenship, the *levée en masse*, the politics of mass involvement, not to mention its educational policies and the destruction of regional languages and cultures, were not the anachronistic revivals of a past practice of citizenship, but harbingers of the new politics of nationalism and identity. Indeed, once the fusion of culture and politics is established, then it is possible to wonder whether some form of cultural identity was not presupposed in earlier classical models of citizenship.[52]

When I act according to my national identity, I express what I, in some essential sense, have come to be. In this respect the concept of national identity is analogous to that of classical citizenship. Freedom is the expression of a pre-given essence. But there are major differences. Classical citizenship was appropriate for the politically active élite in societies where most of the population were allowed no political role. It was sustained by activity: each citizen was engaged in politics, and this engagement could plausibly be conceived in terms of self-rule. Politics was not merely about the exercise of power and the distribution of benefits, but was a way of life with its own pleasures and rewards. Citizenship needed to be demonstrated by participation in that life; in principle at least, it was this participation which formed the culture of the State. National identity, on the other hand, is characteristic of large-scale, anonymous societies. It provides the accent and the tone in which everyday life is carried on, but it rarely provides its central focus or content. It is an aspect of our lives, a latent quality available to be mobilised as and when necessary. The key difference between the republican and the national conceptions of citizenship lies in the relationship of the individual to the political realm. For the republican, the relationship is ideally one of *agency*: citizens *form* the State through their political activity. For the nationalist, the relationship is one of *mimesis*: citizens *recognise* themselves in the State. National subjects find their identity affirmed in the political realm, and for this reason make themselves available to its demands.

In practice, the difference between republicanism and nationalism is one of degree. Different political communities encourage more or less participation by citizens in political affairs. In one notable case, the United States of America, certain republican ideals have found their way into significant constitutional documents and have a significant place in the national culture.[53] As we have seen, a healthy political life requires a degree of political participation, so there is good reason to encourage a greater level of political participation in all countries, and to the extent that this becomes an aspect of a national culture, then there will be partial fusion of the two doctrines. However, it is important to recognise that, in the social and political conditions which have obtained in the modern world, there must always be a significant gap between the activities and concerns of the citizen and the realm of politics, and that every state will rely on cultural *mimesis* to fill that gap. The citizen's relationship with the State – the nation-state – is constituted by his or her national identity. It is this which provides the commitment, both to one's fellow citizens and to the political institutions, necessary for public life. It also provides the motivation for some level of participation. Even though modern citizenship is largely a passive affair, as we have seen, it is never completely so. It still requires a certain minimal level of civic engagement in everyday life, as well as the more extreme commitments demanded in times of crisis. It involves a measure of identification with the political community to which one belongs, and a readiness to override one's more private and local concerns in order to act on behalf of that community. In the modern world, it has been the nation which has provided the requisite identity and motivation. Becoming a citizen has involved acquiring the appropriate cultural identity. In certain cases, citizenship may be a matter of choice, as in voluntary migration, and a choice which may be made for purely self-interested reasons. But the responsibilities incurred go beyond the purview of the original decision. Ultimately, it is a responsibility to acquire a new identity, one which is not experienced as a matter of choice.[54]

The rhetoric of national liberation has been a familiar part of world politics for some hundred years now. However, political theorists and philosophers have paid little attention to the notion of freedom involved, perhaps because they have judged it to be both confused and dangerous. No doubt there is good reason for caution here. It is all too easy to catalogue the instances where appeals to national liberation have justified oppression and worse. Still, there is a legitimate thread to the rhetoric and it is important to draw it out. Clearly, it is not equivalent to the liberal notion of freedom of choice, even though the way of nationalism has been chosen by many. As I have already noted, it is closer to the conception of freedom associated with classical citizenship: when I act according to my national identity I express my essential nature. But it goes beyond this. The freedom – 'liberation' – sought by the nationalist is that of living in a political and social world which corresponds to one's nature. It is the freedom of living with one's fellow countrymen, those who share one's culture and thus one's identity, and of making one's life within institutions and practices which sustain one's own conception of oneself. We have already had occasion to note this conception of freedom in Hegel, and it may well be that it is implicit in the republican tradition. But the nationalist recognises, as the republican did not, the primary role of culture in forming the relationship between the individual and his or her environment. The freedom of modern citizens is not that of making the political order to which they are subject; it is rather that of making and remaking the cultural world which sustains their own identity. To borrow a metaphor that Marx used to describe the relationship between humans and the natural world, there is a 'metabolism' between socially formed individuals and the culture in which they live.[55] The culture provides the necessary support for their identity, and, as they live, they reproduce that culture.

If national identity is not the negative freedom of choice valued by liberals, it does provide the context in which that freedom is exercised. As Will Kymlicka has argued, we do not exercise our freedom of choice in a void. Choosing, especially where the choices concern the kind of life we intend to lead, presupposes the existence of a framework within which various options may be evaluated. It is:

> only through having a rich and secure cultural structure that people can become aware, in a vivid way, of the options available to them, and intelligently examine their value.[56]

This is not a matter of the national culture providing a set of criteria by which options may be ranked against each other. It is rather that it provides the language in which the choices are articulated, the symbols which give significance to various alternatives, and the sense of belonging which sets the boundaries of the choices which one might make. There is, of course, no a priori necessity that this role is played by our *national* culture. In other historical situations it might be played by a religion, a tribal community, or even a form of political activity of the kind envisaged by republicans. However, in the modern world it has been national cultures which have played this role.

National cultures could not provide the context in which freedom of choice is exercised if they did not also restrict that freedom, any more than the nation-state can provide the legal and political conditions necessary for freedom of choice without also restricting it. One way of expressing this is to say that negative freedom cannot exist without negative *un*freedom. But a more perspicuous mode of expression is that negative freedom requires its positive counterpart. For the recognition of the need for these limitations means that they might in principle be accepted – indeed, willed – as conditions of one's freedom.

The sense of freedom appealed to here is not unique to national identity. It arises in all areas in which a deep commitment is experienced as essential to one's conception of what one is. For example, my commitments to my partner, my friends and my children are not as such experienced as matters of choice. Or it may be that I have a commitment to a certain way of life, perhaps through vocation, as on a romantic conception of the artist, or perhaps through habituation. Choice is involved in *how* I fulfil these commitments, not in *whether* I do so. Indeed, when I begin to experience them as matters of choice, this is likely to be a symptom of the waning of the commitment. On some occasions, I acquire these commitments through an act of choice. For example, I get married or choose to have children. Sometimes, however, I incur the commitment in ways which I could not have chosen. For example, the responsibilities I have to my parents or other members of my family. When I act to fulfil these commitments, I do so not because I choose the action from a range of alternatives, but because I feel I must. Of course, in many cases the choice is 'objectively' available: there is no law or even very much social pressure compelling me to act in a certain way. But it is not 'subjectively' present: the alternative is not a presence in my conception of what I might do. That the alternative is objectively available may not be important to us. Indeed, in certain cases we undertake formal commitments which do constrain our future choices just in order to make public the depth of our commitment. To conceive of these as matters of choice is not so much an indication of the high value placed on freedom as a symptom of a lack of depth.

Of course, commitments are subject to change: artists become accountants, devoted spouses form new attachments, and migrants seek to better themselves in foreign lands. It is important – and this is a significant truth in liberalism – that such changes be possible. But it would be superficial to bring these under the rubric of freedom of choice. They involve a change in the determinants of choice – the standards we bring to bear, the aspirations we seek to further, and the meaning we assign to our life as a whole. For the individuals concerned, such transitions do not involve a choice between clearly understood alternatives, but a step – or a leap – from a present which has become unsatisfactory to a murky future. Such transitions are not and *ought not* to be easy. Where we enter legally enforceable commitments we do so partly in order to make future changes difficult. In the case of national identity, for most of us the transition is almost impossible to make completely: our national culture has inescapably formed our voice and our vision. Though here too we may (and certainly ought to) allow the possibility of change, we do not feel that it should be too lightly made.

The role of deep commitments – of *identities* – is analogous to that of constitutions in political life. Normally, the constitution provides the framework for political debate and decision; it is not itself the subject of debate and decision. But in certain situations, it may – and should – become subject to the political process, and the constitution itself should make provision for this. But it will do so in a way which recognises that the changes envisaged are more fundamental than others, and will require more consideration and (perhaps) a greater burden of proof. In other words, there is a distinction between the political change enabled by the constitution and the politics of constitutional change. In an analogous way, our national identity provides one of the contexts in which we exercise our freedom of choice. For this reason, it is not itself subject to that freedom. But this does not mean that it is not subject to change. Debate about the meaning of a nation's past, about the nature of commitments involved in membership of a nation, and about the criteria of membership, are all part of a healthy national culture. The content of a national identity will change as a result of these debates. But these changes are not a matter of individual choice, however much individuals may contribute to them. What an individual may choose to do – a matter of radical choice – is to give up membership of one nation in favour of another. But this is not an easy matter. For most, it is impossible to make the transition completely (though one's children, and children's children may do so); nor is it always possible to leave behind the commitments and responsibilities which go with a national identity. In extreme cases, we have the concept of a *traitor* to remind us of the peculiarly inescapable nature of the responsibilities which go with national identity.

However we construe the notion of freedom involved with national identity, choice is not central to it. Indeed, that it is not usually a matter of choice is what this kind of freedom is about. It is just because our national identity is a nearly inescapable condition of our life that it provides the freedom, not of choice, but of necessity: of acting as we must. But it also promises another form of freedom: that of living in a political and social world which we can identify as our own. When we are free in this sense, we are at home in our world, in a community with others who speak the same language, experience the same emotions, and experience the world in the same terms. It is this sense of individual freedom which underlies the familiar appeal of nationalism – the claim of each nation to be its own State. The force of this appeal lies in the aspiration of members of the national community to live in a society which expresses and sustains their fundamental sense of self. When this aspiration is fulfilled, the social and political environment is not experienced as a constraint on the individual's interests and concerns, but a condition of a worthwhile and satisfying life.

Conclusion

The argument of this chapter has focussed on the concept of freedom. I have argued that the notion of negative freedom – freedom of choice – presupposes a range of more positive conceptions. At a minimal conceptual level, freedom of choice only counts as freedom if the agent has the capacity to make meaningful choices. Negative freedom presupposes freedom as self-determination (or autonomy). However, I have also argued that there are legal and political conditions which are necessary for freedom of choice, and that a practice of citizenship is required if these conditions were to obtain. While at least some aspects of this practice should be required by law, it is also necessary that most citizens undertake the responsibilities of citizenship freely. It is this conception of citizenship as a practice which introduces a conception of positive freedom in the sense most objectionable to Berlin: as a preferred range of activities. There are various ways – not necessarily incompatible – in which this republican conception of freedom might be worked out. However, it is apparent that a practice of citizenship as it was envisaged in the early republican tradition is not available in the modern world. An alternative account is provided by the nationalist emphasis on culture as an aspect of the common political life of citizens. This allows for certain of the freedoms valued by liberals and republicans; and it also provides for a further conception of freedom: that of reconciliation with the social and political world.

At another level the argument was intended to display certain interrelations between political doctrines. I have tried to show that a responsible liberal,[57] that is, someone with a serious concern for the political and legal conditions necessary for liberal values to obtain, should move towards certain characteristically republican views about the life of politics; but also that the only form in which republicanism has been a serious option in the modern world is a nationalist one. Neither liberalism nor republicanism emerge unscathed from the recognition of their dependence. Liberalism has to embrace the sphere of necessity, and to investigate what contributions to political and social life might legitimately be expected of all individuals. The characteristic liberal concern for the rights of the person must be combined with an account of the responsibilities of the citizen. Both liberalism and republicanism have to address the role of culture in political and social life. Liberals must recognise that culture is not irrelevant to issues of political and social freedom but constitutive of them. On the other hand, republicans must recognise the centrality of culture to our understanding of political life. Politics is not merely – or even centrally – about power; it is also about meaning.

These are not small changes. However, they need not involve an abnegation of liberal and republican values. If liberals and republicans need to learn to live with nationalism, it is also the case that an acceptable form of nationalism will be one which incorporates liberal and republican values. Recognition of the need for mutual coexistence is simply the first step in the debate about what the terms of that coexistence should be.

4 Multiculturalism, Aboriginal rights and the nation

The term 'multiculturalism' entered politics in the 1970s – initially in Canada and the United States. The timing is significant. Cultural minorities have existed in almost all modern societies. Sometimes, as with the United States, these have been created by large-scale immigration; in other cases, minority or dissident cultural communities have successfully resisted the pressures towards cultural assimilation characteristic of modernisation. These minorities have almost always enjoyed a second-class status, perhaps tolerated as marginal curiosities and allowed to maintain their cultures as a private indulgence (like the minority religions with which they were often associated), but certainly not expected to take a place in public life alongside the dominant culture. However, after the Second World War, the increasing ease of travel, both within and between states, and the dramatic changes in communication and media, enabled members of minority cultures to keep in touch with each other despite geographical separation and immigrants to remain in contact with the cultures of their home countries. Minority groups were now better able both to resist assimilation and to mobilise in support of greater public recognition of their cultures. There is no doubt that, in the United States and the United Kingdom, an increased sensitivity to the racism which had been endemic to both societies helped create a climate in which the claims of non-racial cultural minorities began to receive a sympathetic hearing.

'Multiculturalism' is often used broadly to refer to the political claims of all cultural minorities. In this chapter, however, I will use the term more narrowly to refer to those issues which arise from the political claims of *immigrant* groups, that is of individuals, families and communities, who have moved from one country to another with the intention of becoming permanent members of the new country, but who resist assimilation to the dominant culture of that country and desire to maintain their old ways of life and identities. I will distinguish multiculturalism in this sense from the claims of *national minorities*, for example the Québécois in Canada, the Scots in the United Kingdom and the Occitans in France, who have a historical association with a certain territory prior to their inclusion within the borders of the existing State. Many national minorities are struggling, not for a place in the dominant culture, but for a form of political independence which recognises their cultural difference and territorial claims. By and large, I will have little to say about the problem of national minorities in general, though some of my discussion will bear on these issues. I will be more concerned with the problems which arise when colonial and postcolonial societies attempt to come to terms with the claims of their indigenous peoples. The issue of indigenous rights arises in countries, such as Canada, the United States, New Zealand and Australia, in which the dominant culture, ways of life and political institutions have been formed by an immigration which has destroyed or marginalised the pre-existing cultures, ways of life and political institutions, and where the indigenous people continue to exist as an alienated minority in what was once their own country. Indigenous peoples are often referred to, particularly in Canada and the United States, as *'first nations'*, and their claims treated as a special case of the claims of national minorities. For reasons which will become apparent later in this chapter, I will avoid this terminology.

I will concentrate on the problems of multiculturalism and indigenous rights as they arise in my own country, Australia. As there are significant differences in the ways these problems arise in Australia and Canada, the United States and New Zealand, I will sketch in some of the relevant history in order to identify some of these differences. No doubt, some of the suggestions I make will reflect the specific historical experience of Australia. However, this in itself may be an important corrective influence in a debate which has been dominated by discussion emanating from Canada and the United States. While there can be no doubt of the importance of these contributions, it may well be that these are slanted by certain features of Canadian and United States political history.[1] Certainly, the issues have taken a rather different form in Australia. Nevertheless, I hope that the themes which I identify and the suggestions I make have more than local significance.

The claims of culture

Shortly after the Second World War, the Australian government initiated a programme designed to encourage large-scale immigration. White Australia had always been conscious of its position as a rich but sparsely populated country on the edge of Asia. This insecurity had been intensified by the Second World War when Japanese forces had reached perilously close to the Australian continent. One of the primary motives for the postwar immigration programme was to build up the population and economic strength of Australia to provide it with a better capacity to resist a future threat from Asia.

The results of this programme have been dramatic.[2] The population of Australia in 1945 was around 7.5 million; it is now over 17 million, and 40 per cent of that increase is due to immigration. The Australia of 1945 was predominantly of English or Irish origin, and the original intention of the immigration programme was to keep it that way.[3] However, though the United Kingdom has remained a major source for immigrants, it quickly proved inadequate on its own. The programme was extended to include the Scandinavian countries and Central and Eastern Europe – people who were considered both racially and politically appropriate for Australia. When this source began to dry up in the 1950s, the programme was extended to include Italy, Greece and Malta. Initially, Asians and Africans were kept out by the 'White Australia' Policy. However, this policy was relaxed in the late 1960s and formally abandoned in 1972, and non-European migration began. Initially, this was a relatively small part of the total intake but, with the acceptance of refugees from Lebanon and Vietnam, the proportion increased, and this increase has continued, partly as a result of a policy which gives some priority to family ties. Somewhere between 35 per cent and 45 per cent of the current immigration intake is from Asia.

Many of the results of the immigration programme are contrary to those originally intended. Instead of securing a culturally homogeneous society, Australia has become one of the most heterogeneous societies in the advanced world. The five million immigrants who have settled in Australia since the war come from around a hundred different countries. Australia now has a greater proportion of its population made up of recent immigrants than any other advanced country (around 40 per cent of Australians were born overseas or have at least one immigrant parent). And instead of the immigration programme protecting a White Australia from Asian incursions, Asia is now one of the most significant sources of new immigrants.

When the term 'multiculturalism' first entered Australian politics, shortly after its debut in North America, it was used to signal a greater involvement of the Government in problems that immigrant communities faced: unemployment, discrimination, educational disadvantage, and so on. However, it quickly came to mean an end to the assumption that immigrants would or should merge into an existing national identity and the adoption of Government programmes designed to recognise and even protect the distinct cultural identities which migrants brought with them. Some form of multiculturalism in this broader sense is now taken for granted in mainstream Australian politics, with both major political parties in Australia claiming to be 'multiculturalist'.[4]

Given the political currency of the term, it would be foolish to assign too precise a meaning to it.[5] Sometimes, it is used simply to assert that Australia is in *fact* a culturally diverse society, consisting of people from a variety of different backgrounds, who are likely to speak different languages, practise different religions, have different social conventions and rituals, eat different foods, and so on. However, those who claim multiculturalism as a fact, usually do so in order to assert multiculturalism as a *value*: that it is a good thing, and that living in a multicultural society allows for a richer and more interesting life than is possible in a culturally homogeneous society, such as Australia before the Second World War. Migrant communities have contributed to Australian life, it is argued, precisely because they have *not* assimilated to a pre-existing Australian identity. Finally, and for present purposes most importantly, multiculturalism is a *political principle* which claims that the Government should act so as to protect and sustain this social diversity: at the very least by preventing discrimination on the basis of culture and not discriminating in its own practices ('negative multiculturalism'), and perhaps also by acting positively to ensure the continued viability of minority cultures ('positive multiculturalism').

One way to defend multiculturalism as a political principle is by reference to multiculturalism as a value. For example, the form of liberalism affirmed in John Stuart Mill's *On Liberty*, or easily derivable from it, identifies variety as a crucial constituent in a conception of a life worth living.[6] For Mill, the choice of one way of life over others is enriched by the awareness of alternatives. Without this awareness, informed choice and commitment is not possible. Social diversity is thus a condition of autonomy, and a liberalism which is committed to autonomy must also value diversity. On this view, multiculturalism as a political principle is derived from multiculturalism as a value. But liberalism of this kind is rejected by many contemporary liberals precisely, if paradoxically, because it is *incompatible* with a proper recognition of the extent of cultural diversity. Mill's liberalism values diversity because it is an intrinsic element in the good life, and for those contemporary liberals influenced by John Rawls, the affirmation of *any* conception of the good life, even one with diversity as a crucial element, is incompatible with those conceptions of the good which do *not* value diversity. Thus, a liberalism based on the value of cultural diversity is too restrictive ('sectarian' is Rawls's phrase[7]) for a multicultural society. Since it is the task of liberalism to seek principles of justice which are as far as possible neutral between different ways of life, it should not favour one conception over another. On this view, the liberal State will be a culturally neutral one, and will treat cultural identity as a private concern, a matter of individual choice or commitment, not a question of public policy. The State should treat culture, as it treats religion, as falling within the sphere of individual right, a sphere which should be protected and not interfered with by the State.

It is important to be clear about what is at stake here. As I have argued in previous chapters, culture exists in the language we use, the forms of social interaction in which we are at home, the symbols we recognise as ours, even in the food we eat and the games we play. The pervasive social culture into which we are born is one of the most significant determinants of our identity. We acquire it through the family, social interaction and education. Normally, we do not choose to acquire a culture, nor can we choose to give it up. It is rather that our cultural identity provides the context within which we choose, and sometimes the criteria on which we choose; it is not itself an object of choice. Culture in this sense is embodied in our sense of who we are and in the social practices within which we exist. Where these two coincide, our individual identity is confirmed and reflected in our social life, and as we express our identity, we reproduce that form of social life.

Will Kymlicka has argued that liberals should recognise the importance of culture just because it is a precondition of individual freedom.[8] In order to exercise our capacity to choose, and in particular to conceive and reconceive our various projects, we need a secure sense of who we are and of the kinds of things which give our lives significance. This is provided by our cultural identity. Kymlicka's argument provides an important reminder of the cultural conditions of autonomy; but it hardly provides a defence of those many forms of culture which do not themselves value or encourage freedom of choice.

It may be, as Kymlicka would argue,[9] that a liberal should not be in the business of defending those cultures which do not value autonomy; but we still need an account which explains why those cultures are so important to their members. Further, Kymlicka's argument does not adequately explain the importance of retaining one's *existing* culture. If culture in general is a precondition of autonomy, then it does not matter (within broad limits) *which* culture an individual has. But much of the moral force and political intensity of multiculturalism resides in the desire of people to retain their own culture.

A better account of the importance of culture lies in the notion of identity. If my identity is formed within a certain culture, then it defines my fundamental perspective on the world, constitutes me as a member of a community, provides me a set of memories and aspirations, and thus with a past and a future, and it gives me a place which is mine. My cultural identity defines who I am; and when I envisage the loss of that identity, I am confronted with the thought that I will lose my sense of self and cease to be what I am. It is important now, and it will be important later, to recognise that such losses can occur – and in certain cases be voluntarily incurred – and that I will in fact continue to exist. However, the loss is a considerable one; and usually carries with it a continuing and deep sense of dislocation and alienation. It is because culture is important to identity, in this sense, that the claim of the individual to his or her own culture has so much force.[10]

To what extent can this claim be met within the framework of a liberalism which claims neutrality between conceptions of the good, and thus, presumably, between the ways of life associated with various cultures? Chandran Kukathas has recently argued that a liberalism of this kind can provide all the protection that cultural identities can reasonably – and legitimately – want.[11] The claims of diverse cultures are, he argues, protected by one of the most fundamental rights in the liberal lexicon, the freedom of association. So long as this right is protected by the Government, it will secure the existence of those cultures which continue to attract the support of their members. Kukathas recognises, of course, that most cultural groups are not associations which people voluntarily join. People are typically born into a culture, and acquire their cultural identity through upbringing, education and social interaction, not through a voluntary act of affiliation. Kukathas argues, however, that just so long as one has as a 'fundamental right', the 'right to be free to leave' the community, then one's association with it can be conceived as voluntary – to a 'small' but presumably sufficient extent.[12] An implication of Kukathas's position is that a liberal polity may include cultural communities which are not themselves liberal. Liberal toleration extends to illiberal groups, just so long as their members are entitled to leave.

Kukathas recognises that many minority cultures are under threat in the modern world, but argues that it is not the appropriate role of governments to protect them, and that, when they attempt to do so, they interfere with the processes of change and development which are necessary for a culture's well-being. Kukathas provides an important reminder that cultures – and the identities they define – are not static features of the social environment, but are subject to change and development, growth and stagnation, and so on. He argues that the health of a culture, and its ultimate survival, depends on the commitments of its bearers; not on Government policy. Kukathas's arguments here are important but overstated. There is no doubt that it is difficult to put in place Government policies which foster a healthy and independent cultural life; but this does not mean that it is impossible. Indeed, one such policy might be to secure the right of internal disagreement and criticism. If the right to leave is the only right of protest that members of a community have, then internal criticism and reform will be stifled.[13]

However, the crucial problem with Kukathas's position is that it does not take into account the effects of cultural inequality. Where there is a dominant culture – the culture, say, of economic life and social interaction – then a marginal culture will be under threat just so long as it remains a matter of private commitment. In practice, most people have little choice but to participate in the dominant culture if they are to have jobs and participate in social and political life, and those who find their identity in a minority culture must be disadvantaged. It is for this reason that members of cultural minorities have asked that the State intervene to protect it from the normal pressures of the economic and cultural market-place, perhaps by the provision of subsidies or by making special legal provision or exemption for them. And to liberals such as Kukathas who are reluctant to allow the State to intervene in this way, they have a powerful response: the State itself is complicit in their cultural marginalisation. No State in the modern Western world is as culturally neutral as the post-Rawlsian liberal argument requires. Almost every state carries on its political and legal affairs in a national language, exercises its authority through rituals and procedures which are imbued with a particular national culture, and administers an educational system which gives priority to one language, one history and – as one might say – one people.[14] So the request for cultural protection is for the redress of an existing imbalance, a redress which – it would seem – can easily be justified in the name of liberal egalitarianism. If the State functions to protect and perpetuate one culture, then surely liberal justice demands that it protect and perpetuate others as well.

But, paradoxically, this argument is too strong: if it exposes an enormous blind spot in one liberal position, it also brings out a limitation in multiculturalism. For the fact that modern states favour one culture over others is not a mere contingency, but is essential to their practice. As I have argued in Chapter 1 (following Ernest Gellner and others), it is likely that *any* State which is appropriate for a modern industrial, market society will provide a unified educational and administrative system which will inevitably favour one culture over others. Further, and this is a separate argument, there are good reasons why this *should* be the case, at least in a liberal and democratic state. Liberalism requires that the State define and protect a range of rights for the citizen; that it provide due legal process through which its members may secure justice; that it conduct its political affairs in ways which are open to scrutiny and criticism; and that it provide an education which allows its citizens to participate in basic social, economic and political activities. In a democratic state, political matters must be open to widespread discussion in which all citizens are able to participate; and citizens must be able to take cognisance of the views and interests of as many other groups as possible. As John Stuart Mill – no enemy of diversity – recognised, it is not possible for a genuinely liberal and democratic state to be culturally neutral.[15] The key connection here is *language*. Where a State is multilingual in its operations (Switzerland is the usual example), it has to make special provisions for this to work (Switzerland has an unusually strong set of civic practices; it works in many ways like a federation, rather than a unified state). Without special provisions – and perhaps other favourable conditions (Switzerland is both small and very wealthy; it runs very tight immigration policies) – multilingualism in the operation of the State would stand in the way of it performing some of the key functions demanded by the liberal. While it is a mistake to identify language with culture, it is clearly a crucial constituent. When one also considers the requirement that the State attract the allegiance and commitment of its citizens, it is hard to imagine a modern state which did not appropriate to itself the further cultural resources necessary for this. The State will exercise authority through symbols and rituals which have a resonance with the traditions of the country; it will legitimise it through a historical narrative and a characterisation of the land and the people which it claims as its own. In other words, the integrity of the body politic, and more especially of a liberal polity, requires the existence of a preferred *public culture*, and this will inevitably occupy a privileged position with respect to other cultures.

It is, perhaps, a further argument – also to be found in Mill – that a modern society requires the elements of a common culture if it is to maintain the minimal level of the trust and fellow feeling necessary for even the most impersonal forms of social life. I would not want to press this argument too far. The demands on social cohesion differ in different contexts; some modern cities show that a semblance of social life can continue without much by way of trust and fellow feeling. However, in circumstances which require commitment, sacrifice or joint action, there will need to be a strong sense of community and common cultural identity. It is no accident that many of the elements of the Welfare State are argued for in the name of the nation (e.g. 'national health'), rather than an abstract principle of social justice. Sensitivity to the plight of fellow citizens is at least in part carried by the sense of a shared national identity, and it is because of this that we have been prepared to empower the State to provide a basic standard of well-being for all citizens.[16]

The idea that the modern State should in principle be neutral between different cultures is a fantasy, though a surprisingly widespread one.[17] It ignores the fact that State power in the modern world necessarily has a cultural dimension. This means that the goal of cultural equality within a society – what David Miller has called 'radical multiculturalism'[18] – is simply not a viable one. The characteristic modern form of the State is the *nation-state*, i.e. the State whose legitimacy depends on its claim to represent a community defined by its culture. This was not always the case. For example, the vast multi-ethnic empires and the cities of the premodern world were at least as 'multicultural' as any modern State.[19] But the nature of State power, the scope of its interventions in the lives of its subjects, and the problem of legitimation are enormously different in the modern world. It is in these circumstances, where the idea of a common culture plays a key role in the practice and the rationale of the State, that the issue of multiculturalism takes on a pertinence that it lacked in the premodern world.

Curiously, Kymlicka, who recognises the cultural dimension of State power, is reluctant to define this culture in terms of the nation. For Kymlicka: '[A] "nation" means a historical community, more or less institutionally complete, occupying a given territory or homeland, sharing a distinct language and culture.'[20] And he concludes from this that many modern states are not genuine 'nation-states', but are multinational in that they include more or less well defined nations within their borders. For example, Canada consists of three nations – the Anglophone majority, the Québécois, and the indigenous people; the United States of many – including various native American communities, Puerto Rico, Hawaii, etc.; Switzerland of three – the French-, German- and Italian-speaking communities; and so on. But Kymlicka does not notice that his 'multinational States' *also* satisfy his criterion of nationhood; indeed, they do so quite as much as his preferred 'subnations'. The United States, for example, is an institutionally complete, historic community with a given territory, and has a distinct public culture and language, even though it also contains smaller nation-like communities within it. So, too, to use an example he does not mention, is the United Kingdom. The point is that cultures, and the communities they define, are not discrete entities, but may overlap, or nest within each other. The fact that Scotland and Hawaii may satisfy the condition of cultural and territorial unity, so as to count as nations on their own, does not mean that they cannot be parts of larger nations (or, for that matter, contain smaller nations within them). The one individual can be *both* Scottish *and* British, or *both* Hawaiian *and* American. The challenge that these 'multinational nations' must meet is that the central State attract or create the cultural resources necessary to service its operations, but this is compatible with a degree of cultural diversity – even nationhood – elsewhere.[21] Of course sometimes multinational nations do not meet the challenge of creating an encompassing national identity, and a national minority will strike out for independence – as the Basques in Spain and France and the Québécois in Canada. But that some multinational nations are under strain does not mean that there are none.

It may be suggested that the main issue here is one of definition, with Kymlicka requiring a high degree of cultural and linguistic homogeneity within a community before it is to be counted as a nation. But, on this definition, it is not clear whether there will be *any* nations. Certainly at least two of Kymlicka's three 'nations' in Canada – the Anglophone majority and the indigenous minority – will not count as such. Nor would the United States, France, the United Kingdom, and even England. It is hard to see the point of using a definition of 'nation' which excludes these central cases. What is more, by employing a definition which fails to recognise the actual diversity of the nation-state, Kymlicka exaggerates the extent of the problems posed by multiculturalism.[22] This is not to deny the problems. The fact that all national cultures allow for diversity (think of the different ways in which Cockneys, Liverpudlians and Oxbridge graduates are all 'English') does not mean that anything goes. The modern State operates through an officially recognised and supported public culture, consisting of a recognised national language, a history, a range of cultural traditions, publicly accepted rituals, and so on. There will be disputes about various aspects of the national culture – for example, about what should be emphasised in the national history, about exclusions and prejudices that are associated with it, and even about the various ways in which one may be a member. Its content is subject to debate and change. A national culture – any culture for that matter – is something like a tradition in Alasdair MacIntyre's sense: it is a story of change and evolution, not a fixed essence.[23] Nevertheless, there will be those, from outside that tradition, whose identity lies elsewhere, members of minority cultures who find themselves without public confirmation of their identity and apparently excluded from the dominant culture. What is their place in the political and social order of the nation-state? Can we provide an understanding of multiculturalism which recognises the significance of this alienation, as well as the need for a dominant public culture?

Let us consider the situation of people who decide to leave a country which, we may suppose, provides the necessary sustenance for their own identity in order to settle in a country which does not. One consequence of this decision is that they can no longer demand the right to have their identity affirmed in the public culture of the country in which they will live. For many this will mean an alienation from the prevailing public culture which may well last their lifetime; and it also means that they will know that their children and grandchildren will grow into a culture which is not theirs. While there is loss, even tragedy in this, it must be regarded as an inevitable consequence of the decision to migrate. Those who make this choice must be aware – and ought to be made aware – of what it means. They, or at least their children, must learn the national language and come to terms with the characteristic forms of social interaction if they are not to be disadvantaged. Of course, the nature and extent of the loss may be much greater than could be envisaged; so the choice to return home should be available (and very many migrants do choose eventually to return to their home countries). But as we have seen, there are strong liberal and democratic reasons why this loss should be borne. A citizen of a democratic country should be able to understand the main issues of political debate and policy; be prepared to participate in political life; to accept – within reasonable limits – the results of the democratic process; and to commit him- or herself to the common causes and responsibilities of the new country. A national identity is not an optional extra to these commitments, but is involved in them. The decision to immigrate must be understood as involving a commitment to share some elements of the identity and culture of the host country. It is, of course, a corollary of this that the host country allow that commitment, and not conceive the immigrants as second-class citizens, forever excluded from full participation in the culture and politics of their new country.

There are complications which will need to be taken into account. The decision to migrate is not always as voluntary as I have pretended. People may choose to leave their own country, not merely because another offers better prospects for them and their families, but because they need to escape from intolerable circumstances. But, whoever is responsible for the circumstances from which they are escaping, it is unlikely to be the Government and people of the country where they intend to settle.[24] A national Government may, and certainly should, accept some refugees, knowing that their identity and commitments will continue to lie with their native country, and that they will not become full members of the host society. But the normal case is where the immigrant desires permanent settlement, and, in this case, they should be treated as potential citizens They should be expected to participate in the public culture of their new country, and provided the means and the opportunity to do so.

This may seem like a return to assimilation. However, a liberal state will also recognise that the process of change should involve the national culture as well. Multiculturalism in the context of the nation-state should be understood as the idea that the cultural identity which informs the political structure be understood in such a way that it both allows for the existence of cultural diversity and is open to influence by that diversity. The dominant public culture – the nation's self-understanding – is susceptible to change, and minority cultures should contribute to that change. This means that cultural groups should be given the freedom to form associations, language schools, lobby groups, and so on. If they are to contribute to public debate, they must be able to sustain a sense of their own cultural identity, and it may well be that the Government should play a role in encouraging and even financing these endeavours. In many cases, including Australia, the contribution of cultural minorities to public life has transformed the national culture beyond recognition. There is, however, a price to pay. If cultural minorities and marginal groups are to contribute to the ongoing debate about the content and meaning of the national culture, they cannot themselves claim that their own cultures and positions should be protected from its outcome. The sphere of public culture is a sphere of conversation, negotiation and occasionally conflict; and what is brought into this sphere cannot be removed from its influence. Sometimes cultural minorities claim that they have a *right* to maintain their culture in an unaltered form. The language of rights serves to present a claim in a non-negotiable form, and thus of isolating it from the effects of public debates. In certain cases this is legitimate. However, its consequences must be understood. If a culture is a non-negotiable right, then it is a matter of private commitment; it is not a participant in public life. Once a culture enters the sphere of politics it loses its protected status. If it is to transform the self-understanding of a nation, it may well find that its own self-understanding is transformed in the process.

There is no doubt that immigrant cultures will contribute to national culture from a position of inequality. The culture to which they are contributing is established and central; theirs is newly arrived and marginal. This is nearly inevitable. Immigrants cannot and should not expect that their culture should take its place on the public stage on an equal footing with the existing public culture. This is not to deny what Charles Taylor has called 'the presumption of equal worth' of cultures.[25] The point here is not that the culture of immigrants is in some sense inferior *as a culture* to that of their host country. Like Taylor, I can make little sense of this idea. The inequality is political and contextual. The immigrants' language is not the language of public debate, their history not taught in schools, and so on. Their culture does not provide the symbols and rituals through which public life is carried on, and it will not enjoy the same level of recognition. Ultimately – and on this point Kukathas must be right – the survival and health of an immigrant culture depends on the commitment of its members. The contextual inequality between the national and the immigrant cultures would of course be reversed if migration took place in the other direction.

Migration inevitably involves alienation. However, it should also carry with it a commitment to participate in the public culture of the nation which will be one's new home, to acquire a new national identity, and also – something I will say more of later – to accept the responsibilities which go with this. This does not rule out the State involving itself in multicultural practices. A liberal state will need to learn the language and cultures of its minorities. Its welfare agencies, education departments, police forces and law courts will have to deal with their ethnic constituencies differently from those of the dominant cultural group if they are to reach some semblance of liberal equality of treatment. But this is, or ought to be, informed by the idea that individuals should be treated equally, not that all cultures are on equal footing.

Behind this argument stands the assumption that states have the right to set the terms of immigration. Legally, the assumption is unproblematic: it is a condition of sovereignty that the State has the right to police its borders and set the terms of entry. But it raises troubling moral issues. There is, at the very least, a tension between the principles of liberalism and the claim that states have the right to control entry.[26] If the freedoms of movement and occupation are important liberal rights, it is not clear why they should stop at state borders. Given the enormous inequalities in the way in which the world is divided up and the differences in life expectations between states, there is little doubt that if people were allowed to move as they wished and work where they found employment there would be a massive movement of the world's population across existing borders. The main thing that stands in the way of this redistribution is the right of states to restrict entry into their territory.

The issue is complex, and I will only touch on one aspect of it here. One of the ideas underlying legal sovereignty is the principle that members of a certain cultural group – a nation – have a privileged relationship with a certain territory. The 'homeland' of each nation is defined by is history, its literature, its music and its art, and it provides – or promises – members of the nation a special place of belonging. It is because of this special relationship that they claim the right to live in their homeland, to travel around it, and – through their state – the right to set the terms under which others can gain entry to it. This principle – the moral sovereignty of the nation – has played an enormous role in the past 200 years and continues to do so. If it has not been properly discussed in philosophy and political theory, this is because of the dominance of a narrowly economic understanding of the relationship between people and their physical environment. Land – whether collectively or individually owned – is conceived to be an object of use or of exchange, not a repository of meaning. This economic understanding is inadequate even for individual property, however. Very few of us conceive of our home and personal possessions primarily as exchangeable objects of utility; all of us have possessions which are tied to our sense of self and which are exchanged only with considerable sense of loss. But the economic understanding is even more inadequate for the sites, areas or territories to which members of various groups claim a special affiliation. It may well be that *every* significant identity carries with it a sense of place and provides its bearers with a special relationship to that place. In the case of nations, the territorial affiliation is obvious and crucial. The nation's homeland is the ground, in a near literal sense, of its members' sense of self. As I have argued in Chapter 1, the extension of territorial identification from locality to national homeland is undoubtedly a product of the modern world, reflecting increased mobility, the emergence of national cultures, and changes in the extent and nature of State power. But although it is historically contingent, this sense of place has a powerful presence in everyday moral consciousness, and it is this which defines England for the English, Australia for Australians and no doubt Kurdistan for the Kurds, and which underlies the claims of a people to sovereignty over their national homeland.[27]

It may be that the doctrine of national sovereignty is no longer sustainable in this form. An exclusive attachment to a homeland is – poignantly and tragically – incompatible with the existence of competing claims to the same national homeland. However, those of us who live in the economically advanced and politically stable countries of the Western world should remember, as we condemn the attempts to apply this principle in the former Yugoslavia and Soviet Union, that we also rely on it to secure a comfortable refuge against the demands of the poor and needy beyond our borders. Though the doctrine rationalises violence and barbarity in the one place, and complacency in the other, it cannot and should not be rejected out of hand. The sense of place has deep cultural and emotional roots, and these need to be explored and understood, not merely dismissed in favour of the deliverances of abstract theory. But theory must have a role in the argument too. Though we should recognise the moral force of national sovereignty, considerations of need and equity also have force. The desire of an existing national community to maintain its relationship to a given territory must be balanced against the needs of those living in conditions of poverty or political repression elsewhere. The claims of national identity deserve a presence in the argument, but they cannot be allowed to settle the issue.

There is no reason to suppose that a morally serious engagement with these issues would not conclude that relatively wealthy and underpopulated countries such as Australia, New Zealand and Canada should substantially increase their rate of immigration, and change the criteria on which potential immigrants are accepted.[28] The doctrine of national sovereignty would play a dual role in this argument. Continuity of an existing national identity might provide grounds to limit immigration; and nation-states could ask that their new members engage with the existing national cultures. Under (unlikely) conditions of large-scale immigration, it might even be necessary to take steps to protect the existing national cultures from being swamped by newly emerging majorities. Under ordinary circumstances, however, no such protection is needed or justified: the existing national culture already holds all the important cards. In this case, what is required is a reasonable and humane policy of multiculturalism: the State should allow – in fact encourage – the practice of cultural diversity, and allow this diversity to contribute to its own cultural self-understanding.[29]

Aboriginal rights

In 1788, White settlers established a colony on the east coast of the Australian continent. They happened to be English, but there is no reason to suppose that, if the English had not arrived, another European power would not have established a colony. Estimates vary as to the number of Aboriginal inhabitants, but it is usually thought to be in the vicinity of 300,000–350,000.[30] These people belonged to some 500 tribal groups, and these ranged over vast areas of what was to become Australia. Archaeological evidence suggests that they had lived there for at least 60,000 years.[31] In terms of any conceivable human experience of time, the Aborigines[32] have been in Australia forever. Over this time, they developed a complex and fascinating culture and mode of living, both with each other and with the environment.

The history of White settlement is the history of the dispossession of these people and their culture. It is also the history of genocide: Aborigines were killed in large numbers, both directly and indirectly as a result of White settlement. At the turn of this century, when the Australian Commonwealth was formed, the Aboriginal population was around 95,000, and by 1930 it was down to 74,000. It was widely expected that they would eventually die out. By 1991, however, it had recovered to around 240,000.[33] Aborigines were denied full citizenship until 1967, and were subject to barbaric and contradictory policies of forced assimilation and social discrimination. Their culture and way of life has been so savagely eroded that in some cases it has disappeared beyond the possibility of recuperation. Today, in terms of every standard measure of well-being (health, life expectancy, alcoholism, property, wealth, employment, education, liability to imprisonment, etc.), Aborigines are the most disadvantaged group in the Australian population.[34]

The broad facts about dispossession and genocide in Australia are similar to those in New Zealand and the Americas. What is perhaps unique to the Australian case is the absence of *any* recognition of a pre-existing legal and political status. The colonial history of North America is littered with treaties made between settlers and indigenous groups. In New Zealand, the Treaty of Waitangi was signed by 500 Maori chiefs and representatives of the British Crown in 1840.[35] While these treaties were invariably broken, they indicate a recognition by the occupying powers of the legal and political rights of the indigenous people, and they have provided a useful point of leverage in contemporary debates and struggles. Nothing like this happened in Australia. No treaties were made. Aboriginal groups were not treated as political societies. Instead, the White advance into the continent was rationalised by the convenient myth of *terra nullius*. It was claimed that the Aboriginal people had no ownership relation with the land, and it was thus available for expropriation without consent or compensation.

The doctrine of *terra nullius* was finally overturned in 1992 in the case of *Mabo vs Queensland* (the 'Mabo Case'), when the High Court of Australia ruled that Australian Common Law included the recognition of pre-existing 'native title'.[36] The Court acknowledged the existence, prior to European settlement, of a complex understanding of the relationship of people to the land, an understanding which included – though it went beyond – a set of rights and duties with respect to its occupancy and use. There was, however, an important limitation to the Mabo judgement. While it established legally that members of Aboriginal communities enjoyed property rights over various portions of the Australian continent, it did not establish that the communities also had rights of political and legal *sovereignty* over that land. Indeed, it explicitly refused to do this. If in one sense ('property'), the Mabo judgement recognised that Australia had once belonged to the Aboriginal people, in another sense ('sovereignty'), it did not. So, when the British Crown claimed sovereignty over Australia (initially over the eastern two-thirds), this meant that the Crown and succeeding legislatures had the right to annul pre-existing ownership as they saw fit. By the time of the Mabo judgement, much Aboriginal land had in fact been legally appropriated and the original title extinguished. In order for an original native title over land to remain in existence, the Aboriginal people must have maintained an ongoing relationship with it. According to one estimate, this meant that over 80 per cent of the Aboriginal population was excluded from the Mabo judgement. And even where native title continues to exist, it can still be nullified by legislation (though compensation will be payable, as with any expropriation by the Crown).[37]

It is a moot point whether it is coherent to recognise pre-existing property rights but to deny sovereignty.[38] However, this a matter of law, and I will not pursue it here. Morally, at least, the issue is straightforward. The five hundred or so tribes which inhabited Australia prior to Western settlement had done so without dispute (except, occasionally, with each other) for many millennia. Though they may historically have gained possession of the land by the dispossession of some other people, this was so long ago as to leave no currently identifiable group with a claim to reparation. Their relationship to the land sustained a unique and complex culture – one which recognised the relationship to the land as crucial to their identity and well-being. Indeed, given the nature of Aboriginal property – that the land was used by individuals in virtue of their membership of tribes; that it was not alienable either by individuals or tribes; and that the relationship between tribes was predicated on an understanding of each tribe's prior rights to certain territories – there is no easy way to distinguish the claim to property from the claim to sovereignty. If we are to translate the Aboriginal relation to the land into Western legal categories with a minimum of distortion, then the concepts of property and sovereignty will both be required. It may be that the Aboriginal people lacked a state – or states – with sufficient power to deter invaders and that their sovereignty was not part of an international framework of reciprocal recognition. But the moral basis of their claim was just as strong as that of every modern state to have its territorial integrity and right to control entry respected. Indeed, the absence of other identifiable claimants suggests that the claim is a good deal stronger than that of the nation-state which has inherited their dispossession. The Aboriginal people were entitled to have their sovereignty recognised in 1788, and it should be retrospectively recognised now.[39]

I have been discussing the nature of the dispossession of the Aborigines because it seems obvious that the history is morally relevant; and that, in considering what is now due to the Aboriginal people, we should not merely take into account their present situation, but also what has happened in the past. This assumption is shared by Aboriginal people themselves. For them it is crucial, both to their own identity and for an understanding of what is due to them, that they are the original inhabitants of Australia.[40] This assertion of the moral relevance of the past is by no means unique to indigenous people: probably every important identity is constructed in terms of a conception of the past, and questions of current well-being will often require that some aspect of the past be addressed by way of compensation, retribution, or reinterpretation. The current situation of Aborigines is partly constituted by the history of their expropriation, and we cannot address that situation without taking that past into account.

Curiously, however, this is denied by Will Kymlicka, who argues that:

> it is a mistake...to put too much weight on historical property rights...[for] the idea of compensating for historical wrongs, taken to its logical conclusion, implies that all the land which was wrongly taken from indigenous people in the Americas or Australia or New Zealand should be returned to them. This would create massive unfairness, given that the original European settlers and later immigrants have now produced hundreds of millions of descendants, and this land is the only home they know. Changing circumstances make it impossible and undesirable to compensate for certain historical wrongs.[41]

But Kymlicka's argument is confused. If the 'logical conclusion' of 'compensating for historical wrongs' would be further 'massive unfairness', then no doubt this should be taken into account in resolving what now ought to be done. But this does not imply that we should ignore or downplay the 'historical wrong'. Rather, we should assess what it is and what might count as addressing it, and *then* consider the costs of so doing. It might well be that the costs in terms of further consequential injustice will severely limit the extent to which compensation is possible. But this should not inhibit the initial inquiry. Indeed the comparison requires that it proceed.

Kymlicka recognises that there is an important distinction between the claims of indigenous people and that of immigrant cultural minorities. Indigenous groups are, he argues, national minorities, i.e. they are more or less self-contained communities with their own culture and territories. What they want, and what they have a right to, is self-determination; that is, some form of political independence. Immigrant groups, on the other hand, do not have a territorial identity (at least, not in their new country), and, while they have certain cultural rights, they do not add up to independence, nor even to cultural equality with the dominant culture.[42] However, there are several problems with this way of distinguishing between the claims of indigenous people and those of immigrants. It is simply not true that national self-determination is desired by all indigenous people. This is certainly not the case in Australia where, as we shall see, there is a vigorous debate about this very issue with most Aboriginal leaders opposed to it. Even when indigenous groups do seek a form of national independence, it is not clear that this is always an appropriate goal. If in the final analysis it is what indigenous people want which should determine their future, it still needs to be discussed what they *ought* to want. This is a substantive and complex political issue, and it needs to be decided by debate amongst the indigenous people themselves. To decide this in advance is to prejudge the outcome of that debate and to limit the options available to indigenous people. It should also be noted that when Kymlicka attempts to justify the moral difference between indigenous and immigrant groups, he appeals – as he must – to their different histories. It is because immigrants (once) chose to leave their own country and settle in a new one that they (and their descendants) may be assumed to have voluntarily incurred their minority status. Their past consent explains why they do not now have a claim to cultural equality. It is because indigenous people were not given a choice, but had their land taken away from them and their culture destroyed or threatened by foreign settlement, that they retain a claim to sovereignty over traditional lands. The lack of past consent explains their present moral claim. This means that, in order to understand the present claims of indigenous people, we have to come to terms with the nature of the historical wrong they suffered.[43]

It is important, though difficult, to contextualise the moral issues involved here. The invasion of the Australian continent and the arrogation of sovereignty by the British Crown and subsequent Australian governments must be placed in the context of what was and is historically possible. It was nearly inevitable that there would be enormous changes to the situation of Aboriginal people. They were hunters and gatherers, and were able to live, and by their own standards to live well, prior to European settlement. But given the agricultural revolution of some 12,000 years before, the Industrial Revolution which was getting under way even as Captain Cook explored the eastern coast of the Australian continent, and the developments in transport, navigation and trade in the sixteenth, seventeenth and eighteenth centuries, there is no way that this way of life could have maintained itself without fundamental change. Nor is it clear that it ought to have. Where between 300,000 and 350,000 indigenous people were able to subsist before White settlement, neither dependent on nor contributing to the rest of the world, a modern agriculture and industry now enable the Australian continent to support countless millions more. These considerations do not justify, excuse or even rationalise the brutality, oppression, exploitation and misery which were the direct and indirect consequence of White settlement in Australia. But one does not have to believe in doctrines of historical progress to think that these should be placed in the context of what was historically possible, and one does not have to be a utilitarian to think that the interests and needs of the many must figure in any argument as to the rights of the few.

The moral sovereignty held by the Aboriginal people in 1788 was not, any more than the sovereignty enjoyed by nation-states today, an absolute right. It covers a range of factors relating to traditional use of the land, its importance to the way of life and the identity of the people, and the absence of other identifiable claimants. Like the national sovereignty claimed by states in the modern world, it must be taken into account in any argument as to the final disposal of that territory. But it should not predetermine the outcome of that argument. If, as I suggested earlier in this chapter, wealthy nations ought to adopt immigration policies which take account of the needs of those outside their borders, so too there are moral as well as historical grounds for suggesting that the Aboriginal inhabitants of Australia could not expect to retain sole occupation of the continent.

These considerations are not intended to diminish the responsibility of present-day Australians for the expropriation of Australian Aboriginal people, but to place the origins of that responsibility within a historical narrative rather than an abstract moral discourse of right and wrong. They also indicate some aspects of the reparation which is due. For example, they place the onus squarely on White settlers to recognise the priority of Aboriginal ways of life and traditions, to respect and learn about Aboriginal culture, and to change their own self-understanding in response to it. As I argued earlier, the conception of national sovereignty at work in the Western world demands no less of immigrants; and there is no reason to diminish these demands in the case of the moral sovereignty which we can retrospectively ascribe to Aboriginal people. It means that all migrants to this country have the responsibility to come to terms with the culture of the Aboriginal inhabitants. It also means that the understanding of Australian national identity must recognise Aboriginality, and this recognition must have a prominent place in all public and official occasions. The symbols and rituals through which Australians identify themselves as Australians, both to themselves and others, must give priority to the history and achievements of those who have the best claim to this identity.

I have already mentioned that there are some Aboriginal leaders and sympathisers who argue that pre-existing sovereignty establishes a claim to national independence.[44] For them, the transformation of non-Aboriginal Australian identity is largely irrelevant. They argue that Aboriginal people possess, not just residual ownership, but also residual sovereignty and that it is appropriate to assert that sovereignty in the form of one or more autonomous Aboriginal states. For example, Henry Reynolds has argued that there is good reason to extend the Mabo judgement to include sovereignty and that national self-determination for Aboriginal and Torres Strait Islander people would complete the logic of that recognition.[45] And, as I have already mentioned, Will Kymlicka and others have argued that the indigenous people of Canada and the United States constitute national minorities and have therefore a right to national independence.[46]

There can be little doubt that there is a strong prima facie case for the national independence of indigenous people. Although there is considerable controversy about the conditions under which a group can claim the right to secede from a state which claims authority over it, there is general agreement that one clear instance of this right is when a group with a legitimate claim to its own territory has been unjustly incorporated into a larger political entity.[47] The right of indigenous people to secede from the political authority of their colonial and postcolonial masters seems to be at least as strong as that of the Latvian, Estonian and Lithuanian people to secede from the old Soviet Union. Despite this, I will suggest that secession and national independence is not an appropriate goal, at least for most Aboriginal people. I will not directly address the question whether they have this right. It seems likely that they do. A more important question is whether they should exercise it.[48]

Now it may well be that some form of sovereignty is appropriate in many areas and for many Aborigines. It is even possible – and this is the policy of the Aboriginal Provisional Government – that these separate areas could together constitute an Aboriginal nation. However, there is an enormous diversity of Aboriginal languages and cultures, and though the depth and complexity of the relationship to the land, together with the shared experience of invasion, resistance and dispossession, are significant common threads, the economic dependence and geographical fragmentation constitute formidable problems to such a project. Except for occasional rhetoric, it is not clear that it is seriously envisaged. What is a much more likely scenario is that certain groups will seek a greater or lesser degree of independence. For example, the Torres Straits Islanders, who are culturally homogeneous and ethnically distinct from mainland Aborigines, might well seek a quasi-independent status from Australia. Even in this case, given the relatively small numbers of people involved and the lack of economic resources and defence capacity, it is not likely that full independence would be possible or sought. Most Aborigines and their sympathisers are sceptical of this programme.[49] What is more likely is that in some regions – in Western Australia, the Northern Territory and Cape York – Aboriginal communities will achieve a considerable measure of autonomy within the Australian Commonwealth, and that this will extend to different systems of laws and law enforcement, control over entry, and the like. Indeed, very strong forms of self-government of this kind are already in place in certain areas, with local Land Councils – usually consisting of tribal elders and traditional leaders – exercising considerable political and juridical authority. While there are formidable political obstacles in the way of the extension of this programme, there are precedents for quite strong forms of indigenous autonomy in Canada and the United States, and there are even some precedents in Australia, for example, the Norfolk and Cocos Islands, and the existing federal structure could accommodate it.

Developments along these lines would not amount to full autonomy, but they would be a partial recognition of the strength of the Aboriginal claim to sovereignty. Their attraction is that they promise the space – in a literal sense – in which tribal Aborigines can continue or recuperate their culture on their own terms and they provide a political form in which the Aboriginal relationship to the land might be sustained or renewed. The operation of Aboriginal law and custom would be separate, in space if not in time, from that of Western law and custom. It is, however, quite misleading to describe this in the language of national independence. These groups are tiny in relation to the rest of the population and dependent upon the Federal or State governments not merely economically, but also in respect to education, health, physical infrastructure, and the like. For good or ill, these communities are very much part of the Australian nation.

Even this option is not available to those Aborigines – almost certainly the majority – who have long been deprived of their traditional land and are living in the cities and towns of Australia. For many, land rights are no longer on the agenda; their land has long been given over to agricultural, industrial or other use, or their own relationship to it has become tenuous and distant. Many have formed a conception of their own lives which does not involve a direct association with their traditional land. For these Aborigines, life involves much closer contact with dominant non-Aboriginal forms, and cultural change and renewal must take place in this context. The interaction between different laws and customs takes place in the encounter between Aboriginal and non-Aboriginal people occupying or competing for the same streets, pubs, jobs, unemployment offices, sports fields and schools. Much more difficult to envisage than land rights and self-government are the conditions which will allow Aborigines the capacity, not merely to sustain past forms of life, but to create new forms of Aboriginal life in a profoundly non-Aboriginal context. The challenge here is to find the political, legal and social forms in which this can take place.

Discussion of Aboriginal rights almost invariably focusses on those rights which are necessary to recreate or sustain some form of traditional life. These rights – which include land rights and rights of self-government – are very important. If they do not add up to national independence as this was traditionally conceived, they constitute a form of self-determination which provides a partial recognition of Aboriginal claims to sovereignty. But Aboriginal self-determination must take other forms as well. Those Aborigines, who are not in a position to form self-governing communities on traditional land or who choose not to do so, have just as much a historical claim as those who are. However important traditional culture is to Aboriginal people, the rights and resources they are provided should not be predicated on the continuance of that culture.[50] And the conceptual and political difficulties in the way of discovering and establishing the legal, social and political forms in which non-traditional Aboriginals can create and recreate their lives are immense. However difficult they will be to achieve in practice, land rights and self-government for Aborigines are less problematic than changes needed in the towns and cities of Australia. The recognition of Aboriginal difference must find a place, not just in the symbols and rituals of the public culture, but in the legal forms and meanings involved in day to day social life. If there is to be a form of Aboriginal self-determination which is an appropriate response to the past abrogation of Aboriginal moral sovereignty, it must take place as part of the life of the Australian people. The challenge which indigenous and non-indigenous Australians must face is to work out ways to live together, a *modus vivendi* which reflects, not the enormous disparity in power, population and wealth of the two groups, but the moral weight of the claims on both sides.

The Mabo judgement has profoundly transformed the relationship between Aboriginal and non-Aboriginal Australians. However, it may be that a second judgement is even more significant. In December

1996, in the *Wik Peoples vs the State of Queensland*, the High Court ruled by the slimmest of majorities (four to three) that for vast areas of land – the so-called 'pastoral leases' – native title coexisted with agricultural title and that the conditions for coexistence have to be worked out on a piecemeal basis.[51] While the political implications of this judgement have yet to be determined, it does locate very precisely the moral problem facing indigenous and non-indigenous people: that of *coexistence*. Just as pastoralists and local Aboriginal groups have to recognise the existence of two (or sometimes more) sets of legitimate claims to the same stretch of land, so too the inhabitants of Australia – and other countries with a similar history – must come to terms with the existence of two (or more) sets of claims to the same country. These claims cannot be neatly ascribed to different territories. They – and the ways of life they represent – must work themselves out together. It is this central issue which is not confronted by the rhetoric of national independence and sovereignty.

If in virtue of their history and current position, Aboriginal people have certain rights, it is important to ask: Who do they have rights *against*. The usual and I think the correct answer to this question is: non-Aboriginal Australians. But it is important to ask why this should be so. After all, most contemporary Australians will never themselves have acted with the intention of harming Aborigines, and most of the worst atrocities were committed in the past.[52] By what line of inheritance do contemporary Australians inherit the sins of the predecessors? And which contemporary Australians? Is it only those of us of Anglo-Celtic stock whose ancestors came to Australia in the nineteenth century? Should we exclude those recent immigrants, especially those whose background is free of the taints of European colonialism and imperialism? And what of those Australians whose ancestors had no choice in the decision to migrate, but were brought over as convicts?

For those of us brought up to believe that we can only be held responsible for what we as individuals have done, there is something mysterious in the idea that we may be morally accountable for actions performed by others, especially when these may have taken place before we were even born. Much of the philosophical puzzlement about 'collective responsibility' is generated by the assumption that individual agency is the ultimate source of moral obligation. As I argued in Chapter 2, in its most general form this doctrine is self-defeating. If it is by my actions that I acquire obligations, this is because I may properly be held accountable for what I do, and *this* principle does not acquire *its* obligatory force as a consequence of my action. The obligation to keep my promises is not created by my promising to keep my promises. There are also moral obligations of a general kind, e.g. the 'natural duties' not to inflict needless pain, not to kill other human beings, etc., which we all have irrespective of whether we have implicitly or explicitly assumed them. However, a moderate and more plausible version of the doctrine of self-acquired obligations limits it to *specific* obligations. It argues that the only way in which I acquire obligations to some that I do not have to all is by an explicit act of some kind. On this view, I acquire specific collective responsibilities in virtue of my undertaking the rights and duties which accrue to membership of an association. This conception of collective responsibilities has its clearest application in cases where we join a club or corporation and assume certain responsibilities as a consequence of this. However, it does not easily apply to our membership of those associations which are not (or not normally) consequent upon acts of choice. I become a member of a family simply by being born into it. In virtue of that membership I find myself entwined in a complex web of mutual affiliations, responsibilities and commitments. In a similar way, I grow up as a member of a nation and come to identify myself in terms of its land, history and culture. Because I have this identity, I am able to take pride in my country's achievements; but I am also implicated in its failures. The point is not that I chose to accept these responsibilities. Indeed, it may be that the burdens of a particular country's history are so great, or its traditions so oppressive and brutal, that I would not have chosen to be a member of that country. But this does not absolve me of the responsibilities inherent in that country's past. I have them, not because of what I have or would have done, but because of what I am.[53]

When we turn to the specific claims of indigenous people, it is tempting to suggest that the issue of responsibility turns on the question of benefit. Those who have a special responsibility to make reparation to the indigenous people of Australia are those who have lived and flourished on the land that was taken from them. Many, perhaps almost all, non-indigenous Australians have benefited in some way from this expropriation, and it is these people who have the issue of reconciliation, compensation and coming to terms with Aboriginal Australia on their moral agenda. Now there is no doubt that this is part of the answer; but it is not all of it. There is a quite distinct moral thread connecting us with the expropriation of the Aboriginal people, and it is important to disentangle it.

In the Australian case, it is difficult to isolate this thread because it intertwined with the issue of benefit. But that they are separate threads becomes clear in other cases. For example, the Holocaust has a specific relevance to Germans just because they are Germans. This may not be just the responsibility to make reparation; it is also the responsibility to remember what happened, and why it happened. Habermas, speaking as a German, puts this well:

> Our own life is linked to the life context in which Auschwitz was possible not by contingent circumstances but intrinsically. Our form of life is connected with that of our parents and grandparents through a web of familial, local, political, and intellectual traditions that it is difficult to disentangle – that is, through a historical milieu that made us what and who we are today. None of us can escape this milieu, because our identities, both as individuals and as Germans, are indissolubly interwoven with it.[54]

This is not a matter of whether present-day Germans have benefited from the past actions of their compatriots. This is highly unlikely. It is because they have a certain identity they acquire certain historical responsibilities, and find themselves implicated in actions which they themselves have not performed and, indeed, might never have performed.

A national identity involves, not just a sense of place, but a sense of history. The history constitutes the national memory, and it provides a way of locating those who share that identity within a historical community. The history is not given, but subject to debate and reinterpretation. For example, Australians of earlier generations grew up with a history of British achievements, the European 'discovery' and 'exploration' of Australia, the trials and triumphs of the early settlers, and so on. It was a history in which Aboriginals were marginal or absent. But this history has been and is being rewritten. It is now recognised that Australia did not come into existence with European discovery; that Aboriginal cultures and ways of life had existed for millennia; that Aboriginal practices had formed the land which was to be appropriated and exploited by the European immigrants; and that Aborigines had with flair and courage resisted White advances into their country. Australian history is now coming to terms with the suffering, destruction and human tragedy consequent upon the European settlement of Australia. The details of this history may be debated, but it cannot be disavowed. Acquiring a national identity is a way of acquiring that history and the rights and the responsibilities which go with it. The responsibility to come to terms with the Australian past is a morally inescapable component of what is to be Australian.

It is in this context that we must understand one of the dangers of multiculturalism. In so far as it involves a diminished sense of Australian historical identity and a strengthened sense of the affiliations which migrant Australians have to the countries of their origin, it also carries with it a weakened sense of the responsibilities which are written into Australian history. Many recent migrants do not feel implicated in it. It is not just that they personally have not been involved with or had direct dealings with Aboriginal people; this is true of most Anglo-Celtic Australians. It is because their cultural identity implicates them in a different history and, perhaps, with a different set of responsibilities. It is only if they have a sense that coming to be an Australian involves coming to share the history that they will recognise that they have acquired the responsibilities which go with that history.

Though all Australians, even recently arrived ones, have a responsibility to come to terms with the Aboriginal past, present and future of Australia and to contribute to the transformation of Australian life that this will require, the agency which will be most involved is, inevitably, the Australian government. Yet it has this task at a time when the capacity of all national governments to undertake major tasks is being undermined. Governments are under increasing pressure, both from international and domestic economic forces, to reduce Government commitments and expenditure. At the same time, there is widespread cynicism – some of it justified – about the capacity of Government policy makers and bureaucrats to carry out effective social interventions, and widespread alienation from the political process. The political climate of the day, in Australia as in most Western countries, is favourable to smaller and less active governments. This provides the context in which multicultural policies have their somewhat contradictory place.[55] Though they call for greater Government involvement in social life, they also help erode the moral basis for that involvement. Governments may legitimately intervene in the business of society only in so far as they have, and are perceived to have, the moral authority to do so. For the past century or so, governments have relied for this on the claim to represent the nation and to embody and protect that culture which forms the day to day life of its citizens. While the legacy of nationalism is a profoundly ambiguous one, it remains one of the few moral and political resources available to combat the erosion of State authority. If the Government ceases to embody the significant identity and thus commitment of its citizens, it will not have the moral capacity to undertake major tasks, especially those which require sacrifice on the part of citizens. If multiculturalism is not to have this effect (and it is in the interests of multiculturalism itself that it does not), the multicultural agenda must be clearly subordinated to the national one.

In this chapter, I have considered the issues of multiculturalism and indigenous rights largely in isolation from the major social and political changes which are taking place in the contemporary world. However, as I suggested at the beginning of the chapter, the changes in media, communication and transport, which have taken place in the past fifty years or so, have played a role in the emergence of multiculturalism as a significant political issue. These changes have also provided the context in which indigenous claims have acquired a new political salience. It is now time to examine the nature and impact of these changes in more detail. As I argued in Chapter 1, nationalism in the modern world has had specific economic, political and cultural conditions, and it may well be that we are beginning to live in a world in which these conditions no longer obtain. If so, the kind of national identity which has for the past few hundred years provided the cultural underpinnings of a liberal and democratic polity may itself be under threat. In these circumstances, the nature of multiculturalism may change. It may no longer be a political principle expressing the claim of immigrant groups seeking an appropriate place in the established public culture, but become a name for the uneasy coexistence of different cultural groups only united by mutual suspicion and antagonism. At the same time, the conception of national identity may no longer be available to provide moral resources for a state ready to intervene in social life, nor as a way in which a contemporary generation inherits responsibilities for past injustices. If the argument of this chapter is correct, this would have profound effects, not merely on the practice of liberal democracy, but on the possibility of our coming to terms with some of the most important and difficult issues of today's world. I turn to these matters in the next chapter.

5   The end of the affair?

> When philosophy paints its grey in grey, a shape of life has grown old, and it cannot be rejuvenated, but only recognized, by the grey in grey of philosophy; The owl of Minerva begins its flight only with the onset of dusk.
>
> (Hegel)[1]

By 'the grey in grey of philosophy' Hegel meant the theoretical comprehension of a 'shape of life', and this is, he is suggesting, only possible *after* the event. It is only when a historical phenomenon has worked itself out that it will cease to be a dynamic and changing reality; only then can the philosopher be confident that it will not assume a new form and escape the conceptual net that has been laid for it. The 'owl of Minerva' – the symbol of theoretical comprehension – is able to take flight only when dusk is already falling on the shape of life it seeks to understand.

One implication of this passage is that the quest for knowledge of any complex and vital historical reality must always run the risk of prematurity. We arrive at a conceptual understanding of a phenomenon on the basis of what it *has* been; but if it continues to exist, it may well undergo transmutations which will take it beyond the scope of the theory which we have so carefully and lovingly constructed. Capitalism, for example, has assumed forms in the late twentieth century which were not provided for in the best nineteenth- and early twentieth-century accounts, those of Marx and Weber. Another – and perhaps more surprising – implication is that the claim to have constructed an adequate concept of a phenomenon assumes that no new forms of it are on the historical agenda, and that its future existence will only involve repetition of what has already been. When the philosopher proposes a theory of a historical phenomenon, he or she is implicitly claiming that it has just about run its course.

Theoretical comprehension is only available on what is historically – if not chronologically – past.[2]

This does not mean that we should withdraw from the enterprise of theoretical comprehension. However, we should understand its risks and limitations. As Hegel remarked, it 'is just as foolish to imagine that any philosophy can transcend its contemporary world as that an individual can overleap his own time'.[3] We cannot but speak from a perspective formed by our own historical present; it must therefore always be a gamble to suppose that the present will provide an overview of the phenomenon we seek to understand. We must be aware that transmutations may take place which will render our conceptual models obsolete. We should not refrain from making large claims; however, the larger the claim, the greater the possibility that we have unsuccessfully tried to 'overleap' our own time.

One of my aims in this book has been to provide a conceptual understanding of nationalism. If Hegel is right, then this project involves the claim that no new forms of it are on the historical agenda. There is therefore some consistency – though perhaps a hint of circularity also – in the fact that I will now argue that we are able to envisage the end of nationalism. In this chapter, I will suggest that the economic, political and cultural conditions which have created and sustained the nationalist project over the past four to five centuries are in the process of irreversible change and that the circumstances of the contemporary world – the world of 'late modernity' – are antithetical to nationalism.

This claim may seem more than foolhardy at a time in which we are witnessing the eruption of especially intense and sometimes violent forms, not just in the post-Soviet world, but in many parts of the economically advanced Western world as well. It is also a chastening thought that ever since nationalism was clearly identified around 200 years ago, some of the major theorists of modernity – including Kant, Hegel and Marx – have predicted its demise. What reason can we have now to suppose that we have a greater historical knowledge? David Miller's warning is apposite:

> Premature reports of the death of nationality have abounded in the twentieth century, and those who deliver them have constantly been caught off guard by the actual course of historical events.[4]

The risk of being shown to be wrong is, however, unavoidable. My view is that those who anticipated the end of nationalism often correctly identified trends in the modern world which were antithetical to the nationalist enterprise. To some extent, their mistake was one of prematurity: these trends have taken much longer to work themselves out than they anticipated. A more important mistake was that they did not recognise the significance of other trends which have encouraged nationalism. Because they did not recognise that there has been an intimate, indeed symbiotic, relationship between nationalism and modernity, they were inclined to see nationalism as an atavism, destined to be marginalised by the main tendencies of modern life. In this, they were badly mistaken. As I argued in Chapter 1, the modern world has proved to be especially and perhaps uniquely hospitable to nationalism.

However, this is not the end of the story. In this chapter, I will suggest that the conditions which have sustained nationalism are now in the process of irreversible change, and these changes are not merely inhospitable, but hostile to nationalism. My thesis is that the social, economic, political and cultural circumstances which have sustained nationalism over the past three or more centuries are changing irrevocably, and that the main features of a later modernity are antithetical to it. Nationalism is part of the pathology of early modernity. This claim is not incompatible with the continued existence of singularly virulent forms of nationalism. The very historical forces which are undermining its viability also generate intense reactions, so it is not surprising that the end of nationalism is accompanied by eruptions, disruptions and conflicts. However, contemporary struggles are not harbingers of a new era of nationalism in world history, but more like, in Gramsci's phrase, 'morbid symptoms' of a historical period in which the old cannot be reinvigorated, but the new is not yet ready to emerge. In the period of late modernity, it may well be that the nationalist project can only be sustained by political movements which are prepared to turn their backs on mainstream political, economic and cultural life.

I have put the argument bluntly. However, Hegel's warning remains. The final judgement is that of history. It may be that nationalism will take on new forms which take it beyond the arguments presented in this chapter. If so, nationalism might not only survive, but even flourish, though in a transmuted form. Once again, history will have shown theory that it is master.

The end of nationalism

In Chapter 1, I developed an explanation of what I called 'primary' nationalism in terms of three main factors. First: The development of market relations eroded earlier forms of self-sufficient rural life and created a network of interdependence and mobility, initially in more or less well defined territories. This provided the social space within which a conception of the nation could take root. Second: The State was increasingly able to monopolise coercive power within a defined area; it also developed new forms of administration and intervention. It became a constitutive presence in almost all aspects of social life. Third: The development of vernacular print language and the new printing technologies and forms of media allowed for the development of public spheres in which national cultures were developed and disseminated.

Let me now review some of the relevant changes in these three dimensions of social life. Market relations are now more massively and visibly global than ever before. Networks of ownership and control mean that large corporations are no longer based within established states, but are multinational – not merely in their operations – but in their identity. The organisation of material production cuts across state borders, as corporations make use of cheap labour in one place, an educated labour force in another, and a compliant government somewhere else. The production and circulation of information and other non-material commodities are even more resistant to organisation along national lines. The labour market itself is increasingly multinational. Many of the established national economies depend upon a large presence of non-national labour, of a legal, semi-legal or illegal kind. Divisions within the labour force have allowed, or even encouraged, cultural differentiation, so that many migrant workers have no need to assimilate into the dominant language and culture, and meet resistance if they try to. It is likely that these patterns will continue. Most national borders are porous, and industries grow up which are dependent upon the availability of cheap migrant labour. If the world continues to move towards a free and open market in the products of labour, it seems inevitable that this market will eventually encompass labour itself.

Second, there is the diminishing authority of the nation-state itself. In the modern world, no state can turn its back on economic development, except at immense cost to stability and strength. This imperative has meant a progressive loss of national independence and state sovereignty. National governments have come to depend on the good will of a number of international financial institutions (the World Bank, the OECD, etc.) and are hostage to a variety of international agreements. Financial deregulation has ceased to be a matter of choice for national governments, but a condition of receiving economic assistance, credits, investment and the like, and this has meant that national policies are now much more subject to global forces than they ever were before. In order to placate financial markets, states have often removed key areas of economic policy from political decision by handing them over to independent authorities (e.g. reserve banks). Of course, the nation-state retains an enormous amount of power. It is responsible for security, welfare, education, and provision of infrastructure within its own borders, and in many cases retains the capacity for the effective use of force on a wide scale. But in the long term, states – even the most powerful – have little choice but to exercise their control in these areas within the constraints imposed on it by the global market. The traditional nationalist ideal of self-sufficiency has become an obvious illusion.

Paradoxically, however, the very processes which are eroding the position of the nation-state also seem to make resurgent nationalisms of a traditional kind much more viable. The nineteenth- and early twentieth-century idea that there was a threshold size for a viable nation is no longer persuasive.[5] A situation in which even the larger nation-states must give up their claim to economic independence, provides a context in which national minorities can make a claim to their own state. Québécois and Scottish claims to secession are a good deal more plausible in the context of the North America Free Trade Association and the European Union than they were previously. It is now possible for new putative nations to assert the political aspirations of their own petty cultures, reviving old feuds and memories of past betrayals to legitimise their claims to a now largely rhetorical political sovereignty. There are now many tiny island states in the Pacific region, and – at least for the moment – quite a few in Eastern Europe and the erstwhile Soviet Union. That relatively small units can make a plausible claim for political independence is an index, not of the devolution of effective political power, but its evaporation. And, however tiny the nation, it will find that it has its own minorities, and will remain vulnerable to cultural fragmentation and diversity.

At least as significant as these economic and political changes are the changes in the sphere of media, communication and culture. When Marx predicted the end of nationalism in *The Communist Manifesto*, he did so on the basis of an assumed correspondence between material and cultural production:

> In place of the old local and national seclusion and self-sufficiency, we have intercourse in every direction, universal interdependence of nations. And as in material, so also in intellectual

production. The intellectual creations of individual nations become common property. National one-sidedness and narrow-
mindedness become more and more impossible, and from the
numerous national and local literatures, there arises a world literature.[6]

There is certainly something in this. Patterns of exchange and work do
have a cultural dimension. The increasing number of people in the
world whose lives are organised around the capitalist market must
learn to assess objects in terms of their price and to operate with
money as a universal measure of value; to come to terms with the fact
that, in market transactions, no one is especially concerned with the
well-being of others; and to learn to govern their transactions by the
norms of instrumental rationality. The market assigns certain
meanings to the objects with which it deals and imposes a certain
identity on those who deal with these objects.[7] As the market has
pervaded the world, so these meanings and identities have become
universal. Buyers and sellers understand the rules of the market game,
and communicate – in whatever language – on the assumption of a
shared understanding. In this sense, Marx was right: there is now a
global culture.

When we consider areas of cultural production less immediately
involved in economic transactions, there are developments which
also suggest a movement towards global homogeneity. If there is
not yet a world literature, there are international styles in shopping
malls, fast-food outlets, airports, business and commercial architecture, high fashion, and so on. However, to construe these as signs
of an emerging global culture would be a mistake. In fact, they are
symptoms of a quite contrary development. What the global market
has made possible is a massive *diversification* of cultural forms.
Think, for example, of various kinds of music (classical, jazz, pop,
country, as well as subgroupings), subcultural styles of dress, film,
literature, body building and fashions in intellectual life. The
'international style' in architecture, fashion, etc. is merely one of the
various forms which coexist or compete in the cultural market-
place. There is a multiplicity of cultural forms available to
individuals, and it is largely a matter of choice which they
participate in. Very few of these cultural forms are organised on
anything remotely like national lines, and most resist being
subsumed within existing national cultures. The various 'imagined
communities' of devotees created by these cultural forms cut across
national lines.

No doubt these tendencies towards diversification have always been present in the market; however, they have intensified in the late twentieth century. Underlying this has been the development of new forms of communication, information technology and media. If sound and image have not displaced language as crucial cultural determinants, they have come to play an increasing and, in some spheres, dominant role, largely because of the new technological possibilities available. The new cultural forms have themselves spawned a variety of public spheres, and associated groups of intellectuals concerned to ponder, celebrate, differentiate, evaluate and popularise their particular speciality. A brief visit to the magazine section of the local newsagent or a slightly longer time spent on the World Wide Web will provide evidence of the enormous proliferation of publications, conversations and other activities devoted to one or other specialised form of cultural life.

No doubt a first language still plays a crucial role in shaping the identities which are available to most people. However, it no longer provides the foundations for – what is imagined to be – a unitary national culture. Many of the most popular cultural forms – music, sport, movies – do not work through an established print language. The growing importance of oral and visual media has lessened the need for individuals to become more than minimally literate in the existing national language.[8] In many areas, a simplified form of English provides the lingua franca of world communication. Even where a common print language exists, it is not so much a source of identity as a condition of diversity. That teenagers and their parents, urban African-Americans and rural fundamentalist Christians, understand the same script does not diminish the vast cultural differences contained in the way they speak and in the codes and signifiers they employ. A common print language no longer provides the foundation on which writers and authors construct a conception of a community to which only (and perhaps all) users of that language belong. As I pointed out in Chapter 1, a common language does not by itself constitute a community. The users of a language might only conceive of themselves as related by an indefinitely extended web of relationships, and not form the conception of a community which makes these relationships possible. To form such a conception was the task of the national public spheres which emerged in the period of early modernity. These spheres still exist, especially with regard to more traditional cultural forms (e.g. the novel, poetry, theatre). But they are becoming increasingly fragmented, and the public spheres associated with the new cultural forms and technologies rarely define themselves or their audiences along national lines.

Nor have traditional intellectuals, artists and writers been insulated from these developments. Novelists, artists and poets now seek – and their publishers and agents demand – an international audience, whilst academics find that their own particular speciality has become just another of the proliferating cultural forms which are competing on the world market for acolytes, subsidies and audiences. Most intellectuals find that they have more in common with those who share their disciplinary or subcultural affiliation, than with other intellectuals from their own national culture. The ease of international travel for the relatively privileged, and the number of occasions for it, all contribute to a lessening of the links between even the traditional intellectual and his or her local culture. It may well be that the decline in adherence to national cultures is greater amongst intellectuals and other élites than amongst the mass of the population. However, it is not simply an élite or intellectual phenomenon. The new forms of media and communication have pervaded all sections of society in almost all countries. Even if it were an intellectual and élite phenomenon, this would be significant. These groups have played a key role in creating and sustaining national cultures, and their defection from the national cause is itself an important symptom of its decline.

Of course there are reactions against these tendencies, as well as Government policies which try to counter them. But what is clear is that in the economically advanced countries, the national public spheres which played such a key role in the development and sustenance of national cultures are of declining importance. Consequently, though there is a vast amount of cultural production with a diversity of audiences, it is enormously fragmented, and does not provide an integrated framework of representations through which its audience can identify themselves as members of the nation.

Patterns of social movement and migration have meant that many of the great urban centres – London, Paris, New York, etc. – have changed character in ways which have weakened their links with traditional national cultures. In many cases, they have generated new identities based on location, ethnic origin, social class, sexual preference or whatever. The diversities and inequalities of modern urban life have resisted assimilation into an imagined national unity. In this, they exemplify an extreme form of the tendencies towards cultural diversity and fragmentation which is characteristic of almost all large societies in the economically advanced world. If immigrants of the nineteenth and for much of the twentieth century had little choice but to make their lives with only a distant and tenuous relationship to their country of origin, the immigrants of the late twentieth century may often be in constant communication with their home country and remain involved in its affairs. As I have argued in the previous chapter, conceptions of national identity allow for a considerable degree of cultural diversity, and many immigrants – and their children – are ready to participate in the cultural and political life of their new country. However, the emergence of multiculturalism as a political issue does indicate a tension in the relationship between culture and polity which is at the heart of modern nationalism. The task of nation-building, of creating a sense of community able to contain the cultural diversity present in all countries, was relatively (though only relatively) easy when people had little alternative. Late twentieth-century developments have provided all too many alternatives. Unless national states are able to mobilise sufficient cultural resources to compete successfully with, contain or displace other forms of cultural life, then we are moving into the post-nationalist era.

Probably the key point about the future of nationalism in the late modern world was made by Eric Hobsbawm:

> [T]here is one major respect in which the phenomenon today is functionally different from the 'nationalism' and the 'nations' of nineteenth and earlier twentieth-century history. It is no longer a major vector of historical development.[9]

For the past 200 years, the nation has been the central political focus of the major historical transformations which have taken place. It has provided an organising principle within which most social, cultural and even economic activity went on. Most political projects were formulated in terms of the nation-state, and those which were not, such as socialism, were quickly reformulated in national terms. But the nation no longer enjoys this centrality. The main political, economic and cultural projects of the contemporary world do not involve the nation as an organising principle. Indeed, many are incompatible with it. Much of the remaining strength of the nation – and a not inconsiderable strength – lies in its past: the history, culture and traditions which it has appropriated to itself. Nationalism no longer projects a future.

Of course, where nationalism remains the name of the game, it will continue to generate counter-nationalisms. Real or imagined opposition has always been one of the most powerful sources of nationalism. When one's cultural traditions – of religion, language, custom, or whatever – are subject to attack, one can often only resist by finding the political means to defend that culture. Almost inevitably, resistance to cultural oppression turns into nationalism. Many nationalisms, which might not survive the more mundane pressures of day to day life in the modern world, flourish in conditions of conflict. The fierceness of the struggle is not an effect of the intensity of the nationalist feelings involved, but their cause. In the former Yugoslavia, for example, it was primarily the use of nationalism on behalf of Serbian aggrandisement which generated various counter-nationalisms. Cultural identities which had coexisted peacefully enough for many years and had, in many cases, been actively fostered by Government policies, had little alternative but to take a nationalist form. The nation-state becomes the only obvious vehicle to protect the religious or ethnic identity under threat. Once roused, of course, it would be naive to expect nationalist animosities to diminish quickly, especially if the short-term settlement is widely regarded as inequitable. But there is little reason to suppose that these nationalist struggles are the way of the future.

Whatever account is finally given of the resurgence of nationalisms in the post-Communist world, few would dispute that the circumstances are highly atypical.[10] For many, the flourishing of secessionist nationalist movements in the more economically advanced Western world provides more convincing evidence of the enduring nature of the nationalist project. Certainly, the durability and dynamism of, for example, the Québécois and Catalan cultures are impressive. But at least some of the intensity of the recent struggles rests on a misidentification of the threat to these cultures. It may well be that the main threats to Québécois or Catalan cultural integrity do not come from the central governments of Canada or Spain. Indeed, in recent years these governments have fallen over backwards not to provoke anxiety. It is rather that these local cultures are subject to the same global influences that are impacting on all nation-states. But, in these cases, the influences tend to work through the structures of the dominant community, and are interpreted by the minority as the effects of that dominance. (This is similar to the way in which the influence of international cultural forms on national ones is interpreted by many defenders of the national culture as evidence of 'Americanisation'. This interpretation confuses the game with the main player.) In the West as well as in the post-Soviet world, nationalism tends to escalate as each struggle generates further intensity and counter-intensity. It will be interesting to see how long these nationalisms survive once the struggle is over, more especially if secession takes place.

If my argument is along the right lines, we are now in a position to envisage the end of nationalism. But the force of this conclusion should not be exaggerated. Many of the tendencies I have mentioned will take a long time to work themselves out. The State still has enormous resources at its disposal, and retains responsibility in extremely significant areas including defence, education and welfare. States are not unaware of the importance of nationalism in sustaining their own authority and of the threats to it, and have mobilised considerable resources on its behalf through cultural programmes, educational policies, advertising, sporting subsidies, and the like. National cultures do survive, and distance from other centres and sense of place often combine to generate cultural agendas which are specific to particular countries. Especially in the older nation-states, such as the USA, Britain, France, etc., there are diverse and rich cultural traditions which have been appropriated on behalf of the nation, and these often have a depth and an appeal lacking in the new cultural forms. Most important of all, perhaps, is the threat experienced by many at the fragmentation of national identity. The nation has provided its members with a glimpse of power, triumph and excitement denied in everyday existence. It has provided a sense of belonging to a vast community spread over space and time which is not otherwise available. It has been a source of meaning in a world which otherwise denies it. Given that the pressures which are eroding national identity do not themselves provide an alternative, it is not surprising that they provoke strong and sometimes violent reactions.

As I suggested at the beginning of this chapter, there is a certain circularity to my argument. It is predicated on the assumption – the leap of faith if you like – that the present era provides a perspective from which it is possible to provide an overview of nationalism. But that perspective is only available if nationalism itself has ceased to be a dynamic historical reality, and is available, as Hegel would put it, to be 'grasped in thought'. This assumption may well turn out to be unjustified, and nationalism may assume forms which take it beyond the account offered here. The possibility of historical refutation is the hostage to the future which every social theory must provide. And even if the account I have provided – or one like it – proves to be correct, it still leaves open the question of what, if anything, will take the place of nationalism. Nationalism and the nation-state have played key roles in world history over the past 200 or more years, and it is simply not possible to do more than guess at the shape of a world without them. All we can do is try to understand the place that nationalism has occupied in the modern world, and the strength and some of the achievements of national identity, as well as its all too obvious catastrophes. We may then begin to have an understanding of what we are losing, even if we have no idea of what will take its place. In this respect, as in others, we are very much in the position of Walter Benjamin's angel of history. We are continuously impelled into the future by the winds of time; but we are impelled backwards, only able to survey the past. We have only our knowledge of what *has* happened to provide us with a hint of what is to come.[11]

Three forms of cosmopolitanism

The world today faces immense problems: a large percentage of the world's population live in conditions of absolute poverty and many are starving; there is massive and increasing inequality in the quality of life and use of the world's resources; short sighted developmental policies continue to inflict immense environmental damage; non-renewable resources are being run down; military conflict is endemic to large parts of the world; and in many countries the most basic human rights are constantly violated. Action on a global scale is required even to begin to confront these issues; much of this will involve interference with matters which have traditionally been regarded as falling within the authority of individual states. Reflecting on these problems, many would welcome the conclusion of the previous section. Nationalism has, it is argued, restricted our attention to the needs and concerns of our compatriots and encouraged us to ignore more urgent requirements outside our borders. It has legitimised oppressive and barbaric policies within state borders, and stood in the way of intervention. It has promoted a politics of national self-interest, in which the wealthy and powerful nations have flourished at the expense of the weak and the poor, and where no one is concerned for the plight of the world as a whole. As the world becomes increasingly interdependent, the nation-state is, not merely a historical, but also a moral anachronism. What is required is the displacement of the nation by more global communities, of the nation-state by institutions better able to reflect the new global reality and to respond appropriately to the world's problems, and of national identity by a more cosmopolitan moral consciousness.

It may well be that cosmopolitanism is the way of the future. However, before we embrace this too readily, we must investigate what it involves.

Thomas Pogge has drawn an important distinction between *legal* and *moral* cosmopolitanism:

> *Legal* cosmopolitanism is committed to a concrete political ideal of a global order under which all persons have equivalent rights and duties, that is, are fellow citizens of a universal republic. *Moral* cosmopolitanism holds that all persons stand in certain moral relations to one another: we are required to respect one another's status as ultimate units of moral concern – a requirement that places limits on our conduct and, in particular, upon our efforts to construct institutional schemes.[12]

Later in this section, I will introduce a third notion of cosmopolitanism which is, I will suggest, as important. But for the moment, let us concentrate on these two senses.

The basic doctrine of *moral* cosmopolitanism is not controversial – at least, it will not be controverted here. The assumption of the equal worth of all persons is common ground to all mainstream moral theories, so it may well be argued that contemporary moral theory is, in principle, cosmopolitan. What *is* controversial is the question of precisely what this doctrine requires, both in terms of basic political institutions and our individual moral practice. *Legal* cosmopolitanism may be conceived as one possible answer to the question: What political institutions are most likely to realise the ideal of cosmopolitanism? But once the distinction between the two kinds of cosmopolitanism has been drawn, it becomes a moot point whether a world Government is the only, or the best, way to achieve recognition of all.[13] I will return to this issue later.

What are the requirements of moral cosmopolitanism on our individual moral practice? If we assumed, for example, that the recognition of the equal moral worth of all requires that we conceive of everyone as having an equal claim on us, then this is at odds with those forms of everyday morality which allow – even prescribe – special preference to those who are close, for example, friends or family. Fortunately, most moral cosmopolitans do not interpret their doctrine so austerely as to rule out special preferences of this kind. According to Henry Shue, for example, 'We not only do not ordinarily criticize people morally for displaying priority for intimates, but we would be extremely suspicious of anyone who did not display it.'[14] However, it is important to spell out, as Shue does not, precisely why a commitment to a universalistic morality does *not* have this consequence.

The argument might go like this: It is necessary for the emotional and physical development of children that they be given nurture, care and love; it is also an important part of the well-being of many people that they be able to have and raise children, and this includes giving them the nurture, care and love they need. Indeed, given the extreme vulnerability and dependency of young humans, it is not clear that the species could survive without some complementarity of this sort. So there is good reason to suppose that some form of the family will play a role in any morally acceptable form of social life, and therefore that a morality concerned with the well-being of all will affirm the right to a reasonable family life as a component in that well-being. However, family life is constituted by a network of special affections and attachments. This means that the most impartial morality must provide for the special commitments involved in the family. A somewhat similar argument would take as its starting point the importance of friendship in most people's conception of a worthwhile existence, and would show that friendship also requires a range of special commitments and responsibilities. These arguments would show that even a cosmopolitan morality committed to the equal worth of all, is not only compatible with, but will require the existence of relationships of mutual priority, i.e. relationships based on the fact that those within the relationship have greater commitment to each other than they have to those outside the relationship. Of course, there ought to be limits on the preference which parents may give their own children, or friends may give to each other; however, within these limits a degree of moral priority is appropriate and justified.

These examples show that there need be no inconsistency between affirming the cosmopolitan ideal and also recognising the importance of particular attachments and the commitments they carry with them. But can we carry this argument beyond the (relatively) uncontroversial examples of the family and friendship?

Shue himself is sceptical of this. He argues strongly against an 'almost irresistibly natural-seeming image' in which we conceive:

> our duties from the point of view of a pebble dropped into a pond: I am the pebble and the world is the pond I have been dropped into. I am the center of a system of concentric circles that become fainter as they spread...My duties are exactly like the concentric ripples around the pebble: strongest at the center and rapidly diminishing towards the periphery.[15]

Shue does not deny what he calls 'the priority of intimates', i.e. that our strongest moral responsibilities are towards our family and friends:

> What is wrong with the concentric-circle image of duty is not that it has a center which is highlighted. What is wrong is the *progressive* character of the decline in priority as one reaches circles farther from the center...Once the center has been left behind...I see insufficient reason to believe that one's positive duties to people in the next country...are any greater than one's positive duties to people on the next continent.[16]

No doubt Shue is right to reject the concentric circle image: moral relations do not map neatly onto geographic ones. But he is wrong to assume that impersonal egalitarian morality takes over once we leave behind the sphere of the intimate and familial (the 'center'). Personal relations and impersonal morality are not the only sources of responsibility. Another significant source is human association. As we enter into relationships and institutions, or find ourselves involved in them, we discover that we are implicated in complex networks of moral commitment and obligation to others in those relationships and institutions.

The issue of what our specific moral responsibilities are is partly determined by the relationships and institutions within which we exist. To some extent, these responsibilities are independent of the moral value of the institutions and relations themselves. Even thoroughly evil institutions give rise to reasonable expectations, and sometimes it would not be morally appropriate to disappoint these expectations. (For example: A committed socialist might believe that private property was evil; this would not absolve her of the responsibility to pay for a book she ordered.) But if we put these cases to one side, then the individual responsibilities which we acquire through membership of an association derive from the moral quality of the association. For the moral cosmopolitan, this will be evaluated in terms of the contribution of the association in the specific circumstances in which it exists to the well-being of all. Many institutions will do so in two ways. They will contribute directly to that goal, and also they will provide for their members the opportunity to develop their capacities, work with others, and lead a fulfilling life. They could do neither of those things if they did not also involve a network of special responsibilities. For example, the glory of a modern civil society is the number of non-State organisations which it enables to flourish. These include trade unions and professional associations, community groups, local churches, political parties and special interest lobbies, charity organisations, and so on. Some of these are local, others geographically based, but increasingly these include associations which cut across national borders. The point is that whatever the nature of a particular grouping, membership will *always* involve specific commitments and responsibilities. The legitimacy of these relationships and institutions does not depend upon their satisfying the quite impossible demand that they involve no assumptions of moral priority. This would preclude almost all human associations and relationships. The important question is whether they are aspects of a good and complete life for human beings.

Moral cosmopolitanism, indeed, any form of moral universalism, must come to terms with difference. However, this does not mean that all the forms of difference and all the ways in which we give priority to the claims of those with whom we have special relationships are justified. As I have already noted, it is only because we think that some form of the family is necessary for human life that the commitments it embodies have a claim on us. This does not mean that all forms of the family are defensible. It is apparent, for example, that most historical forms of the family have involved the oppression of women and a good deal of mistreatment of children. Nor does it mean that there are no limits to the preference one is entitled to give to members of one's immediate family. Here, as elsewhere, there is room for moral debate, criticism, and change. A good deal of the moral life consists in evaluating particular forms of relationship and of adjudicating the importance of different claims upon us. There is no doubt that the basic doctrine of moral cosmopolitanism, that all individuals are ultimately of equal moral worth and have an equal right to lead a worthwhile and satisfying life, should have a place in public debate and private reflection on how we should lead our lives.

The extent to which cosmopolitanism must come to terms with different and formally unequal patterns of moral responsibility becomes more apparent when we begin to consider the political conditions under which the equal moral worth of all might be recognised, i.e. we move from *moral* to *legal* cosmopolitanism. The ideal of a world State – a 'universal republic' – uniting the natural and the political orders (*cosmos* with *polis*[17]) may have appealed in the Hellenistic or Roman worlds, but – as Kant came to realise – is neither a plausible nor an attractive option in the modern world.[18] If we are to approach a cosmopolitan political order, it must allow for, and indeed will express, something of the diversity and fragmentation characteristic of late modernity. Cosmopolitan theorists such as Thomas Pogge and David Held have recognised this, and have argued for a political order in which the cluster of powers traditionally claimed by the modern State is broken up into institutionally distinct and operationally diverse spheres, where people have – and are encouraged to have – multiple affiliations, where civil associations cut across traditional state borders, where there are different levels and forms of political authority and economic power, and where there are legal and political avenues to protect the fundamental rights of all individuals.[19] Whether or not Pogge's or Held's specific suggestions are viable is not directly relevant here. The point is that, as soon as we begin to envisage a network of overlapping, complementary but sometimes conflicting spheres of authority, we must also recognise the existence of different – and formally unequal – patterns of moral priority. Each of us will find ourselves involved in or subject to particular institutions, and contributing to the life of these institutions will require specific commitments, both to the institutions themselves and to other members. For example, cosmopolitanism will require the existence of organisations through which redistribution takes place in order to eliminate starvation and improve the conditions and prospects of the very poor. These organisations will have to engage the energies and commitments of full-time professionals as well as volunteers. If their members are to work effectively together, there will need to be a shared sense of loyalty to the institution and to each other. Organisations require fellow feeling and commitment, and that cannot exist unless there is a reciprocal sense that members have a greater commitment to each other – at least in respect to a range of activities – than they have to those outside the institution. This commitment need not – and ought not – be absolute. But unless it exists as part of the shared understanding of those who belong to the institution, then it will not function effectively. The organisations will also need to call upon, indeed probably demand, contributions from those in a position to make them. In general, people are more likely to contribute to the well-being of others if we know that their contribution is part of an organised and effective programme of aid. They also need some assurance that others are doing their bit as well. Whatever form these organisations take, it must be the case that those who are required to make sacrifices on behalf of cosmopolitan ideals feel some commitment to the decisions made by the relevant institutions. The institutions must attract the allegiance of those subject to them. When we consider bodies of any size, especially those whose members may never encounter each other, this shared understanding and commitment will be carried by the cultural self-understanding, both of members of the organisation and those subject to its demands.

Put this another way. Once we move beyond the conception of a single world State, we must recognise that moral cosmopolitanism will require a network of moral communities, that is, bodies constituted by a shared self-understanding which carries with it a range of mutual responsibilities. This self-understanding will be carried by the culture of the group, and those who become members of it will acquire the relevant cultural identity. This means that, as with any network of significant human relations, those involved will have special responsibilities and commitments to fellow members, and perhaps to the group itself, which they do not have to those outside. This self-understanding must also be conveyed to other individuals and groups who must respond to and support the operations of the organisation. There will, in other words, be a specific kind of cultural affiliation associated with each of the various bodies through which a cosmopolitan moral order must operate.

Moral cosmopolitans are wary of special commitments because they leave the way open for inequality. In the name of special responsibilities, families accumulate wealth to themselves without regard to the desperate plight of others, nations pursue imperialist and colonial policies, professions achieve high rewards for their members regardless of the social costs, and so on. But special commitments are essential for any collective activity, even that directed towards cosmopolitan goals. What ought to be important for the cosmopolitan is not the existence of special commitments as such, but the extent to which these are compatible with broader moral demands and the role of the specific organisation in a wider social context. No doubt there should be mechanisms to limit the extent to which communities can pursue their own goals to the detriment of the needs and rights of others. But communities themselves are an essential part of the moral life.

It should not need saying that the existence of special responsibilities is not incompatible with a belief in the fundamental equality of all. That I have a special commitment to the members of my family does not mean that I believe they are morally more important or better than members of other families. If I have a special responsibility for my compatriots, I need not believe that my country is better than others. Indeed, if I believe that my responsibility includes that of atoning for what has been done in the past, then I may even believe that my nation is somewhat worse than others. Part of the justification of these commitments lies simply in the fact that they are mine – they are aspects of my identity and my life. Of course that is not the whole story. The other part of the justification is the claim that these bodies play an valuable role in human life and that the particular forms of commitment and responsibility they embody are themselves morally defensible.

By and large, cosmopolitans have seen the nation-state as part of the problem, not the solution.[20] However, as soon as it is fully recognised that a single world State is not an option, and that any conceivable cosmopolitan order will be characterised by institutional and cultural diversity, it becomes a moot point whether some form of the nation-state might not play a role. Certainly, there is nothing in a nationalism which respects liberal principles which is incompatible with an adherence to cosmopolitan values.[21] Although the nation is of declining importance in the world, it does offer the cosmopolitan cultural and political resources that he or she can ill afford to neglect. It has provided the context in which the *only* half-way successful experiments in large-scale democracy in the modern world have been carried out. It has provided a self-understanding which has encouraged its members to make considerable sacrifices for what they conceived to be a common good. Even if the nation is not the way of the future, it remains to be seen whether the institutions necessary to realise a cosmopolitan moral order can create or attract to themselves the political and cultural resources necessary to carry out their tasks. It is noteworthy that the most effective transnational institutions – the multinational corporation, the major financial bodies – have so far proven remarkably resistant to democratic control and have shown little sign of concern for the equal moral worth of members of the world community.

Earlier in this section, I made use of Thomas Pogge's distinction between legal and moral cosmopolitanism. There is, however, a *third* sense of the term which may be of even more importance in the post-national world. Kai Nielsen captures this sense well:

To be a cosmopolitan…is to identify with and have a commitment to and a concern for all of humankind and not just for some subunit of it *and* it is, as well, to have some reasonable understanding of, to prize and to take pleasure in, humankind's vast, and sometimes creative, diversity. It is not just that a cosmopolitan will grudgingly accept, as an intractable fact, the great variety of forms of life, practices, art-forms, languages, religions, cuisines and the like that the world has to offer, but she will take pleasure in the very existence of them, feel at home with a goodly number of them and wish to see them prevail where their prevailing does not harm others. Above all she will take an active interest in them, be reasonably knowledgeable about them and wish to see all of them flourish that are respectful of the rights of others, including, of course, alien others.[22]

To be a cosmopolitan in Nielsen's sense is to be someone who is at home in a wide variety of social, political and cultural contexts. As Nielsen argues, this is not incompatible with having a greater knowledge of and a primary attachment to one's own social, political and cultural milieu. One's self-understanding may well be rooted in a specific country and its language, history, literature, political institutions, and the like, and these may define a range of moral responsibilities and commitments which are all but inescapable. However, one will also be knowledgeable and appreciative of the different responsibilities and commitments of others. Indeed, unless one had one's own primary attachments, it is unlikely that one would be able properly to appreciate the primary attachments of others. For this reason, the 'rootless cosmopolitan' of populist mythology would only be capable of a superficial understanding of different cultures, including his or her own. For the 'rooted cosmopolitan', one's commitment to what is one's own will be tempered by the awareness that others have precisely the same commitment to what is theirs, and that it is only the accident of birth and upbringing which determines which set of responsibilities and commitments one has.[23]

Cosmopolitanism in this sense has long been a privilege, only available to an élite – those who have the resources necessary to travel, learn other languages, and absorb other cultures. For the majority of the population, living their lives within the cultural space of their own nation, cosmopolitanism has not been an option (hence perhaps the popular suspicion of cosmopolitanism). However, in the contemporary world, cultural and linguistic diversity is omnipresent, and the capacity to communicate with others and to understand their cultures is available to everyone. Too often, circumstances are not conducive to this. Members of other cultural groups are conceived of as threats, undermining established ways of life and competing for all too scarce employment prospects and welfare resources. In these circumstances, the temptation towards closure may be overwhelming: to assert one's own cultural identity against the real or imagined threat of the other. In a context of uncertainty, barriers and defences may well appear to be the only way to protect one's own identity. Yet it is also the route towards cultural stagnation. Cosmopolitanism is the hard won and difficult to sustain virtue of living with and appreciating diversity. It is perhaps the primary virtue necessary if some semblance of communal social life is to be maintained in the late modern world.[24]

Cosmopolitanism in this sense is not incompatible with the moral cosmopolitan's insistence on the fundamental equality of all, nor with the legal cosmopolitan's project of creating institutional and organisational structures through which this equality can be recognised and protected. It is, however, an important corrective to the austere universalism to which philosophical cosmopolitans are often drawn, where particular attachments and affinities are regarded as impediments to, rather than constituents of, a global moral order. It is only if the virtue of cosmopolitanism is widespread in the relevant communities that there will be any chance of realising cosmopolitan ideals. If cultural diversity is the necessary outcome of globalisation, then cosmopolitanism is the virtue of this necessity.

Living with diversity

As I remarked in Chapter 3, Hegel was no nationalist. Yet, in many ways, his *Philosophy of Right* provides a good account of the moral geography of a world in which, for most people, most of the time, the borders of the state were also the borders of the moral universe. The sense of belonging to the one nation, or for Hegel, of being citizens of the one state, provided the moral context within which people lived their lives, and the State was the ultimate authority within its borders.[25] In the relatively unusual case of travel to or residence within a foreign country, the citizen became subject to the laws of that country. Normally, however, the individual was not him- or herself directly involved in moral relations with citizens of other states. Moral relations with people or groups outside the borders could be left to the State. Life in the State defined a moral division of labour:[26] within the state, moral responsibility fell ultimately on the individual; in the world at large, it fell on states. Of course, Hegel did not identify the State as the nation-state, and he underestimated the role of culture in constituting the community represented by the State and differentiating that community from others. But his account provided a fairly accurate map of the spheres of moral relationship. If the division of labour was never carried through with perfect consistency, it provided a sufficient approximation to everyday experience to allow individuals to find their moral bearings within the enlarged modern world.

Whatever our final judgement on the Hegelian scheme, we have now left its possibility far behind. We live in a world of overlapping identities and affinities. Most of us have a range of different commitments – to families and friends, to professions, to political programmes, to religions, to cultural affiliations, a sense of national identity (which may or may not correspond with political member-ship), and so on. Each of these will provide an identity which is important to us, and these identities will intersect and conflict at various points and in various ways. The world no longer provides us with an overarching framework in terms of which we can order these various responsibilities and adjudicate demands between them. The demands of the State no longer bear the stamp of an overriding moral authority; they are more likely to be experienced as the burdens imposed by a petty and inefficient bureaucracy. The nation has become only one of the competing cultural presences in our lives; not the inescapable environment in which other cultural activities take place. Most of us find ourselves involved in moral relationships with those outside the borders of our state, if not through association, at least through the knowledge of their plight conveyed in the newspa-pers and television news.

When Nietzsche announced the death of God it was not as the loss of belief, or even of faith; it was the loss of *location* and *direction*:

> Who gave us the sponge to wipe away the entire horizon? What were we doing when we unchained this earth from its sun? Whither is it moving now? Away from all suns? Are we not plunging continually? Backward, sideward, forward in all direc-tions? Is there still any up or down? Are we not straying through an infinite nothing? Do we not feel the breath of empty space?[27]

The death of God has, of course, proved to be a much more drawn out business than even Nietzsche anticipated. So too, with the death of the nation. Despite my arguments earlier in this chapter, I am aware that the nation is likely to be around for a few years yet. However, as with the nineteenth-century crisis in religious belief to which Nietzsche was giving exemplary expression, there is at the end of the twentieth century a foreboding sense of an absent centre, or better, of the loss of a significant orientation point in our moral experience. As the nation loses its power to move us, as it ceases to provide one of the relatively stable reference points in public debate, then we move one step further towards a moral world of merely competing interests, of struggles in which power is not only the only effective weapon, but also the only voice to be heard.

Martha Nussbaum has argued that we should follow the Stoics and:

think of ourselves not as devoid of local affiliations, but as sur-
rounded by a series of concentric circles. The first one encloses the
self, the next takes in the immediate family, then follows the extended family, then, in order, neighbours or local groups, fellow
city-dwellers, fellow countrymen – and we can easily add to this
list groupings based on ethnic, linguistic, historical, professional,
gender, or sexual identities. Outside all these circles is the largest
one, humanity as a whole.[28]

The concentric circle metaphor is an attractive, but ultimately
misleading, one. It provides no explanation of why the area of our
ultimate moral concern should be defined by the largest circle. Henry
Shue, who presented a similar metaphor in order to criticise it,
assumed that it was the smallest of the concentric circles that had the
greatest moral weight, and this is just as plausible as Nussbaum's
assumption that it is the largest. But, when it comes to the point, we
might just as well opt for a middle one. There is nothing in the model
which justifies one choice rather than another. But, more importantly,
the topographical image simply assumes the existence of a single moral
space, and this is precisely the question most at issue. As every
geographer knows, mapping requires agreement as to co-ordinates,
and the moral situation of the contemporary world is the progressive
loss of agreement as to what these co-ordinates should be. Even if we
allowed the metaphor, there is no reason to think of the 'circles' as
concentric, rather than having different centres; overlapping rather
than intersecting; and located on a single plane, rather than a
multidimensional one. There is no one moral space, but many; and
there can be no one map which charts these many terrains.

If Hegel provided a map of the moral world of modernity, it may be
that Nietzsche provides a guide of the post-national world of late
modernity. But it is early days yet. If the loss of morally authoritative
voices – God, the nation – is the inevitable outcome of economic
globalisation and cultural diversification, then answers to moral
questions must be sought elsewhere. If cosmopolitanism can be
understood as a way of living with diversity – and with the loss of
certainty which is its corollary – then cosmopolitanism may be an
important part of the answer. But the problem of creating social
practices and institutions through which diversity can flourish
remains. There is little which suggests that those which are coming
into existence will do a better job than the nation-state.

Notes

Introduction

1 Goodin and Pettit, 'Preface' to *A Companion to Contemporary Political Philosophy* (Oxford and Cambridge, MA, Blackwell, 1993), p. ix.
2 Goodin and Pettit, 'Introduction' to *A Companion to Contemporary Political Philosophy*, p. 3.
3 There was a brief entry on nationalism in Paul Edwards (ed.), *Encyclopedia of Philosophy* vol. 5 (New York, The Macmillan Company & The Free Press; London, Collier-Macmillan, 1965) by Stanley Benn. Benn distinguished a moderate nationalism, which is more or less equivalent to democratic self-determination, from 'blood and soil' nationalism, which 'it would be absurd to treat as if it invited serious rational criticism'.
4 For a glimpse of the literature now available on nationalism and related themes, see the bibliographical essay, 'The state of the nation', at the end of this volume.
5 See Will Kymlicka, 'Community', and Allen Buchanan, 'Secession and Nationalism', both in Goodin and Pettit (eds), *A Companion to Contemporary Political Philosophy*. It should be noted that Buchanan emphatically rejects the claims of national self-determination to provide a ground for secession.
6 Yael Tamir, *Liberal Nationalism* (Princeton, Princeton University Press, 1993; second edition 1995), p. 14.
7 David Miller explicitly rejects the idea of 'sanitising' nationalism by focussing on 'good' versions of it; however, his defence of nationalism inevitably does just that. See *On Nationality*, op. cit., pp. 9–10.
8 Yael Tamir, *Liberal Nationalism*, op. cit., ch. 1, entitled 'The idea of the person'.
9 At least this is the argument of Liah Greenfeld's *Nationalism: Five Roads to Modernity* (Cambridge, MA and London, Harvard University Press, 1992), ch. 1, an argument which I endorse below.
10 See my *Morality and Modernity* (London and New York, Routledge, 1991) for some suggestions as to how such an account might proceed.

1 The coming of nationalism

1 *Nations and Nationalism* (Oxford, Basil Blackwell, 1983), p. 1. See also Elie Kedourie: '[Nationalism] pretends to supply a criterion for the determination of the unit of population proper to enjoy government exclusively on its own, or the legitimate exercise of power in states, and for the right organisation of a society of states' (*Nationalism*, first published 1962; fourth expanded edition Oxford and Cambridge, MA, Basil Blackwell, 1993, p. 1). Kedourie's formulation is equivalent to Gellner's just so long as we change his 'or' into an 'and'.

2 Benedict Anderson, *Imagined Communities: Reflections on the Origin and Spread of Nationalism* (London and New York, Verso, 1983; revised edition 1991), pp. 5–6.

3 Anderson, *Imagined Communities*, op. cit., p. 6.

4 Anderson, *Imagined Communities*, op. cit., p. 6.

5 Anderson, *Imagined Communities*, op. cit., p. 6.

6 Anderson's presentation of this issue is made more obscure than it might be by an unfortunate choice of terminology and tendentious illustrations. He writes: 'We may today think of the French aristocracy of the *ancien régime* as a class; but surely it was imagined this way only very late' (*Imagined Communities*, op. cit., pp. 6–7). In a footnote, he adds: 'Hobsbawm, for example, "fixes" it by saying that in 1789 it numbered about 400,000 in a population of 23,000,000....But would this statistical picture of the noblesse have been imaginable under the *ancien régime*?' The answer to Anderson's rhetorical question is of course 'Yes'. Sieyès, writing in late 1788 or early 1789, estimated the number of the First Estate as 110,000, and there is no indication that, in trying to 'fix' the number of the nobility, he was doing anything unusual (the fact that he provides a different numerical 'fix' to Hobsbawm is irrelevant). See Emmanuel Joseph Sieyès, *What is the Third Estate?*, trans. M. Blondel (London and Dunmow, Pall Mall Press, 1963), ch. 3, pp. 82–3. Elsewhere, Anderson writes that the cohesion of the *ancien régime* as class was 'as much concrete as imagined' (*Imagined Communities*, op. cit., p. 77). The implied contrast between 'concrete' and 'imagined' is particularly unfortunate.

7 As far as I can tell, little in Anderson's own account of the nation depends upon his misleading presentation of the key concept. However, it has misled others. See, for example, David Archard, 'Should nationalists be communitarians?', *Journal of Applied Philosophy* vol. 13 (1996), pp. 215–20, especially p. 217, where he ascribes to Anderson a 'contrast between "real", meaning physically contiguous, and "imaginary", meaning conceived across physical distance'. For Archard, 'any group, larger than one that permits face-to-face contact, is (and must be)' imaginary. My view is that (in the relevant sense) all social relations are imagined; but that only some involve a conception of the group as a component of the imagining; and that this distinction has little to do with size.

8 Anderson, *Imagined Communities*, op. cit., p. 9.

9 Raymond Williams, *Keywords* (New York, Oxford University Press, 1976), p. 76.

10 The term '*Bildung*' is itself an enormously rich one. My use here is modelled on Hegel's, who emphasises the idea of individuals educating themselves into forms of social life. See *Elements of the Philosophy of*

Right, trans. H.B. Nisbet (Cambridge, Cambridge University Press, 1991), Part Three, Section Two, § 187, pp. 224–6. I discuss it in more depth in Chapter 3 below.

11 This was recognised by early theorists of the nation such as Herder and Fichte who argued that language is a fundamental constituent of national identity. It is also well realised by nationalist politicians, administrators and ideologues. Even as I write, hard to come by intellectual and material resources are being expended in the new nations of Eastern Europe and Asia in order to create national languages able to cope with the complexities of the modern world from the residues of half forgotten local dialects. I have learned much of the importance of language in this context from Peter Hill.

12 We may pick out two stages in the evolution of the modern concept of culture. The first was when the word 'culture' began to be used on its own, and not with an attendant noun phrase indicating *what* (e.g. the body, the intellect) was being cultivated. According to Williams, this took place in the late seventeenth and early eighteenth centuries in England, and somewhat later in France. The second, which took place around a century later, was when it began to be used in contrast to 'civilisation'. See again the discussion in Williams, *Keywords*, op. cit.

13 I here follow the account provided by Norbert Elias, *The Civilizing Process: The History of Manners* (Oxford, Basil Blackwell, 1983), especially ch. 1. However, Elias (along with many others) emphasises the motive of *ressentiment* in the way in which the relatively backward Germans gave a higher value to (German) 'culture' over (French/English) 'civilisation'. I am not persuaded by this argument. At the very least, it needs to take into account the fact that the concept of culture allows for a diversity precluded by the initially absolutist notion of civilisation.

14 See the discussion of the term in Émile Benveniste, *Problèmes de linguistique générale* (Paris, Gallimard, 1966), ch. 28. According to Benveniste, the word was coined almost simultaneously in France and England. See also the entry under 'Civilisation' in Raymond Williams, *Keywords*, op. cit.

15 A point emphasised to me by Barry Hindess.

16 Hugh Seton Watson, *Nations and States: An Enquiry into the Origins of Nations and the Politics of Nationalism* (London, Methuen, 1977), p. 5; see also E.J. Hobsbawm: 'Neither objective nor subjective definitions [of the nation] are...satisfactory, and both are misleading', in *Nations and Nationalism since 1780: Programme, Myth, Reality* (Cambridge, Cambridge University Press, 1990), p. 8.

17 Simon Schama, *Landscape and Memory* (New York, Alfred A. Knopf, 1995), p. 16: 'National identity...would lose much of its ferocious attachment without the mystique of a particular landscape tradition: its topography mapped, elaborated, and enriched as a homeland.' Schama himself provides an exhilarating account of some of these traditions, e.g. of the role of the woodland in German national identity, the oak tree for the English, and so on.

18 See Anderson, *Imagined Communities*, op. cit., ch. 10. This chapter was added to the second edition.

19 See the discussion in Anderson, *Imagined Communities*, op. cit., pp. 9–11. One of the reasons that the armed services play a special role in the

celebration of the nation is that they symbolise the willingness to make that sacrifice.

20 Anderson, *Imagined Communities*, op. cit., p. 7. The importance of equality in the nation is also emphasised by Liah Greenfeld; see Greenfeld, *Nationalism: Five Roads to Modernity* (Cambridge, MA and London, Harvard University Press, 1992), *passim*.

21 According to Hans Kohn, 'Nationalism is inconceivable without the idea of popular sovereignty', *The Idea of Nationalism: A Study in its Origins and Background* (first published 1944; reprinted Toronto, Collier-Macmillan, 1969), p. 5. The suggestion in the text is that the converse is also true.

22 At least elegance and power were a feature of Gellner's early work on nationalism; see especially *Nations and Nationalism*, op. cit. However, in his later work, he shifts ground in some important – and unacknowledged – ways. See, for example, his *Encounters with Nationalism* (Oxford and Cambridge, MA, Blackwell, 1994) and *Conditions of Liberty: Civil Society and Its Rivals* (New York, Allen Lane: The Penguin Press, 1994), especially chs 13–18. In his posthumous *Nationalism* (London, Weidenfeld & Nicolson, 1997), Gellner combines his earlier theory with a quite incompatible historical account. By and large, I will focus on the earlier – *Nations and Nationalism* – theory. I will keep track of the most significant shifts in the notes.

23 Gellner, *Nations and Nationalism*, op. cit., pp. 37–8.

24 Gellner, *Nations and Nationalism*, op. cit., p. 38.

25 See the criticisms of Gellner by John Breuilly, 'Reflections on nationalism', *Philosophy and Social Science* vol. 15 (1985), pp. 65–75, especially pp. 69, 73; and by Miroslav Hroch, 'From national movements to fully-fledged nation', *New Left Review* no. 198 (March/April 1993), pp. 3–20, especially p. 10.

26 Probably Hans Kohn was the first proponent of this orthodoxy: 'Nationalism as we understand it is not older than the second half of the eighteenth century', *The Idea of Nationalism: A Study in its Origins and Background*, op. cit. See also Kedourie: 'Nationalism is a doctrine invented in Europe at the beginning of the nineteenth century', *Nationalism*, op. cit., p. 9; Hugh Seton-Watson: 'The doctrine of nationalism dates from the French Revolution', *Nations and States* (London, Methuen, 1992), p. 6. Benedict Anderson dates the beginning of nationalism 'towards the end of the eighteenth century', *Imagined Communities*, op. cit., p. 14.

27 For example, Linda Colley, *Britons: Forging the Nation 1707–1837* (New Haven and London, Yale University Press, 1992), argues for a British nationalism early in the eighteenth century. Liah Greenfeld, *Nationalism: Five Roads to Modernity*, op. cit., finds evidence of an English nationalism in the sixteenth century. I discuss some aspects of Colley's and Greenfeld's work below.

28 See John Breuilly, 'Reflections on nationalism', op. cit., pp. 73–4, Eric Hobsbawm, *Nations and Nationalism*, op. cit., especially pp. 123–30, 182.

29 Eugen Weber, *Peasants into Frenchmen* (Stanford, California, Stanford University Press, 1976). A partial response to Weber's argument would be to point out that almost all theories of nationalism (including Gellner's) would imply that its initial impact would be much greater on urban

dwellers than on more insulated and localised agricultural workers. For some empirical evidence and tentative conclusions about England at the beginning of the nineteenth century, see Linda Colley, *Britons: Forging the Nation 1707–1837*, op. cit., pp. 291–300.

30 Linda Colley, *Britons: Forging the Nation 1707–1832* , op. cit.

31 For example, Hans Kohn cites a passage in John Milton's *apologia* for the execution of Charles I, in which he appeals to the unique privileges and responsibilities of Englishmen: 'a Nation not slow and dull, but of a quick, ingenious, and piercing spirit, acute to invent, subtle and sinewy to discourse', 'a Nation chosen before any other' to 'begin some new and great period in his [God's] Church'. See Hans Kohn, 'The genesis and character of English nationalism', *Journal of the History of Ideas* vol. 1 (1940), pp. 69–94, see pp. 84–5. There is an apparent inconsistency between Kohn's recognition of the presence of English nationalism in the seventeenth century, and his view cited above (note 26) that nationalism 'is not older than the second half of the eighteenth century'.

32 Richard Helgerson, *Forms of Nationhood: The Elizabethan Writing of England* (Chicago and London, The University of Chicago Press, 1992).

33 Liah Greenfeld, *Nationalism: Five Roads to Modernity*, op. cit., especially ch. 1.

34 In a footnote, Gellner notes 'the early emergence of nationalist sentiment in England' (*Nations and Nationalism*, op. cit., pp. 91–2 fn.), and suggests that this might be connected with the fact that in that country 'the individualist, mobile spirit preceded by many centuries…the coming of industrial order…' It is hard to understand, still less to share, Gellner's confidence that this does not contradict his thesis about that industrialisation *explains* both individualism and nationalism. In an earlier passage, Gellner suggests that 'by accident' on Europe's Atlantic seaboard 'a dynastic state…corresponded, more or less, with a language and a culture' (pp. 39–40). But he goes on to say that the 'fit was never very close', apparently (on this occasion, Gellner's customary lucidity deserts him) because of the diversity of local cultures and the cosmopolitan nature of élite cultures. In the later *Conditions of Liberty*, op. cit., Gellner again mentions cases on 'the Atlantic coast of Europe' in which 'strong dynastic states…roughly, even if very roughly, correlated with cultural areas' (p. 113). This time, however, he does not repeat his earlier grounds for scepticism about the degree of correlation. Indeed, he goes on to say: 'History has made a present to nationalism of a broad region where the nationalist imperative was already, at least in a considerable measure, satisfied before the event' (p. 113). In *Nationalism*, op. cit., he again notes the existence of areas of Western Europe where the union of culture and polity had been established 'long before the internal logic of modern society decreed that the couple were meant for each other' (p. 51). These concessions present enormous problems for Gellner's account. The notion of a 'cultural area' coinciding ('even if very roughly') with the bounds of an established state is quite inconsistent with the claim that premodern popular culture was diverse and élite culture cosmopolitan. If 'cultural areas' of this size existed – or were coming into existence – at the beginning of the modern world, then industrialisation is clearly not the explanation for the homogenisation of culture. In my view, the early Gellner was right to insist upon the diversity of premodern cultures, and right to search for an explanation

for the apparent homogenisation of culture associated with the nation. He simply chose the wrong explanation.

35 This point is also made by Breuilly; see 'Reflections on nationalism', op. cit., p. 69.

36 Gellner refers to Hume and Kant as providing philosophical expositions of the two principles; what he does not recognise is that Kant's conception of practical reason (reason as universality) was presented as a critique of the Humean notion of 'reason as the slave of the passions' (roughly, instrumental reason). As Kant recognised, the two principles will conflict.

37 Gellner, *Nations and Nationalism*, op. cit., p. 21.

38 Gellner effectively concedes this point in *Nationalism*, op. cit., ch. 10, pp. 66–71, where he locates the source of nationalist doctrines in the Romantic reaction against the Enlightenment. However, he makes no attempt to link this recognition with the thesis that industrialisation is the cause of nationalism.

39 Part of the reason for Gellner's dismissal of the intellectual content of nationalism is his low opinion of the intellectual merits of nationalist thinkers: 'the prophets of nationalism were not anywhere near the First Division, when it came to the business of thinking', and their 'precise doctrines are hardly worth analyzing'. See *Nations and Nationalism*, op. cit., p. 124. This low opinion is shared by almost all recent theorists of nationalism. For example, Anderson writes of the 'philosophical poverty and even incoherence' of nationalism, and the fact that it has 'never produced its own grand thinkers', *Imagined Communities*, op. cit., p. 5. In fact nationalists could field quite an impressive team, not just including Herder, Fichte and List, but also Rousseau, Montesquieu and J.S. Mill, and perhaps even Max Weber. It should be noted that the later Gellner softens his stance somewhat; see his sympathetic remarks on Herder in *Nationalism*, op. cit., p. 69.

40 Gellner, *Nations and Nationalism*, op. cit., p. 125.

41 See Raymond Williams, *Keywords*, op. cit., pp. 88–90.

42 Immanuel Wallerstein is pre-eminent amongst those who argue for the international nature of the developing capitalist system. It is, however, a crucial part of his argument that the 'world system' must be divided into individual nation-states, and he emphasises the role of the States in securing or failing to secure the conditions for economic expansion. See *The Modern World System [I]: Capitalist Agriculture and the Origins of the European World-Economy in the Sixteenth Century* (New York and London, Academic Press, 1974), and *The Modern World System II: Mercantilism and the Consolidation of the European World Economy, 1600–1750* (New York and London, Academic Press, 1980).

43 For a succinct account of the development of the modern State, see David Held, *Democracy and the Global Order: From the Modern State to Cosmopolitan Governance* (Cambridge, Polity Press, 1995), Part II. See also Giovanni Poggi, *The Development of the Modern State: A Sociological Introduction* (Stanford, California, Stanford University Press, 1978).

44 See Eugen Weber, 'What rough beast?', *Critical Review* vol. 10 (1996), pp. 285–98; especially p. 287.

45 Benedict Anderson refers to the explosion in the availability of printed material as 'print capitalism'; see *Imagined Communities*, op. cit., chs 2–3. The term 'capitalism' is misleading in this context, given the small size of

most of the printing shops and the key role played by the printer/entrepreneur. In classical Marxist terms, this was petty commodity production, not capitalism proper. Still, the term does capture the orientation towards profit. Anderson's main source is Lucien Febvre and Henri-Jean Martin, *The Coming of the Book*, trans. David Gerard (London, New Left Books, 1976). But see also Elizabeth L. Eisenstein, *The Printing Press as Agent of Change: Communications and Cultural Transformation in Early Modern Europe* (Cambridge, Cambridge University Press, 1979; reprinted 1994).

46　See Anderson, *Imagined Communities*, op. cit., *passim*. However, Anderson has very little to say about the crucial early developments in England, France and Germany. This may be partly due to his special concern with postcolonial nationalism, but is also due to his reluctance to recognise that seventeenth- and eighteenth-century European nationalisms existed well before the 'Creole' nationalisms of the New World.

47　Jürgen Habermas, *The Structural Transformation of the Public Sphere: An Inquiry into a Category of Bourgeois Society* (first published 1962, English translation by Thomas Burger, Cambridge, MA, The MIT Press, 1989); see especially Parts II and III. For discussion, see Craig Calhoun (ed.), *Habermas and the Public Sphere* (Cambridge, MA and London, The MIT Press, 1992); of particular relevance to the issues discussed here is the chapter by Geoff Eley, 'Nations, publics, and political cultures: Placing Habermas in the nineteenth century'.

48　See the discussion of different discursive spaces in eighteenth-century England in Peter Stallybrass and Allon White, *The Politics and Poetics of Transgression* (Ithaca, New York, Cornell University Press, 1986), especially ch. 2. If we followed Henry Fielding, we would also include barber's shops, for, 'You there see foreign affairs discussed in a manner little inferior to that with which they are handled in the coffee-houses; and domestic occurrences are much more largely and freely treated in the former than in the latter'. Fielding goes on to suggest that 'for the females of this country, especially those of the lower order' there is the 'chandler's shop, the known seat of all the news; or, as it is vulgarly called gossiping, in every parish in England'. See *The History of Tom Jones: A Foundling* (New York, Barnes & Noble, 1967), vol. One, Book II, ch. IV, pp. 74–5.

49　See Stallybrass and White, *The Politics and Poetics of Transgression*, op. cit., pp. 84–118.

50　Jonathan Swift's remark on some now forgotten Whig opponents is an apt criticism of Habermas: 'It is the Folly of too many, to mistake the Eccho of a *London* Coffee-house for the Voice of the Kingdom.' See 'The conduct of the allies, Nov., 1711', in Jonathan Swift, *Political Tracts 1711–1713*, ed. Herbert Davis (Oxford, Basil Blackwell, 1964), p. 53.

51　See Emmanuel Joseph Sieyès, *What is the Third Estate?*, op. cit.

52　Quoted and discussed by Rogers Brubaker, *Citizenship and Nationhood in France and Germany* (Cambridge, MA and London, Harvard University Press, 1992), p. 6, pp. 46–7, and pp. 192–3.

53　*Imagined Communities*, op. cit., p. 50. See also the Preface to the Second Edition, p. xiii, where Anderson complains that 'his original plan to stress the New World origins of nationalism' had been ignored by commentators.

54 See Bernard Bailyn, *The Ideological Origins of the American Revolution* (Cambridge, MA, Harvard University Press, 1965); see also Michael J. Sandel, *Democracy's Discontent: America in Search of a Public Philosophy* (Cambridge, MA and London, Harvard University Press, 1996), especially ch. 5.

55 See Seton Watson, *Nations and States*, op. cit., p. 148.

56 See John Breuilly, *Nationalism and the State* (Manchester, Manchester University Press, 1982).

57 See Partha Chatterjee, *Nationalist Thought and the Colonial World: A Derivative Discourse* (Zed Books, London, 1986), p. 30.

58 I am indebted to Philip Gerrans, 'Colonising nationalism', *Political Theory Newsletter* vol. 7.1 (July 1995), pp. 35–41, for forcing me to reconsider my views on this issue. See my 'How European is nationalism? A response to Philip Gerrans', *Political Theory Newsletter* vol. 7.1 (July 1995), pp. 60–6, for an initial rejoinder to Gerrans's argument.

59 This is one possible reading of Anthony D. Smith's argument that premodern ethnic communities – *ethnies* – both preceded and provided the foundation for modern nations; see his *The Ethnic Origins of Nations* (Oxford and Cambridge, MA, Blackwell, 1986). I discuss some of Smith's views more fully below. See also John A. Armstrong, *Nations before Nationalism* (Chapel Hill, University of North Carolina Press, 1982).

60 David Miller, *On Nationality* (Oxford, Clarendon Press), p. 24; see also p. 30.

61 As pointed out to me by Jack Barbalet.

62 Gerrans suggests that the thousand year long Vietnamese resistance to China was nationalist in character. See 'Colonising nationalism', op. cit., pp. 36–8.

63 Gellner, *Nationalism*, op. cit., pp. 20–1.

64 Ernest Renan, 'What is a nation?', trans. Martin Thom, in Homi K. Bhabha (ed.), *Nation and Narration* (London and New York, Routledge, 1990). This was first given as a lecture in 1882.

65 Harry Beran, 'Border disputes and the right of national self-determination', *History of European Ideas* vol. 16 (1993), pp. 479–86, p. 480.

66 See the passage which is used as an epigraph for this section. Renan's views are approvingly discussed by Brian Barry, 'Self-government revisited', in David Miller and Larry Siedentop (eds), *The Nature of Political Theory* (Oxford, Clarendon Press, 1983). Beran also cites Bertrand Russell, *Political Ideals* (first published 1917; reprinted London, Allen & Unwin, 1963) as a proponent of this view.

67 See Jean Jacques Rousseau, *Considerations on the Government of Poland*, in *Political Writings*, translated and edited by Frederick Watkins (Madison, University of Wisconsin Press, 1986), especially chs I–IV.

68 Miller argues that 'national identities are not all-embracing, and the common culture they require may leave room for many private cultures to flourish within the borders of the nation'. This underestimates the extent to which the 'common culture' embraces difference. See *On Nationality*, op. cit., p. 26.

69 This is a major theme of Colley, *Britons*, op. cit. See also Linda Colley, 'Britishness and otherness: An argument', *Journal of British Studies* vol. 31 (1992), pp. 309–29.

70 Cp. Linda Colley: 'historically speaking, most nations have always been culturally and ethnically diverse', *Britons*, op. cit., p. 5.

71 See Hugh Trevor-Roper, 'The invention of tradition: The Highland tradition of Scotland', in Eric Hobsbawm and Terence Ranger (eds), *The Invention of Tradition* (Cambridge, Cambridge University Press, 1983).

72 David Miller gives an excellent account of the relationship between English and British identities in *On Nationality*, op. cit., pp. 165–76.

73 Michael Walzer, *What it Means to be an American* (New York, Marsilio, 1992); see also his 'Pluralism: A political perspective', in Stephen A. Thernstrom (ed.), *The Harvard Encyclopedia of American Ethnic Groups* (Cambridge, MA, Harvard University Press, 1980); reprinted in Will Kymlicka (ed.), *The Rights of Minority Cultures* (Oxford and New York, Oxford University Press, 1995).

74 William H. McNeill, *Polyethnicity and National Unity in World History* (Toronto, University of Toronto Press, 1986), p. 34.

75 Walker Connor, 'A nation is a nation, is a State, is an ethnic group, is a...', *Ethnic and Racial Studies* vol. 1 (1978), pp. 379–88; reprinted in abbreviated form in John Hutchinson and Anthony D. Smith (eds), *Nationalism* (Oxford and New York, Oxford University Press, 1994).

76 Anthony D. Smith, *The Ethnic Origins of Nations*, op. cit. See also Smith, *National Identity* (Harmondsworth, Penguin, 1991).

77 Smith, *Ethnic Origins of Nations*, op. cit., p. 17.

78 Daniel Defoe, *The True-Born Englishman*, Part I, in *Selected Writings of Daniel Defoe*, ed. James T. Boulton (Cambridge, Cambridge University Press, 1965; reprinted 1975). This passage is used by Benedict Anderson as an epigraph to *Imagined Communities*, op. cit. A different passage with a similar message is quoted by David Miller, *On Nationality*, op. cit., p. 25.

79 Smith, *National Identity*, op. cit., p. 29.

80 See Hans Kohn, *The Idea of Nationalism*, op. cit., especially pp. 329–34; Michael Ignatieff, *Blood and Belonging: Journeys into the New Nationalism* (London, BBC Books and Chatto & Windus, 1993), especially pp. 3–6. Rogers Brubaker, *Citizenship and Nationhood in France and Germany*, op. cit., provides an interesting study of the different practices in France – a 'civic' or 'territorial' nation – and in Germany – an 'ethnic' nation. Variants of the distinction are provided by John Plamenatz, 'Two types of nationalism', in Eugene Kamenka (ed.), *Nationalism: The Nature and Evolution of an Idea* (Canberra, Australian National University Press, 1975, and by Liah Greenfeld, *Nationalism*, op. cit., pp. 1–26, etc. Curiously, Anthony Smith also subscribes to the ethnic/civic distinction; see *Ethnic Origins of Nations*, op. cit., especially pp. 134–52, and *National Identity*, op. cit., especially pp. 8–15, 82–3, 123–42, etc. At first sight, Smith's thesis that nations have an 'ethnic core' is not easily conjoined with the claim that there is an important distinction between ethnic and non-ethnic nationalisms. However, the two are compatible so long as one is careful (as Smith is not) to interpret the first as a historical thesis that nations are in fact permutations of pre-existing ethnic communities and the second as a distinction between those national cultures which emphasise ethnic elements and those which do not.

81 See Rogers Brubaker, *Citizenship and Nationhood in France and Germany*, op. cit., for a detailed discussion of the differences between Germany and France.

82 See Kohn, *The Idea of Nationalism*, op. cit., pp. 329–32. For similar views, see Plamenatz, 'Two Types of Nationalism', op. cit., and Greenfeld, *Nationalism*, op. cit.

83 See Hobsbawm's Introduction to Hobsbawm and Ranger (eds), *The Invention of Tradition*, op. cit.

84 See Will Kymlicka, 'Misunderstanding nationalism', *Dissent* (winter 1995), pp. 130–7, especially p. 131.

85 Anderson, *Imagined Communities*, op. cit., p. 145.

2 National and other identities

1 Erik H. Erikson, *Childhood and Society* (New York, W.W. Norton & Co., first published 1950; revised and enlarged edition 1963), p. 282. Erikson goes on to say that the 'study of identity…becomes as strategic in our time as the study of sexuality was in Freud's time'.

2 Philip Gleason, 'Identifying identity: A semantic history', *Journal of American History* vol. 69 (1983), pp. 910–31 provides a useful discussion of the proliferation of 'identity' talk in the social sciences. See also Perry Anderson, 'Fernand Braudel and national identity', in *A Zone of Engagement* (London and New York, Verso, 1992), especially pp. 266–70.

3 For a discussion of Erikson's role, see Gleason, 'Identifying identity', op. cit., pp. 914–15.

4 The seminal work here remains Louis Althusser's attempt to enlist Lacanian psychoanalysis in the service of Marxist structuralism in 'Ideology and ideological State apparatuses: Notes for an investigation', in *Lenin and Philosophy and Other Essays* (London and New York, New Left Books, 1971). See also 'Marx and Freud' in the same volume. For significant recent work, see Judith Butler, *Gender Trouble: Feminism and the Subversion of Identity* (New York and London, Routledge, 1990) and Wendy Brown, *States of Injury* (Princeton, Princeton University Press, 1995).

5 Sometimes this assumption is explicit. For example, Avishai Margalit and Moshe Halbertal distinguish between the 'metaphysical individual' – which they identify with the 'person' – and the 'anthropological individual' – the 'personality'. For Margalit and Halbertal, an identity is a culturally defined 'personality'. See their 'Liberalism and the right to culture', *Social Research* vol. 61 (1994), pp. 491–510; especially pp. 501–2. In similar vein, Philip Pettit distinguishes between the 'personal self' and the 'process by which an agent takes on a larger identity' – an 'identification'; see *Republicanism: A Theory of Freedom of Government* (Oxford, Clarendon Press, 1997), pp. 257–60. Judith Butler puts the implicit assumption here very nicely: 'Within philosophical discourse itself, the notion of 'the person' has received analytic elaboration on the assumption that whatever social context the person is 'in' remains somehow externally related to the definitional structure of personhood.' See *Gender Trouble*, op. cit., p. 16.

6 See Marcel Mauss, 'A category of the human mind: The notion of person; the notion of self', in Michael Carrithers *et al.* (eds), *The Category of the*

Person: Anthropology, Philosophy, History (Cambridge, Cambridge University Press, 1985), especially pp. 14–17. The lecture was originally given in 1939.

7 Except for the comments on Hobbes, I rely in this paragraph on the entry on 'Person' in *The Compact Edition of the Oxford English Dictionary* vol. II (Oxford, Oxford University Press, 1987). However, I do not always follow the distinctions which the *OED* draws between various senses of the term.

8 Thomas Hobbes, *Leviathan*, ed. Michael Oakeshott (Oxford, Blackwell, n.d.), Part I, ch. XVI, p. 105.

9 John Locke, *An Essay concerning Human Understanding* (Oxford, Clarendon Press, 1984), Book II, ch. XXVII, 26.

10 Locke, *Essay*, op. cit., II, XXVII, p. 18.

11 *Essay*, op. cit., II, XXVII, 6: 'The Identity of the same *Man* consists…in nothing but a participation of the same continued Life, by constantly fleeting Particles of Matter, in succession vitally united to the same organized body.'

12 See *Essay*, III, XI, 16.

13 *Essay*, II, XXVII, 9.

14 This is, of course, the nub of Butler's famous objection to Locke that 'consciousness of personal identity presupposes, and therefore cannot constitute, personal identity, any more than knowledge…can constitute truth, which it presupposes'. See Joseph Butler, *The Analogy of Religion*, Dissertation I: 'Of personal identity' (London, Longmans & Co., 1834), p. 308.

15 Thanks to Sandra Lynch for discussion of these issues.

16 David P. Behan, 'Locke on persons and personal identity', *Canadian Journal of Philosophy* vol. 9 (1979), pp. 53–75. For some criticisms of Behan in other respects, see Ross Poole, 'On being a person', *Australasian Journal of Philosophy* vol. 74 (1996), pp. 38–56.

17 *Essay* II, I, 11, emphasis added; see also II, I, 12.

18 *Essay* II, XXVII, 16, emphasis added; see also II, XXVII, 24.

19 Kant, *The Metaphysical Elements of Justice* (being Part I of *The Metaphysics of Morals*), trans. John Ladd (Indianapolis, Bobbs-Merrill, 1978), Introduction, IV, p. 223.

20 Kant, *The Doctrine of Virtue* (Part II of *The Metaphysics of Morals*), trans. Mary J. Gregor (Philadelphia, University of Pennsylvania Press, 1971) Part One, Book I, ch. II.

21 'Freedom of the will and the concept of a person', *Journal of Philosophy* vol. 68 (1971), pp. 5–20; see p. 6. Frankfurt goes on to say that we generally suppose – 'either rightly or wrongly' – that the essential characteristics of being a person are uniquely human, but this supposition plays no role in his further argument.

22 For example, Daniel Dennett writes:

I am a person, and so are you. That much is beyond doubt. I am a human being, and *probably* you are too…At this time and place human beings are the only persons we recognise, and we recognise almost all human beings as persons, but on the one hand we can easily contemplate the existence of biologically very different persons – inhabiting other planets, perhaps – and on the other hand we

recognise conditions that exempt human beings from personhood,
or at least some very important elements of personhood.
('Conditions of personhood', in Amélie Oksenberg
Rorty (ed.), *The Identity of Persons* (Berkeley,
University of California Press, 1976, p. 175)

For Graham Nerlich, the distinction between person and humans is an
orthodoxy to be noted rather than defended:

I follow a familiar path in claiming that not every human being is a
person, and, perhaps, not every person is a human being.
(*Values and Valuing: Speculations on the Ethical Life
of Persons*, Oxford, Clarendon Press, 1984, p. 6)

23 I should note three honourable exceptions to this tendency. Richard
Wollheim argues in *The Thread of Life* (Cambridge, MA, Harvard University Press, 1984), especially ch. I, that if a being is to be a person it must
be in virtue of its species life:

species are selected as persons-species, either in reality or in fiction,
on the basis of how their members live, or how they lead their lives:
of how they live in virtue of being members of that species. (p. 9)

In other words, we are persons in virtue of being human and participating in the way of life which is characteristic of humans. If there were to
be non-human persons, they would be such in virtue of a way of life
specific to the species to which they belonged. Wisely, Wollheim spends no
time on this fantasy.
According to Annette Baier in *Moral Prejudices: Essays on Ethics*
(Cambridge, MA and London, Harvard University Press, 1995), ch. 13: 'A
naturalist view of persons':

[We] naturalists see persons as intelligent, talkative, playful mam-
mals who have become conscious of ourselves, or our mammalian
nature, its possibilities and the constraints it imposes. (p. 325)

And Amélie Rorty concludes a fascinating discussion of persons in
Mind in Action (Boston, Beacon Press, 1988), Part I, by arguing for an
approach to persons which attempts to see:

how the cultural history of the various versions of the concept of a
person has been modified by and has in turn modified its biological
base. (p. 98)

It is however testimony to the domination of the term 'person' in contemporary philosophy that Wollheim, Baier and Rorty all retain the term
as their preferred designation of what we centrally are.
24 Hegel, *Elements of the Philosophy of Right*, trans. H.B. Nisbet
(Cambridge, Cambridge University Press, 1991), Part One, § 35, Addition.
In *The Phenomenology of Spirit*, trans. A.V. Miller (Oxford, Oxford

178 *Notes for pp. 54–9*

University Press, 1977), § 187, Hegel had argued that humans had to rise above natural existence by risking their life in order to attain 'the truth of this recognition' as persons.

25 See also the remark in *The Phenomenology of Spirit*, op. cit., § 480, that 'to describe an individual as a "person" is an expression of contempt'. The pejorative connotations of the German '*Person*' are more marked than the English 'person', which makes Hegel's point easier to make in that language. The *Oxford English Dictionary* does note a derogatory use, but it seems largely dormant in contemporary English. That a derogatory sense of the French '*personne*' is alive and well is indicated by Simone Weil's discussion in 'Human personality', in *Simone Weil: An Anthology*, ed. Sîan Miles (London, Virago, 1986).

26 *Philosophy of Right*, op. cit., Part One, § 36.

27 Kant himself was aware of this problem. For him, the rigorous morality of law and duty was not self-sufficient, but presupposed a religious narrative involving God, personal redemption and immortality. His point here was not, as unsympathetic critics have charged, to renege on the austerity of the moral law by providing a guarantee of the ultimate concomitance of virtue and individual happiness. It was rather to provide the individual with the resources to make sense of his or her own particular existence. Without some such story, the Kantian morality – and the concept of a person which is its creature – fails to have a purchase on human life. For Kant, the final identity that we need to make sense of our lives is a Christian one. For Hegel, this was a desperate attempt to overcome problems caused by Kant's failure to recognise the moral resources available within the modern world. Life in the family and the State involves ethical frameworks which are not reducible to abstract right; the identities of family member and of citizen are not that of personhood, and they provide glimpses of a richer and more satisfying conception of the self than personhood.

28 'On the genealogy of morals', Essay Two, § 1, in *On the Genealogy of Morals; Ecce Homo*, ed. Walter Kaufmann (New York, Vintage Books, 1969).

29 *On the Genealogy of Morals*, Essay Two, § 1.

30 *On the Genealogy of Morals*, Essay Two, § 2.

31 *On the Genealogy of Morals*, Essay Two, § 3.

32 *On the Genealogy of Morals*, Essay Two, § 14. Nietzsche goes on to argue that the institution of punishment actually impedes the development of feelings of guilt in the criminal because he sees exactly the same characteristics for which he is being punished (e.g. cruelty) being exercised in the name of justice.

33 *On the Genealogy of Morals*, Essay Two, § 3.

34 *On the Genealogy of Morals*, Essay Two, § 16. See also Nietzsche's own comment in *Ecce Homo* that the *Genealogy* showed that the conscience was 'the instinct of cruelty that turns back after it can no longer discharge itself externally' (*On the Genealogy of Morals; Ecce Homo*, p. 312).

35 See *On the Genealogy of Morals*, Essay Two, §§ 6–7, especially the remark, directed against 'good old Kant', that 'the categorical imperative smells of cruelty'.

36 *On the Genealogy of Morals*, Essay Two, § 5.

37 Taylor uses this phrase as the title for ch. 2 of *Human Agency and Language: Philosophical Papers 1* (Cambridge, Cambridge University

Press, 1985). See also the Introduction and Chapters 1 and 4 of this volume, and *Sources of the Self: The Making of the Modern Identity* (Cambridge, Cambridge University Press, 1989), especially Part I. As will be obvious to anyone familiar with his work, the following account draws considerably on Taylor's work. However, the borrowing has been rather eclectic. For example, I have made little use of his concept of 'strong evaluation' and I have not followed him into some of the more speculative reaches of his theory of the self (e.g. the material on 'hypergoods', 'moral sources', etc.). A more substantial difference is that Taylor shows a certain fondness for the conception of the person as a fundamental identity underlying all others and, perhaps as a consequence, does not recognise the irreducible plurality of identities.

38 Taylor, 'Self-interpreting animals', op. cit., p. 58.

39 See Bernard Williams, 'Internal and external reasons', in *Moral Luck: Philosophical Papers 1973–1980* (Cambridge, London and New York, Cambridge University Press, 1981), especially p. 102 and p. 105.

40 See 'Internal and external reasons', op. cit., p. 104.

41 I discuss some aspects of family morality in *Morality and Modernity* (London and New York, Routledge, 1991), ch. 3.

42 The focus on the moral world of persons which is characteristic of liberalism makes it very difficult to come to terms with the notion of collective responsibility. I discuss this issue in the 'National identity' and 'National identity and moral philosophy' sections below, and again in ch. 4.

43 See the discussions of the family in *The Phenomenology of Spirit*, op. cit., especially §§ 451–2, and *The Philosophy of Right*, op. cit., Part Three, Section One, especially §§ 173–80.

44 Breyten Breytenbach, *Return to Paradise* (New York, Harcourt Brace, 1992), quoted in J.M. Coetzee, 'Resisters', *New York Review of Books* (2 December 1993), pp. 3–6.

45 J.G. Herder, *J.G. Herder on Social and Political Culture*, translated and edited by J.G. Barnard (Cambridge, Cambridge University Press, 1969). It should be noted here that Herder seemed not to have envisaged a political role for the nation.

46 See the discussion in Chapter 1, in the section entitled 'The nation: imagination and culture'.

47 It is not hard to discern this as an implicit presence in Anthony D. Smith's argument for the ethnic core of modern nations. See *The Ethnic Origins of Nations*, op. cit., and *National Identity*, op. cit.

48 See Anderson, *Imagined Communities*, op. cit., especially ch. 1, on this theme. However, we need to emphasise – as Anderson does not – that what is provided is not survival in any very strong sense. If it were, then giving up one's life could hardly count as sacrifice.

49 See, for example, Robert Goodin, 'What is so special about our fellow countrymen?', *Ethics* vol. 98 (1988), pp. 663–86. Goodin notes that at least sometimes we have more stringent obligations to aliens, e.g. to respect their rights, than we have to compatriots.

50 This point is emphasised by Samuel Scheffler in an important series of papers on (his terminology) 'special responsibilities'. See 'Individual responsibility in a global age', *Social Philosophy and Policy* vol. 12 (1995), pp. 219–36; *Families, Nations and Strangers*, The Lindley Lecture

(Lawrence, University of Kansas, 1995); and 'Relationships and responsibilities', *Philosophy and Public Affairs* vol. 26 (1997), pp. 189–209.

51 I return to this issue in Chapter 5.

52 See Miller, *On Nationality*, op. cit., ch. 3, where Miller provides a powerful defence of 'the ethics of nationality' against universalistic criticisms.

53 It is a weakness of Miller's defence of nationalist ethics that he focusses on our special responsibilities to attend to the needs of our co-nationals, and all but ignores the responsibility for what they do.

54 See Yael Tamir, *Liberal Nationalism*, op. cit., pp. 97–8.

55 As Hannah Arendt comments, we properly feel guilt about something that we as individuals have done or failed to do: 'Guilt, unlike responsibility, always singles out; it is strictly personal.' Arendt's use of the adjective 'personal' in this context is significant. See Hannah Arendt, 'Collective responsibility', in *Amor Mundi: Explorations in the Faith and Thought of Hannah Arendt*, ed. James W. Bernauer (Boston, Martin Nijhoff, 1987), p. 43.

56 The distinction between guilt and shame deserves much more discussion than I can provide here. For a key recent discussion, see Bernard Williams, *Shame and Necessity* (Berkeley, Los Angeles and London, University of California Press, 1994), especially ch. IV and Endnote 1. Williams does not however explore the extent to which one can appropriately feel shame, but not guilt, for what others have done. This distinction has been pressed in Australia in the context of indigenous issues by Raimond Gaita; see especially 'Not right', in Peter Craven (ed.) *Best Australian Essays 1998* (Melbourne, Bookman Press, 1998). See also Desmond Manderson, 'Unutterable shame/unuttered guilt: Semantics, Aporia and the possibility of Mabo', *Law, Text, Culture* vol. 4.1, Special Issue: *In the Wake of Terra Nullius* (ed. Colin Perrin), pp. 234–44.

57 Renan, 'What is a nation?', op. cit., and Miller, *On Nationality*, op. cit., pp. 34–42.

58 I will return to this issue in Chapter 4, when I will be specifically concerned with the responsibility of postcolonial nations such as Australia, Canada and the United States, to come to terms with the expropriation of their indigenous people.

59 Yael Tamir presents a persuasive case for the importance of identity and (what she calls) 'connectedness'. See *Liberal Nationalism*, especially ch. 5.

60 On this difference between the enterprise of moral (or in his terminology 'ethical') theory and the natural sciences, see Bernard Williams, *Ethics and the Limits of Philosophy* (London, Fontana/Collins, 1985), especially ch. 8.

61 This principle was clearly enunciated by David Hume and will always be associated with him. See *A Treatise of Human Nature*, ed. L.A. Selby-Bigge (Oxford, Clarendon Press, 1975), Book III, Part I, Section 1, especially pp. 456–7. It is distinct from (unless ultimately incompatible with) his other view that 'reason is utterly impotent' with respect to motivation.

62 See John Rawls, *A Theory of Justice* (Cambridge, MA, Harvard University Press, 1971), especially pp. 20–1, 48–51.

63 See 'The independence of moral theory', *Proceedings and Addresses of the American Philosophical Association* vol. 47 (1974/75), pp. 5–22. My understanding of the conception of reflective equilibrium draws on

Norman Daniels, 'Wide reflective equilibrium and theory acceptance in ethics', *Journal of Philosophy* vol. 76 (1979), pp. 256–82, and on Kai Nielsen, 'Reflective equilibrium and the transformation of philosophy', *Metaphilosophy* vol. 20 (1989), pp. 235–46. According to Daniels, the broader conception ('wide reflective equilibrium') was already implicit in *A Theory of Justice*.

64 For example, it may well be that certain – otherwise attractive – forms of small-scale life are not possible given industrialisation, population increase, and the multiplication of desires. It is possible to argue that the changes should not have taken place, but it is difficult to maintain that they could at this point of world history be reversed. Serious moral debate must take facts like this into account.

65 As Rawls remarks, with characteristic understatement, 'it is doubtful whether one can ever reach this state'. See *A Theory of Justice*, op. cit., p. 49.

66 'How to Become What One Is' is the subtitle for Nietzsche's philosophical autobiography, *Ecce Homo*. See *On the Genealogy of Morals; Ecce Homo*, op. cit.

67 Scheffler, 'Relationships and responsibilities', op. cit., p. 191.

68 See Scheffler, 'Relationships and responsibilities', op. cit., p. 202.

69 My position here is close to that of Scheffler who argues that 'one's relationships to other people give rise to special responsibilities when they are relationships one has reason to value' ('Relationships and responsibilities', op. cit., p. 197). For an interestingly different position, see Yael Tamir, *Liberal Nationalism*, pp. 101–2.

3 Three concepts of freedom: liberalism, republicanism and nationalism

1 See Richard Mulgan, 'Liberty in Ancient Greece', in Zbigniew Pelczynski and John Gray (eds), *Conceptions of Liberty in Political Philosophy* (London, The Athlone Press, 1984), especially p. 8. Mulgan notes the existence of various derivative senses of freedom operative in the ancient world. See also Joel Feinberg, *Social Philosophy* (Englewood Cliffs, New Jersey, Prentice-Hall, 1973), p. 4. Feinberg cites C.S. Lewis, *Studies in Words* (Cambridge, Cambridge University Press, 1961), pp. 111ff.

2 Gender is a significant subtext of the discussion in this chapter – and indeed, elsewhere in this book. Since almost all theorists confined citizenship to men, the masculine gender is usually appropriate for personal pronoun and generic terms. Where the conception under discussion is inclusive of women as well as men, I use 'his or her' and other gender-neutral terms.

3 Aristotle, *Politics*, with translation by H. Rackham (London, Heinemann and Cambridge, MA, Harvard University Press, 1967), Book I, ch. I, § 8, p. 9.

4 See Michael Walzer, 'Citizenship', in Terence Ball *et al.* (eds), *Political Innovation and Conceptual Change* (Cambridge, Cambridge University Press, 1989). A broadly similar account is offered by J.G.A. Pocock, 'The ideal of citizenship since classical times', *Queens Quarterly* vol. 99 no. 1 (spring 1992), pp. 33–55. The distinction between two conceptions of citizenship is a commonplace in recent discussion. See, for example, Lolle

Nauta, 'Changing conceptions of citizenship', *Praxis International* vol. 12 (1992), pp. 20–34; Will Kymlicka and Wayne Norman, 'Return of the citizen: A survey of recent work on citizenship theory', *Ethics* vol. 104 (1994), pp. 352–81.

5 G.W.F. Hegel, *Elements of the Philosophy of Right*, op. cit., Part Two, Section 2, § 124, p. 151.

6 'The liberty of the ancients compared with that of the moderns', in *Political Writings*, ed. Biancamaria Fontana (Cambridge, Cambridge University Press, 1988), p. 316.

7 See Perry Anderson, *Passages from Antiquity to Feudalism* (London, New Left Books, 1974), ch. 1, especially p. 27.

8 After noting the criticism of modern (American) slavery by Benjamin Franklin and Tocqueville that it rendered slave owners unfit and unwilling to work, Moses Finley commented, 'No ancient moralist would have thought it harmful to be unfit for getting a living by industry; on the contrary, that was precisely the ideal for the truly free man' (M.I. Finley, *Ancient Slavery and Modern Ideology*, London, Chatto & Windus, 1980, p. 100).

9 This address was originally given in 1958. References here will be to the somewhat revised version in Isaiah Berlin, *Four Essays on Liberty* (Oxford, Oxford University Press, 1969). See also Berlin's Introduction to this volume.

10 It should be noted that here and elsewhere I follow Berlin and use 'freedom' and 'liberty' interchangeably.

11 Berlin, *Four Essays on Liberty*, op. cit., Introduction, p. xxxix.

12 Berlin, *Four Essays on Liberty*, op. cit., p. 131.

13 Berlin, *Four Essays on Liberty*, op. cit., p. 134.

14 See Charles Taylor, 'What's wrong with negative liberty', in Taylor, *Philosophy and the Human Sciences: Philosophical Papers 2*, op. cit.

15 Jean Jacques Rousseau, *The Social Contract* (New York, Meridian, 1974), Book I, ch. 7, p. 31.

16 In the following discussion, I draw on Quentin Skinner, 'Machiavelli on the maintenance of liberty', *Politics* vol. 18.2 (November 1983), pp. 3–15; 'The idea of negative liberty: Philosophical and historical perspectives', in Richard Rorty *et al.* (eds), *Philosophy in History* (Cambridge, Cambridge University Press, 1984); 'The paradoxes of political liberty', *Tanner Lectures on Human Values* vol. 7 (1986), pp. 227–50, reprinted in David Miller (ed.), *Liberty*; and 'The republican ideal of political liberty', in Gisela Bock *et al.* (eds), *Machiavelli and Republicanism* (Cambridge, Cambridge University Press, 1990).

17 See Philip Pettit, *Republicanism: A Theory of Freedom and Government* (Oxford, Clarendon Press, 1997); see especially chs 1 and 2.

18 In his earlier work on freedom, Pettit was concerned to defend an explicitly negative conception. See, for example, Philip Pettit, 'Negative liberty, liberal and republican', *European Journal of Philosophy* vol. 1 (1993), pp. 15–38; and 'Freedom as antipower', *Ethics* vol. 106 (1996), pp. 576–604.

19 It certainly goes beyond Berlin's conception of negative freedom: for Berlin, 'it is perfectly conceivable that a liberal-minded despot would allow his subjects a large measure of personal freedom' (*Four Essays on Liberty*, op. cit., p. 129). However, it seems to me that Berlin is simply

mistaken here. It might well be argued that my negative freedom *now* includes my freedom to plan for the *future*. It is certainly the case that many of my present actions (including writing this sentence) are future directed. If this is the case, then my negative freedom at a time is affected by uncertainty of how things will be at a future time, for example, if the 'liberal-minded' despot is replaced by a nasty one, or if the marriage becomes conflictual. In which case, freedom from coercion will *require* freedom from domination. At the very least, the two conceptions will tend to merge into each other.

20 I misunderstood Pettit on this point in an earlier contribution to this topic; see 'Freedom, citizenship, and national identity', *The Philosophical Forum* vol. 28 (1996/97), pp. 125–48; see especially pp. 132–3. Thanks to Philip Pettit for pointing this out.

21 See Pettit, *Republicanism*, op. cit., especially ch. 6.

22 What is missing in Berlin's polemic against positive freedom is the recognition that almost all the theorists he attacks concede that some conception of free choice is a necessary aspect of freedom. For example, T.H. Green, who is castigated by Berlin for his claim that 'the ideal of true freedom is the maximum of power for all...to make the best of themselves', also insists, only a few sentences previously, that 'there can be no freedom among men who act not willingly but under compulsion'. See T.H. Green, 'Liberal legislation and the freedom of contract', in David Miller (ed.), *Liberty* (Oxford, Oxford University Press, 1991), especially pp. 22–3. And, as we shall see, both Hegel and Karl Marx provide accounts of freedom which recognise the role of choice.

23 Machiavelli, *The Discourses*, trans. L.J. Walker and Brian Richardson (Harmondsworth, Penguin, 1978), Book I, ch. iii, p. 112.

24 Walzer, 'Citizenship', op. cit., p. 217.

25 'The liberty of the ancients compared with the moderns', op. cit., p. 326. To be fair, it has to be noted that Berlin himself makes one of his few – and uncharacteristic – concessions to positive freedom on this point. He writes: 'Perhaps the chief value for liberals of political – "positive" – rights, of participating in the government, is as a means for protecting what they take to be an ultimate value, namely individual – "negative" – liberty.' ('Two concepts', op. cit., p. 165).

26 Skinner, 'The paradoxes of political liberty', op. cit., pp. 198–9.

27 Charles Taylor provides a compelling statement of a form of republicanism which emphasises political commitment, not merely as necessary condition of freedom, but as a *form* of freedom, in 'Cross-purposes: The liberal-communitarian debate', in Nancy L. Rosenblum (ed.), *Liberalism and the Moral Life* (Cambridge, MA and London, Harvard University Press, 1989).

28 See, for example, Marx, *Economic and Philosophical Manuscripts of 1844* in Karl Marx and Friedrich Engels, *Collected Works, Vol 3: 1833–1844* (London, Lawrence & Wishart, 1975), especially the manuscript entitled 'Estranged labour'.

29 Karl Marx, *Capital Vol. III*, trans. David Fernbach (Harmondsworth, Penguin Books, 1981), ch. 48, p. 959.

30 Hegel, *The Philosophy of Right*, op. cit., Part Three, § 153, p. 196.

31 G.W.F. Hegel, *The Encyclopaedia Logic: Part I of the Encyclopaedia of the Philosophical Sciences*, trans. T.F. Geraets, W.A. Suchting and H.S. Harris (Indianapolis, Hacket, 1991), p. 58.

32 It is plausible to present Hegel's philosophy of the State as the final episode in the civic republican tradition before it was hidden from view by the dominance of liberal, socialist and nationalist doctrines in the nineteenth and twentieth centuries. See the brief but illuminating discussion in Laurence Dickey, *Hegel: Religion, Economics and the Politics of Spirit* (Cambridge, Cambridge University Press, 1989), pp. 227–30.

33 Hegel, *The Philosophy of History*, trans. J. Sibree (New York, Dover Publications, 1956), Part II, ch. 3, p. 252.

34 See Hegel, *Elements of the Philosophy of Right*, op. cit., § 268, pp. 288–9; § 324, p. 361.

35 The canonical discussion of the epistemological principles underlying this form of reasoning is Hegel's Introduction to *The Phenomenology of Spirit*, op. cit., pp. 46–57.

36 Hegel provides an account of the logic of this process in *The Philosophy of Right*, op. cit., Part Three, Section 2, § 187, pp. 224–6.

37 *The Philosophy of Right*, op. cit., Part Three, Section 2, § 186, p. 224.

38 Hegel, *The Philosophy of Right*, op. cit., Introduction, especially §§ 14–18, pp. 47–51.

39 Hegel, *The Philosophy of Right*, op. cit., Introduction, § 10: 'Only when the will has itself as its object is it *for itself* what it is *in itself*.' See also § 22.

40 *The Philosophy of Right*, op. cit., Part Three, §§ 146–7, pp. 190–1.

41 See Aristotle's characteristic depiction of life outside the *polis* in *Politics*, op. cit., Book I, ch. I, § 8, p. 9.

42 For some discussion of the notion of rationality required to understand this process, see Ross Poole, 'Living with reason', *Inquiry* vol. 35 (1992), pp. 199–217.

43 The classical account of the institutions of what has come to be called 'civil society' (in a sense related to Hegel's, but not equivalent to it) is Alexis de Tocqueville, *Democracy in America*, 2 vols (New York, Vintage Books, 1990).

44 Compare Taylor, 'Cross-purposes', op. cit., p. 170.

45 Hegel, *The Philosophy of Right*, op. cit., Part Three, Section 3, § 301, p. 341.

46 Hegel does provide an odd, though strangely prescient, argument to the effect that particularity will find some satisfaction in the largely symbolic role of the constitutional monarch; see *The Philosophy of Right*, op. cit., Part Three, Section 2, especially § 279, pp. 320–1.

47 And also with some modern republicans. The conception of self-rule plays no part in Skinner's presentation of Machiavelli nor in Pettit's rational reconstruction of the republican tradition.

48 It is therefore deeply ironic that Hegel's political philosophy is sometimes interpreted as an apologia for nationalism. For a – surely definitive – refutation of this legend, see Shlomo Avineri, 'Hegel and nationalism', in Walter Kaufmann (ed.), *Hegel's Political Philosophy* (New York, Atherton Press, 1970).

49 Yael Tamir, *Liberal Nationalism*, especially ch. 5.

50 The key texts here are *Considerations on the Government of Poland* and *Constitutional Project for Corsica*, both in Rousseau, *Political Writings*, ed.

Frederick Watkins, op. cit. For an account of the reception and influence of Rousseau in pre-Revolutionary France, see Simon Schama, *Citizens: A Chronicle of the French Revolution* (London, Penguin Books, 1989), Part I, ch. 4. The title of the chapter, 'The cultural construction of a citizen', sums up my theme very nicely.

51 See the extract from *Ideas for a Philosophy of History* in *J.G. Herder on Social and Political Culture*, op. cit., pp. 317–26; see also the discussion in F.M. Barnard, *Herder's Social and Political Thought*, op. cit., pp. 80–1.

52 As suggested by Barry Hindess, 'Multiculturalism and citizenship', in Chandran Kukathas (ed.), *Multicultural Citizens* (St Leonards, NSW, Centre for Independent Studies, 1993). It is significant in this context to recall Walzer's suggestion that Roman citizenship became a more formal matter of entitlement not of participation, as it was extended to culturally distinct peoples.

53 See Michael Sandel, *Democracy's Discontent: America in Search of a Public Philosophy* (Cambridge, MA and London, Harvard University Press, 1996). Sandel argues that a liberal understanding of American national culture has displaced a previously dominant republican understanding.

54 I discuss immigration and the acquisition of citizenship in Chapter 4.

55 See Marx, *Capital* vol. 1 (Harmondsworth, Penguin, 1976), ch. 7, p. 283.

56 Will Kymlicka, *Liberalism, Community and Culture* (Oxford, Clarendon Press, 1989), p. 165. It should be noted that Kymlicka does not identify the 'rich and secure cultural structure' with a specifically *national* culture.

57 The relevant notion of responsibility is of course Max Weber's: see 'Politics as a vocation', in *From Max Weber*, eds H.H. Gerth and C. Wright Mills (London, Henley & Boston, Routledge & Kegan Paul, 1977).

4 Multiculturalism, Aboriginal rights and the nation

1 Will Kymlicka has suggested that discussions in the United States have downplayed the problem of national minorities because of the dominance of the experience of racism and multiculturalism ('American multiculturalism in the international arena', *Dissent* (fall 1998)). He may well be right about this. However, it is also possible that the Canadian treatment of indigenous groups as national minorities is influenced by the centrality of the issue of Quebec secession in Canadian politics. No doubt my own discussion here is influenced by the claim of most Australian Aboriginal leaders that neither the multicultural nor the national minority agenda is appropriate for most Australian indigenous people.

2 The information in the following paragraphs is largely drawn from Stephen Castles, *The Challenge of Multiculturalism: Global Changes and the Australian Experience* (Wollongong, NSW, Centre for Multicultural Studies, University of Wollongong for the Office of Multicultural Affairs, Department of the Prime Minister and Cabinet, 1992), ch. 1, and Uldis Ozolins, 'Immigration and immigrants', in Judith Brett, James Gillespie and Murray Goot (eds), *Developments in Australian Politics* (Melbourne, Macmillan, 1994).

3 According to Castles, the first Minister for Immigration, Arthur Calwell, 'promised the Australian public that there would be ten British immigrants for every "foreigner" ', *The Challenge of Multiculturalism*, p. 8.

4 There is disagreement about the extent to which the policy is accepted by the population at large (opinion polls giving different results depending on the questions asked), and attempts are often made to challenge the consensus in the name of 'ordinary Australians'. The most intellectually respectable of these was the historian Geoffrey Blainey's *All for Australia* (North Ryde, NSW, Methuen Haynes, 1984). Recently, strong opposition to multiculturalism has been voiced by elements within the conservative Government and by some independent members of parliament. While the Government is maintaining an official – though somewhat muted – commitment to multiculturalism, it is taking the opportunity to cut back on multicultural programmes.

5 See David Miller, *On Nationality*, op. cit., pp. 130–40, for an excellent discussion of these issues.

6 See John Stuart Mill, *On Liberty*, in *Utilitarianism; Liberty; Representative Government* (London, Everyman Library, 1957), especially chs 2 and 3. For some discussion of Mill in this context, see C.L. Ten, 'Multiculturalism and the value of diversity', in Chandran Kukathas (ed.), *Multicultural Citizens: The Philosophy and Politics of Identity* (St Leonards, NSW, The Centre for Independent Studies, 1993).

7 See John Rawls, 'The idea of an overlapping consensus', *Oxford Journal of Legal Studies* vol. 7 (1987), pp. 1–25; see p. 6. The distinction between 'toleration' liberalism and 'autonomy' liberalism is criticised in Will Kymlicka, *Multicultural Citizenship* (Oxford, Clarendon Press, 1995), ch. 8. The passage from Rawls is cited and discussed on pp. 163–4.

8 See Will Kymlicka, *Liberalism, Community and Culture* (Oxford, Clarendon Press, 1989), ch. 8. Kymlicka reiterates this position in *Multicultural Citizenship*, op. cit., ch. 5, pp. 80–94, but in the exposition moves towards the position – discussed below – that culture is important for our sense of identity.

9 As mentioned above (note 7), Kymlicka argues elsewhere against 'toleration liberalism' that autonomy should be the fundamental value for liberals; so that, for him, liberal toleration should not be extended to those cultural minorities which restrict the civil liberties of their members. See Kymlicka, *Multicultural Citizenship*, op. cit., ch. 8. While I am sympathetic to this argument, there are some difficulties in applying it. It may be that a cultural group (e.g. a religion) does not restrict the *civil* liberties of its members; but because it controls certain resources which are of profound importance to their members (i.e. the promise of salvation), it is able to restrict their liberty in important ways. A culture may not only determine the importance of individual liberty, but may also determine what counts as a constraint on it (e.g. the threat of damnation hardly affects a non-believer).

10 For persuasive accounts of the importance of culture to identity, see Avishai Margalit and Joseph Raz, 'National self-determination', *Journal of Philosophy* vol. 87 (1990), pp. 439–61, and Avishai Margalit and Moshe Halbertal, 'Liberalism and the right to culture', *Social Research* vol. 61 (1994), pp. 491–510. Margalit and Halbertal draw a distinction between the 'metaphysical individual' – identified by them with the 'person' – and the 'anthropological individual' – the 'personality'. In their terminology, when I lose a certain cultural identity I cease to be the same 'personality' though I remain the same 'person'. In Chapter 2 above, I argued against

the reification of the concept of a person, and suggest that the concept should not be understood as designating a metaphysical substratum (what we essentially are beneath various social identities), but rather as one of the social identities which are available to us. If anything, this strengthens the case for the importance of culture.

11 See Chandran Kukathas, 'Are there any cultural rights?', *Political Theory* vol. 20 (1992), pp. 105–39; reprinted in part in Will Kymlicka (ed.), *The Rights of Minority Cultures* (Oxford, Oxford University Press, 1995). Page references here will be to the latter.

12 Kukathas, 'Are there any cultural rights?', op. cit., p. 238.

13 Kukathas, 'Are there any cultural rights?', op. cit., pp. 234–7.

14 As Will Kymlicka notes, the analogy between religion and culture does not work: 'It is quite possible for a state not to have an established church. But the state cannot help but give at least partial establishment to a culture when it decides which language is to be used in public schooling, or in the provision of state services' (*Multicultural Citizenship*, op. cit., p. 111).

15 See John Stuart Mill, *Representative Government*, in *Utilitarianism; Liberty; Representative Government*, op. cit., ch. 16, p. 361: 'Free institutions are next to impossible on a country made up of different nationalities. Among a people without fellow feeling, especially if they read and speak different languages, the united public opinion, necessary to the working of representative democracy, cannot exist...The same books, newspapers, pamphlets, speeches, do not reach them.'

16 These points are well made by David Miller; see *On Nationality*, op. cit., ch. 3, especially pp. 70–3.

17 For example, Joseph Raz writes: 'A political society, a state, consists – if it is multicultural – of diverse communities, and belongs to none of them.' See 'Multiculturalism: A liberal perspective', *Dissent* (winter 1994), pp. 67–79, p. 69. Jürgen Habermas argues that the liberal-democratic state – the proper object of 'constitutional patriotism' – should be differentiated both in theory and practice from the cultural community – the object of nationalist sentiments; see 'Citizenship and national identity: Some reflections on the future of Europe', *Praxis International* vol. 12 (1992), pp. 1–19. Chandran Kukathas does discuss the issue of Australian national identity, and – not surprisingly – argues for a 'weak' understanding of this notion – comprising a 'shared history and common legal and political institutions'. See Kukathas, 'The idea of an Australian identity', in Kukathas (ed.), *Multicultural Citizens*, op. cit. But even this 'weak' understanding (which ignores language) is incompatible with the demand of liberal neutrality.

18 See Miller, *On Nationality*, op. cit., pp. 131–40. See also Yael Tamir, *Liberal Nationalism*, op. cit., pp. 147–9, and the work of Clifford Geertz, *The Interpretation of Cultures* (New York, Basic Books, 1973), discussed by Tamir.

19 As argued by William H. McNeill, *Polyethnicity and National Unity in World History* (Toronto, University of Toronto Press, 1986).

20 Kymlicka, *Multicultural Citizenship*, op. cit., p. 11.

21 As I suggested in Chapter 1, it was one of the great imperial achievements of the English to create a concept of 'Britishness' which encompassed,

and to a certain extent even fostered, subordinate Scottish and Welsh identities.

22 In 'The crisis of identification: The case of Canada', in John Dunn (ed.), *Contemporary Crisis of the Nation State?* (Oxford and Cambridge, MA, Blackwell, 1995), James Tully makes a powerful case for the recognition of cultural diversity. The case is weakened (though not fatally) by his exaggeration of the extent to which the traditional conception of the nation imposed cultural uniformity.

23 For MacIntyre's account of tradition, see *After Virtue*, second edition (Notre Dame, University of Notre Dame Press, 1984), ch. 15, and *Whose Justice? Which Rationality?* (London, Duckworth, 1988), ch. 18. It should be noted that MacIntyre himself would not count a national culture as anything more than a debased tradition; see 'Is patriotism a virtue?', *The Lindley Lectures*, The University of Kansas, 1984.

24 See Kymlicka, *Multicultural Citizenship*, op. cit., pp. 98–9.

25 Charles Taylor, 'The politics of recognition', in Charles Taylor *et al. Multiculturalism: Examining the Politics of Recognition* (second edition, Princeton, Princeton University Press, 1992), pp. 66–73.

26 Liberal arguments for a radical easing of restrictions on entry are presented by Joseph H. Carens, 'Aliens and citizens: The case for open borders', *Review of Politics* vol. 49 (1987), pp. 251–73; slightly abridged version reprinted in Will Kymlicka (ed.), *The Rights of Minority Cultures*, op. cit. See also the papers in the collection, Brian Barry and Robert E. Goodin (eds), *Free Movement: Ethical Issues in the Transnational Migration of People and Money* (New York, London, etc., Harvester/Wheatsheaf, 1992). For a fuller and more nuanced account, but one which is similar to the position sketched in here, see Michael Walzer, *Spheres of Justice: A Defence of Pluralism and Equality* (New York, Basic Books, 1983), ch. 2.

27 It is puzzling that Margalit and Raz's sensitive discussion of cultural identity in 'National self-determination', op. cit., makes little reference to this. But the relationship of national identity to territory is a crucial component in the claim to self-determination.

28 In Australia, for example, the criteria for admission give priority to economic and social criteria (e.g. education, skill, language, financial considerations). This policy discriminates against those in greatest need.

29 It also needs to be emphasised that if considerations of national identity provide grounds for relatively affluent countries to limit immigration, they provide no reason why these countries should not transfer resources and provide other forms of assistance to countries in need. See the discussion in Robert E. Goodin, 'If people were money...', in Barry and Goodin (eds), *Free Movement*, op. cit.

30 The *Encyclopedia of Aboriginal Australia*, ed. David Horton (Aboriginal Studies Press for Australian Institute for Aboriginal and Torres Strait Islanders Studies, 1994) gives the figure of 314,500 for the Aboriginal population in 1788 (Appendix, p. 1299). However, in *Aboriginal Sovereignty: Reflections on Race, State and Nation* (St Leonards, NSW, Allen & Unwin, 1966), Henry Reynolds remarks that an 1838 estimate of 1,400,000 Aborigines 'may have been too high, but ...was probably closer to present-day assessments than the figure of 300,000 accepted from 1930 until recently' (p. 20). This would put the figure as closer to 900,000.

31 Astonishing evidence has recently been presented which dates a rock carving discovered at Jinmium in the Northern Territory as 75,000 years old and other human traces as between 120,000 and 176,000 years old. See Richard Fullager, Lesley Head and David Price, 'Early human occupation of Northern Australia: Archaeology and thermoluminescence dating of Jinmium rock shelter, Northern Territory', *Antiquity* vol. 70 (1996), pp. 751–73. Even if this dating is accepted, however, it does not establish continuity with contemporary Aboriginals. There have been invasions and other large population movements since then.

32 Strictly, I should speak here of Aborigines and Torres Strait Islanders which are the two major indigenous groupings in Australia. As will emerge later, the interests of the two groups may diverge on certain issues.

33 Figures from the *Encyclopedia of Aboriginal Australia*, op. cit., p. 1299. It should be noted that in recent years there has been a marked increase in the number of those who identify themselves as Aboriginal, and this is reflected in census returns.

34 For example: median income of Aborigines and Torres Strait Islanders was two thirds of the national figure; mortality rates are over two and a half times the national average; life expectancy is fifteen to seventeen years less than that of the whole population; infant and perinatal mortality rates are three times the national average; rate of imprisonment is eighteen times that of non-Aboriginals; unemployment rates are 35 per cent against the overall rate of 9 per cent; etc. Figures are from the 1991 census, and are contained in Ian Castles (ed.), *Year Book Australia 1994* no. 76 (Canberra, Australian Bureau of Statistics, 1994), pp. 411–16.

35 See Andrew Sharp, *Justice and the Maori: The Philosophy and Practice of Maori Claims in New Zealand since the 1970s* (Auckland, Oxford University Press, 1990; second edition 1997), pp. 15–20 and *passim*.

36 Eddie Mabo was in fact a Torres Strait Islander and his particular claim concerned land on Murray Island. Although there are major differences between (and amongst) the mainland Aborigines and Torres Strait Islanders in their use of and relation to the land, the High Court explicitly extended the judgement to cover *all* indigenous land.

37 On these points, see Tim Rowse, 'Aborigines: Citizens and colonial subjects', in Judith Brett, James Gillespie and Murray Goot (eds), *Developments in Australian Politics* (Melbourne, Macmillan, 1994), especially p. 184. The claim that five sixths of Aboriginals would not qualify for native title was made by Michael Mansell; see 'The court gives an inch but takes another mile: The Aboriginal Provisional Government assessment of the Mabo case', *Aboriginal Law Bulletin* 2: 57 (August 1992).

38 The argument that it is not coherent to separate the issue of sovereignty from that of property in this way, and that the Australian courts should recognise pre-existing Aboriginal sovereignty is powerfully made in Henry Reynolds, *Aboriginal Sovereignty*, op. cit.

39 These point are well made in Janna Thompson, 'Land rights and Aboriginal sovereignty', *Australasian Journal of Philosophy* vol. 68 (1990), pp. 313–29.

40 See, for example, Kevin Keefe, *From the Centre to the City: Aboriginal Education, Culture and Power* (Canberra, Aboriginal Studies Press, 1992), p. 192; Rowse, 'Aborigines: Citizens and colonial subjects', op. cit., p. 186.

The retention by indigenous people of the title 'Aboriginal' is one index of the significance of this claim to their identity.

41 Kymlicka, *Multicultural Citizenship*, op. cit., pp. 219–20. In a section omitted from the cited passage, Kymlicka argues that claims for compensation do not 'by themselves justify the self-government rights which are his preferred option for dealing with the claims of indigenous people'. He writes: 'Many groups have been wrongfully dispossessed of property and other economic opportunities, including women, blacks, and Japanese immigrants....Each of these groups may be entitled to certain forms of compensatory justice, but this does not by itself explain or justify granting powers of self-government.' This argument confuses questions of property with those of sovereignty. I will say something about the self-government option later in this chapter. After the passage quoted, Kymlicka argues that indigenous people may themselves have acquired land by expropriation of prior claimants. Whatever the force of this argument in some cases, it has no application to the Australian case.

42 Kymlicka, *Multicultural Citizenship*, op. cit., pp. 11–26, pp. 61–9, etc. At the risk of multiplying terminology, I have not followed Kymlicka's use of the terms 'ethnic', 'polyethnic', etc., to refer to the cultural diversity generated by immigration. In part this is due to the worries I raised in Chapter 1, in the section entitled 'The nation: imagination and culture'. But it is also because some relevant immigrant groups, e.g. Muslims, are not ethnic groups at all, but religious ones. See the discussion of this point in Joseph H. Carens, 'Liberalism and culture', *Constellations* vol. 4 (1997), pp. 35–47.

43 A different but analogous case is that of African-Americans whose past is one of forced immigration and slavery. It may be that behind Kymlicka's decision to marginalise the issue of historical wrong is the fear that the very enormity of the crime and its consequences may serve to inhibit moral reflection and action. This is a real worry, especially when the results of relatively abstract argument are pitted against the comfortable certainties of everyday moral reflection and the political problems in the way of practical policy. But the problem is inescapable. The other side of this problem is *ressentiment*: the way in which the identity of an oppressed group is constituted by the image of an oppression so vast that it can never be expiated or diminished. See Wendy Brown, *States of Injury* (Princeton, Princeton University Press, 1995), especially ch. 3. But this problem is one for members of the oppressed group to resolve; not for advice from those implicated in the oppression.

44 See, for example, Paul Coe, 'The struggle for Aboriginal sovereignty', Kevin Gilbert, 'Aboriginal sovereign position: Summary and definition', and Michael Mansell, 'Towards Aboriginal sovereignty: Aboriginal Provisional Government', in *Social Alternatives* vol. 13.1 (April 1994), pp. 10–12, 13–15, 16–18.

45 See Henry Reynolds, *Aboriginal Sovereignty*, op. cit.

46 See Kymlicka, *Multicultural Citizenship*, op. cit., *passim* but especially chs 2 and 4.

47 See Allen Buchanan, *Secession: The Morality of Political Discourse from Fort Sumter to Lithuania and Quebec* (Boulder, Westview Press, 1991), especially pp. 67–70. Buchanan refers to this argument as 'perhaps the simplest and most intuitively appealing argument for secession' (p. 67).

48 Cp. Buchanan, *Secession*, op. cit., where he makes the point that sometimes 'one ought not to do what one has a right to do' (p. 68).

49 See, for example, Noel Pearson, 'To be or not to be – separate nationhood or aboriginal self-determination and self-government within the Australian nation?', *Aboriginal Law Bulletin* vol. 3. 61 (April 1993), pp. 14–17. See also the views of Lois O'Donoghue and of Pat O'Shane as described in Bev Blaskett, Alan Smith and Loong Wong, 'Guest editors' introduction: Indigenous sovereignty and justice', *Social Alternatives* vol. 13 no. 1 (April 1994), pp. 5–8. For a non-indigenous view, see Frank Brennan, SJ, *One Land, One Nation: Mabo – Towards 2001* (Brisbane, University of Queensland Press, 1995).

50 Cp. Paul Patton, 'Mabo and Australian society: Towards a postmodern republic', *The Australian Journal of Anthropology* vol. 6. 1 and 2 (1995), pp. 83–93, p. 89: 'it would be another form of racism to extend protection to indigenous communities only on the condition that they maintained and practiced a traditional form of life'.

51 See Graham Hiley (ed.), *The Wik Case: Issues and Implications* (Sydney, Butterworths, 1997). The legal issues here are complex and I cannot do justice to them here. However, it is worth noting that the High Court rules that in case of conflict, the rights of the pastoral lease override those of native title.

52 Though not very far in the past, from 1937 until well into the 1960s, all mainland Australian States and the Northern Territory administered policies which involved forcibly removing indigenous children from their families to be brought up in institutions or in non-indigenous foster homes. Contact between parents and children was discouraged and often rendered impossible by bureaucratic regulation and vast distance. This policy was justified in the name of assimilation. For details of the experiences of the children and the impact on their lives, see *Bringing Them Home: Report of the National Inquiry into the Separation of Aboriginal and Torres Strait Islander Children from Their Families* (Sydney, Human Rights and Equal Opportunity Commission, 1997).

53 Cp. Yael Tamir: 'Since they [associative obligations] grow from relatedness and identity, they are independent of the normative nature of the association.' See *Liberal Nationalism*, op. cit., p 101.

54 Jürgen Habermas, *The New Conservatism: Cultural Criticism and the Historians' Debate* (Cambridge, MA, MIT Press, 1989), p. 232–3. It is not clear to me that this passage is consistent with Habermas's 'constitutional patriotism' and universalistic 'discourse ethics'.

55 For an enlightening account of the tension between multiculturalism and special recognition of the Maoris of New Zealand, see Richard Mulgan, 'Multiculturalism: A New Zealand perspective', in Chandran Kukathas (ed.), *Multicultural Citizens*, op. cit. Mulgan brings out very clearly the way in which multicultural and separatist agendas tend to erode the cultural basis for extensive State intervention.

5 The end of the affair?

1 G.W.F. Hegel, *Elements of the Philosophy of Right*, trans. H.B. Nisbet (Cambridge and New York, Cambridge University Press, 1991), Preface, p. 23.

2 Nietzsche's well known claim that 'only that which has no history is definable' is not strictly true. Nietzsche's point was that everything historical (and for Nietzsche, this was everything) is subject to change and is *for that reason* indefinable. However, this overlooks those historical items which no longer exist. A more plausible version would read 'only that which has *ceased to have* a history is definable'. See Friedrich Nietzsche, *On the Genealogy of Morals*, Essay Two, Section 13, in *On the Genealogy of Morals; Ecce Homo*, trans. Walter Kaufmann and R.J. Hollingdale (New York, Vintage Books, 1989).

3 G.W.F. Hegel, *Philosophy of Right*, Preface, pp. 21–2.

4 David Miller, *On Nationality*, op. cit., p. 184.

5 Hobsbawm, *Nations and Nationalism since 1780*, op. cit., pp. 31–2.

6 Karl Marx and Friedrich Engels, *Manifesto of the Communist Party*, in Marx and Engels, *Collected Works Volume 6: 1845–48* (London, Lawrence & Wishart, 1976), p. 488.

7 I have discussed this in *Morality and Modernity*, op. cit., ch. 1.

8 See E.J. Hobsbawm, *Nations and Nationalism since 1780*, op. cit., p. 162, note 29. Hobsbawm cites David Riesman's Introduction to Daniel Lerner, *The Passing of Traditional Society* in support of the view that modern oral and visual media do not demand literacy. Whether or not this is true, a more significant point is that the diversification of media sources (e.g. of radio and television stations) allows cultural minorities access to news, information, entertainment, and so on, *in their own language*.

9 Hobsbawm, *Nations and Nationalism since 1780*, op. cit., p. 163.

10 See Rogers Brubaker, *Nationalism Reframed: Nationhood and the National Question in the New Europe* (Cambridge, New York and Melbourne, Cambridge University Press, 1996). Brubaker argues that post-Soviet nationalisms are largely the product of Soviet policies ('Nationalist in form, socialist in content').

11 Walter Benjamin, 'Theses on the Philosophy of History', in *Illuminations*, trans. Harry Zohn, ed. Hannah Arendt (London, Fontana Press, 1973; reprinted 1992), p. 249.

12 Thomas W. Pogge, 'Cosmopolitanism and sovereignty', *Ethics* vol. 103 (1992), pp. 48–75; see p. 49.

13 Kant's writings move from legal cosmopolitanism (a world republic) towards something weaker (a federation of states). He does not, of course, waver from a commitment to moral cosmopolitanism. See 'Idea for a universal history with a cosmopolitan purpose' (1784), 'On the common saying: "This may be true in theory, but it does not apply in practice" ' (1793), and 'Perpetual peace: A philosophical sketch' (1795), all in *Political Writings*, ed. Hans Reiss, second edition (Cambridge and New York, Cambridge University Press, 1991). A fuller discussion of cosmopolitanism would need to address Kant's work. See James Bohman and Matthias-Lutz Bachmann (eds), *Perpetual Peace: Essays on Kant's Cosmopolitan Ideal* (Cambridge, MA and London, MIT Press, 1997).

14 Henry Shue, 'Mediating duties', *Ethics* vol. 98 (1988), pp. 687–704, p. 692.

15 Henry Shue, 'Mediating duties', op. cit., p. 691.

16 Henry Shue, 'Mediating duties', op. cit., p. 692.

17 See Stephen Toulmin, *Cosmopolis: The Hidden Agenda of Modernity* (New York, The Free Press, 1990), especially pp. 67–9.

18 See Note 13 above. Alexandre Kojève is one of the few twentieth-century theorists to have advocated a world State. Kojève's *Introduction to the Reading of Hegel* (trans. James H. Nichols, Jr., Ithaca and London, Cornell University Press, 1986) implausibly attributes to Hegel the view that the goal of history is the '*universal* and *homogenous* State' (see, for example, p. 95). It is significant that Kojève ended his life in the service of the (then) European Economic Community.

19 See Thomas Pogge, 'Cosmopolitanism and sovereignty', op. cit.; and David Held, *Democracy and the Global Order: From the Modern State to Cosmopolitan Governance* (Cambridge, Polity Press, 1995), especially Parts III and IV, and 'Democracy: From city-states to a cosmopolitan order?' in Robert E. Goodin and Philip Pettit (eds), *Contemporary Political Philosophy: An Anthology* (Oxford, Blackwell, 1997).

20 See, for example, Henry Shue, 'Mediating duties', op. cit., p. 698; Martha Nussbaum, 'Patriotism and cosmopolitanism', in Martha Nussbaum *et al.*, *For Love of Country: Debating the Limits of Patriotism* (Boston, Beacon Press, 1996), especially pp. 4–5.

21 See Jocelyne Couture and Kai Nielsen, with Michel Seymour, 'Liberal nationalism: Both cosmopolitan and rooted', in Jocelyne Couture *et al.* (eds), *Rethinking Nationalism* (Calgary, University of Calgary Press, 1998). I make use of the 'rooted' and 'rootless' metaphor below.

22 Kai Nielsen, 'Cosmopolitan nationalism', *The Monist* (forthcoming). Nielsen would, of course, reject the argument of this chapter that nationalism is on the way out. For a not dissimilar characterisation of cosmopolitanism, see Jonathan Rée, 'Cosmopolitanism and the experience of nationality', *The Philosophical Forum* vol. 28 (1996/97), pp. 167–79. *Contra* Nielsen, Rée argues that cosmopolitanism in this sense is incompatible with nationalism.

23 I take it that it is this aspect of one's attachments that Richard Rorty intends to capture with his (somewhat idiosyncratic) use of the term 'irony'. See his *Contingency, Irony and Solidarity* (Cambridge, Cambridge University Press, 1989), especially pp. 73–4.

24 A key virtue of the eighteenth-century Enlightenment – especially the Scottish Enlightenment – was *civility*: the capacity to share the same social space as and even to appreciate those with different interests, ways of life, and so on. *Cosmopolitanism* may be thought of as civility writ large enough to encompass profound differences in culture.

25 Hegel was uncomfortably aware of the tendency of civil society to extend across State borders; see *The Philosophy of Right*, op. cit., Part III, § 246, pp. 267–8. It is not clear that he resolved the problems this created for his account of the State.

26 I borrow this useful term from Henry Shue; see 'Mediating Duties', op. cit., p. 87–91.

27 Nietzsche, *The Gay Science*, trans. Walter Kaufmann (New York, Vintage, 1974), Book 3, § 125, p. 181.

28 Martha C. Nussbaum, 'Patriotism and cosmopolitanism', op. cit., p. 9.

Bibliographical essay
The state of the nation

My aim in this essay is to provide an account of the literature on nationalism and related topics which might prove useful to students and scholars, mainly but not only in political and moral philosophy. Philosophers, having arrived late, tend to investigate the terrain as if it were *terra incognita*, ignoring the knowledge of inhabitants and earlier explorers. In fact, there is a considerable body of literature on nationalism in other disciplines, much of which bears on the issues discussed by philosophers and raises philosophical issues in its own right. So I will include work on nationalism by historians, sociologists, cultural theorists and others, as well as from philosophy. Though I have tried to be ecumenical in my selection (though not in my comments), no doubt the suggestions I make reflect my own predilections. However, anyone who begins to explore the list will find references which will take him or her a good deal further. To make fuller exploration easier, I have marked those works which contain useful bibliographies with an asterisk. To keep this essay to a reasonable length, I have concentrated on books and collections, and have only mentioned journal articles when they seemed to be of special relevance or merit.

On nationalism

In 1983, two books transformed the study of nationalism. Benedict Anderson's *Imagined Communities: Reflections on the Origin and Spread of Nationalism* (London and New York, Verso, 1983; expanded edition 1991) is a sympathetic and highly suggestive account of nationalism and its cultural roots. Ernest Gellner's very different *Nations and Nationalism* (Oxford, Basil Blackwell, 1983) provided a sparse and elegant explanation of nationalism in terms of the needs of industrial societies. John Breuilly, 'Reflections on nationalism',

Philosophy and Social Science vol. 15 (1985), pp. 67–75, is an excellent review of both books. Anderson and Gellner continued to write on the topic. Gellner's posthumous *Nationalism* (London, Weidenfeld & Nicolson, 1997) shows his reluctance to give up a beautiful theory in the face of overwhelming difficulties. Anderson's *The Spectre of Comparisons: Nationalism, Southeast Asia and the World* (London and New York, Verso, 1998) adds detail and nuance to the earlier account, without changing the substance. However, it seems to take a rather gloomier view of nationalism.

Neither Gellner nor Anderson spend much time evaluating the work of predecessors. However, Hans Kohn, *The Idea of Nationalism: A Study in its Origins and Background* (first published 1944; reprinted Toronto, Collier-Macmillan, 1969) and Elie Kedourie, *Nationalism* (first published 1962; fourth expanded edition, Oxford and Cambridge, MA, Basil Blackwell, 1993) are still worth reading. Also worth noting is Karl W. Deutsch's *Nationalism and Social Communication: An Inquiry into the Foundations of Nationality* (first published 1953; reprinted Cambridge, MA and London, MIT Press, 1966). Despite his addiction to the almost unreadable social science jargon of the day, Deutsch's attempt to explain the emergence of nationalism in terms of networks of social communication was a considerable advance on anything else available at the time.

Of more recent work, Eric J. Hobsbawm's *Nations and Nationalism since 1780: Programme, Myth, Reality** (Cambridge, Cambridge University Press, 1990; second expanded edition, 1993) is enormously valuable, despite (or perhaps because of) his lack of sympathy with the nationalist project. Anthony D. Smith is undoubtedly the most prolific writer on nationalism in the English-speaking world. His *The Ethnic Origins of Nationalism* (Oxford and Cambridge, MA, Blackwell, 1986) contains fascinating material, though its overall argument suffers from near-terminal conceptual unclarity. *National Identity** (London, Penguin, 1991) provides a more succinct and accessible introduction to his work. Liah Greenfeld, *Nationalism: Five Roads to Modernity* (Cambridge, MA and London, Harvard University Press, 1992), argues that the modern world is to be explained by nationalism (and not the other way around), and provides an impressively detailed and original (indeed, idiosyncratic) account of the emergence of the idea of the nation in England and the United States ('good nations'), and France, Germany and Russia ('bad nations') to illustrate this thesis. Linda Colley, *Britons: Forging the Nation 1707–1837* (New Haven and London, Yale University Press, 1992), is much less ambitious: indeed, it does not claim to advance a theory of nationalism at all. However, it provides an absorbing and insightful account of the emergence of the idea of 'Britain', and in so doing demolishes some persistent myths about nationalism (that it is based on ethnicity, that it requires cultural homogeneity, etc.). Paul James, *Nation Formation: Towards a Theory of Abstract Community** (London, Thousand Oaks, CA and New Delhi, Sage Publications, 1996) provides an excellent critical survey of the literature on nationalism in the course of advancing his own account. Rogers Brubaker has written two fine studies combining historical detail and theoretical reflection: *Citizenship and Nationhood in France and Germany* (Cambridge, MA and London, Harvard University Press, 1992), a detailed study of 'civic' and 'ethnic' elements in conceptions of the nation; and *Nationalism Reframed: Nationhood and the National Question in the New Europe* (Cambridge, New York and Melbourne, Cambridge University Press, 1996), which develops an account of the nation as the product of contingent institutional and political practices in the course of analysing nationalism in the post-Soviet world. Finally, and of particular interest to academics, Bill Readings, *The University in Ruins* (Cambridge, MA and London, Harvard University Press, 1996) charts the changing role of universities in constructing national cultures.

There are two recent and interestingly different anthologies. John Hutchinson and Anthony D. Smith (eds), *Nationalism** (Oxford and New York, Oxford University Press, 1994) contains selections from a broad range of mainly twentieth-century writers. Omar Dahbour and Micheline R. Ishay (eds), *The Nationalism Reader* (New York, The Humanities Press, 1995) ranges as far back as Rousseau, Kant and Sieyès, and contains a more interesting collection of authors. Unfortunately, it does not provide a bibliography. Both anthologies tend to abbreviate the texts they reprint, and, sometimes, the extracts do not give a very good sense of what the writer is on about (and the use of '...' to mark too frequent omissions merely added to this reader's irritation). A more rigorous selection would have allowed justice to be done to the more significant extracts.

Marxism and nationalism

Marxism has always had difficulties – both of a theoretical and a political kind – in coming to terms with nationalism. However, perhaps for this reason, the contributions of many writing in or against the Marxist tradition have a good deal of interest. Karl Marx and Friedrich Engels, *The Communist Manifesto* (first published 1847; available in any selection of Marx's writings) is the obvious place to start. Shlomo Avineri (ed.), *Karl Marx on Colonialism and Modernisation* (London, Anchor Books, 1969) contains a selection of other writings. Joseph Stalin, 'Marxism and the national question', in Bruce Franklin (ed.), *The Essential Stalin: Major Theoretical Writings* (London, Croom Helm, 1973) and V.I. Lenin, 'The right of nations to self-determination', available in any selection of Lenin's writings, formed the basis of twentieth-century orthodoxy. Otto Bauer, 'The nationality question and social democracy', in Patrick Goode and T.B. Bottomore (eds), *Austro-Marxism* (Oxford, Oxford University Press, 1978) might have formed a better starting point. All of the above are in Dahbour and Ishay (eds), *The Nationalism Reader*, op. cit. Tom Nairn, *The Break Up of Britain* (London and New York, Verso, 1977; second edition, 1981) and *Faces of Nationalism: Janus Revisited* (London and New York, Verso, 1997); and Etienne Balibar and Immanuel Wallerstein, *Race, Nation, Class: Ambiguous Identities* (London and New York, Verso, 1991) show that there is still a good deal of life in Marxist approaches. Ephraim Nimni, *Marxism and Nationalism: Theoretical Origins of a Political Crisis** (London and Concord, MA, Pluto Press, 1991) provides a good guide through the Marxist debates.

Philosophers on nationalism

There is a widespread belief that philosophers have not concerned themselves with nationalism. This myth does not survive an even cursory examination of the tradition. Almost all political philosophers from the eighteenth century on have had something to say either for or against nationalism. Here I will only mention more or less explicit discussions of the topic (many of which are to be found in Dahbour and Ishay (eds), *The Nationalism Reader*, op. cit.). David Hume, 'On national characters' (first published 1748; reprinted in *Essays: Moral, Political and Literary*, ed. Eugene F. Miller, Indianapolis, Liberty Classics, 1987); Jean Jacques Rousseau, *The Constitutional Project for Corsica, Considerations on the Government of Poland* (written in 1765 and 1772 respectively; reprinted in *Political Writings*, ed. and trans. J.M. Watkins, Edinburgh, Nelson, 1953); Immanuel Kant, 'Idea for a universal history with a cosmopolitan purpose', 'Perpetual peace: A philosophical sketch' (first published in 1784 and 1795 respectively; both reprinted in *Kant's Political Writings*, second edition, ed. Hans Reiss and trans. H.B. Nisbet, Cambridge, Cambridge University Press, 1991); Johann Gottfried Herder, *J.G. Herder on Social and Political Culture*, ed. F.M. Barnard (selections, mostly from

Reflections on the Philosophy of History of Mankind, first published 1784/85, London, Cambridge University Press, 1969); Johann Gottlieb Fichte, *Addresses to the German Nation* (first published 1808; New York, Harper & Row, 1968); G.W.F. Hegel, *Elements of the Philosophy of Right* (first published 1820; Cambridge, Cambridge University Press, 1991), especially Preface, Part III; John Stuart Mill, *Considerations on Representative Government*, ch. 16: 'Of nationality, as connected with representative government' (first published 1861; reprinted in J.S. Mill, *Utilitarianism; Liberty; Representative Government*, London, J.M. Dent, 1957); John E.E.D. Acton, 'Nationalism' (first published 1862; reprinted in *The History of Freedom and Other Essays*, London, Macmillan, 1922); Ernest Renan, 'What is a nation?' (first published 1882; reprinted in part in Louis L. Snyder (ed.), *The Dynamics of Nationalism: Readings in its Meaning and Development*, Princeton, Van Nostrand, 1964, and in full in Homi Bhabha (ed.), *Nations and Narration*, London and New York, Routledge, 1990); Max Weber, 'The nation' (first published 1922; reprinted in H.H. Gerth and C. Wright Mills (eds), *From Max Weber*, London, Henley and Boston, Routledge & Kegan Paul, 1977).

In the past ten years, there have been at least three excellent philosophical treatments of nationalism. Of these, Yael Tamir's *Liberal Nationalism* (Princeton, Princeton University Press, 1993; expanded edition 1995) was the first and perhaps the most interesting. As an Israeli philosopher, Tamir is well aware both of the force of nationalism and its problems. Sanford Levinson, 'Is liberal nationalism an oxymoron? An essay for Judith Shklar', *Ethics* vol. 195 (1995), pp. 626–45 is a perceptive and searching review (Tamir responds in the second edition of her book). See also the symposium on liberal nationalism in *Constellations* vol. 3 no. 2 (1997). David Miller's *On Nationality* (Oxford, Clarendon Press, 1995) is a systematic and persuasive defence of nationality as a political principle, though his habit of using life in Oxford colleges to illustrate the moral force of nationality diminishes the impact of his arguments. There is a symposium on Miller in *Nations and Nationalism* vol. 2 no. 3 (1996); and the *Journal of Applied Philosophy* vols 11–13 (1994–6) has published a number of articles on Miller's work, and a response by Miller, 'Nationality: Some replies', vol. 14 (1997), pp. 69–82. Margaret Canovan, *Nationhood and Political Theory* (Cheltenham, UK and Brookfield, VT, Edward Elgar, 1996) is a low-key, but incisively argued, exploration of the ways in which nationhood is taken for granted in political theory.

An index of the revival of interest in nationalism is the number of recent collections and/or special issues of journals. These include *Critical Review* vol. 10 no. 2 (spring 1996); Simon Carey, David George and Peter Jones (eds), *National Rights, International Obligations* (Oxford, Westview Press, 1996); *The Philosophical Forum* vol. 28 nos 1–2 (winter 1996/97), Special Issue: *Philosophical Perspectives on National Identity* (ed. Omar Dahbour); Robert McKim and Jeff McMahan (eds), *The Morality of Nationalism* (New York and Oxford, Oxford University Press, 1997); *Canadian Journal of Philosophy* supp. vol. 22 (1996): *Rethinking Nationalism** (eds Jocelyne Couture, Kai Nielsen and Michel Seymour) (Calgary, University of Calgary Press, 1998 [sic]); *The Monist* vol. 83 no. 2 (July 1999), Special Issue: *Nationalism* (ed. Ninad Miskevic); Ronald Beiner (ed.), *Theorizing Nationalism* (Albany, State University of New York Press, 1999). These collections contain articles by most of the major participants in recent debates, and include material on all the themes identified below.

Identity

The concept of national identity is central to the issue of nationalism. Apart from the discussions in Miller, *On Nationality*, op. cit., and Tamir, *Liberal Nationalism*, op. cit., there is surprisingly little discussion of it in the philosophical literature (especially in comparison with the endless debates about 'personal identity'). Two important articles are Avishai Margalit and Joseph Raz, 'National self-determination', *Journal of Philosophy* vol. 87 (1990), pp. 439–61; reprinted in Raz, *Ethics in the Public Domain: Essays on the Morality of Law and Politics* (Oxford, Clarendon Press, 1994); and Avishai Margalit and Moshe Halbertal, 'Liberalism and the right to culture', *Social Research* vol. 61 (1994), pp. 491–510. Jonathan Rée, 'Internationality', *Radical Philosophy* no. 60 (spring 1992), pp. 3–11, argues that the concept is irremediably confused; Ross Poole, 'On national identity: A response to Jonathan Rée', *Radical Philosophy* no. 62 (autumn 1992), pp. 14–19, provides a defence. On identity in general, see Charles Taylor, *Sources of the Self: The Making of the Modern Identity* (Cambridge, Cambridge University Press, 1989), especially Part I. See also Judith Butler, *Gender Trouble: Feminism and the Subversion of Identity* (New York and London, Routledge, 1990); Wendy Brown, *States of Injury* (Princeton, Princeton University Press, 1995); Ernesto Laclau (ed.), *The Making of Political Identities* (London and New York, Verso, 1994); and John Rajchman (ed.), *The Identity in Question* (New York and London, Routledge, 1995).

National identity and the claims of aliens

Significant contributions include Michael Walzer, *Spheres of Justice: A Defence of Pluralism and Equality* (New York, Basic Books, 1983); Robert Goodin, 'What is so special about our fellow countrymen?', *Ethics* vol. 98 (1988), pp. 663–86; Brian Barry and Robert E. Goodin (eds), *Free Movement: Ethical Issues in the Transnational Migration of People and Money* (New York and London, Harvester/Wheatsheaf, 1992), especially the papers by Goodin, Joseph Carey and Barry. Samuel Scheffler has published an important series of articles about special responsibilities; see 'Individual responsibility in a global age', *Social Philosophy and Policy* vol. 12 (1995), pp. 219–36; *Families, Nations and Strangers*, The Lindley Lecture (Lawrence, University of Kansas, 1995); and 'Relationships and responsibilities', *Philosophy and Public Affairs* vol. 26 (1997), pp. 189–209. Forms of cosmopolitanism have been urged against the claims of nationality by Thomas W. Pogge, 'Cosmopolitanism and sovereignty', *Ethics* vol. 103 (1992), pp. 48–75, and Henry Shue, 'Mediating duties', *Ethics* vol. 98 (1988), pp. 687–704.

Multiculturalism

Perhaps not surprisingly, some of the most important contributions to the debates about multiculturalism (and also indigenous rights, secession, and citizenship) have come from Canada. In many ways, Will Kymlicka, *Liberalism, Community and Culture** (Oxford, Clarendon Press, 1989) opened the debate on the extent to which a liberal order is able to recognise the claims of cultural minorities and indigenous people, and he has continued to be a major participant. See his *Multicultural Citizenship: A Liberal Theory of Minority Rights** (Oxford, Clarendon Press, 1995) and *Politics in the Vernacular: Essays on Nationalism, Multiculturalism and Citizenship* (Oxford, Oxford University Press, 1999). There is an excellent symposium on *Multicultural Citizenship*, with a response from Kymlicka in *Constellations* vol. 4 (1997), pp. 35–87. Kymlicka is involved in two indispensable collections: Kymlicka (ed.), *The Rights of Minority Cultures** (Oxford, Clarendon Press, 1995), which reprints a number of key articles on multiculturalism and indigenous rights; and *Nomos* vol. 39 (1997), Special Issue: *Ethnicity and Group Rights* (edited by Kymlicka and Ian Shapiro), which contains new material. James Tully's *Strange Multiplicity: Constitutionalism in an Age of Diversity* (Cambridge, Cambridge University Press, 1995) explores the extent to which Western political and legal thought is able to accommodate cultural difference and – especially – do justice to the claims of indigenous people. Amy Guttman (ed.), *Multiculturalism: Examining the Politics of Recognition* (Princeton, Princeton University Press, 1994), contains an important contribution by Charles Taylor, with comments by Susan Wolf and Michael Walzer, as well as articles by Jürgen Habermas and K. Anthony Appiah. Taylor has also written extensively on Canadian issues; and many of his papers are collected in *Reconciling the Solitudes: Essays on Canadian Federalism and Nationalism* (Montreal and Kingston, London and Buffalo, McGill-Queen's University Press, 1994). Other contributions to the Canadian debate – which ought be read by all concerned with these issues – include: Jeremy Webber, *Reimagining Canada: Language, Culture, Community and the Canadian Constitution* (Montreal and Kingston, London and Buffalo, McGill-Queen's University Press, 1994); Joseph H. Carens (ed.), *Is Quebec Nationalism Just? Perspectives from Anglophone Canada* (Montreal and Kingston, London and Buffalo, McGill-Queen's University Press, 1995); Roger Gibbins and Guy Laforest (eds), *Beyond the Impasse: Towards Reconciliation* (Montreal, Institute for Research on Public Policy, 1998).

Secession

The key contribution to recent discussion is Allen Buchanan, *Secession: The Morality of Political Divorce from Fort Sumter to Lithuania and Quebec* (Boulder, Westview Press, 1991). Many of the collections cited above include articles on this topic, usually taking off from Buchanan's work. See also Kai Nielsen, 'Secession: The case of Quebec', *Journal of Applied Philosophy* vol. 10 (1993), pp. 29–43; David Gauthier, 'Breaking up: An essay on secession', *Canadian Journal of Philosophy* vol. 24 (1994), pp. 357–72; Daniel Philpott, 'In defence of self-determination', *Ethics* vol. 105 (1995), pp. 352–85; and Nielsen again, 'Liberal nationalism, liberal democracies, and secession', *University of Toronto Law Journal* vol. 48 (1998), pp. 253–95. Buchanan's most recent contribution to the topic is 'Theories of secession', *Philosophy and Public Affairs* vol. 26 (1997), pp. 31–61. I have not yet seen Percy Lehning (ed.), *Theories of Secession* (London and New York, Routledge, 1998), which contains a selection of previously published articles. Margaret Moore (ed.), *National Self-Determination and Secession* (Oxford and New York, Oxford University Press, 1998) is a collection of new papers by some of the main participants in previous debates.

Indigenous rights and self-determination

Questions of indigenous rights and self-determination are all too often lumped together with general discussions of multiculturalism, and there is depressingly little work in philosophy and political theory focussed solely on indigenous issues. Much of the work mentioned above, especially the important work of Will Kymlicka and James Tully, does address indigenous claims. See, however, John R. Danley, 'Liberalism, Aboriginal rights, and cultural minorities', *Philosophy and Public Affairs* vol. 20 (1991), pp. 168–85, which criticises Kymlicka's *Liberalism, Community and Culture* for not sufficiently distinguishing indigenous from multicultural issues. David Lyons, 'The new Indian claims and original rights to land', *Social Theory and Practice* vol. 4 (1977), pp. 249–72, was a relatively early contribution to the debate. See also James Tully, 'Aboriginal property and Western political theory: Recovering a middle ground', *Social Philosophy and Policy* vol. 11 (1994), pp. 153–80, and Jeremy Webber, 'Relations of force and relations of justice: The emergence of normative community between colonists and aboriginal peoples', *Osgoode Hall Law Journal* vol. 3 (1995), pp. 624–60. Two books dealing with the New Zealand experience stand out: Richard Mulgan, *Maori, Pakeha and Democracy* (Auckland, Oxford University Press, 1989), and Andrew Sharpe, *Justice and the Maori: Maori Claims in New Zealand Political Argument in the 1980s* (Auckland, Oxford University Press, 1990; second edition 1997). There has been little from Australian philosophers. See, however, the Symposium on Aboriginal Land Rights in the *Australasian Journal of Philosophy* vol. 68 (1990), with contributions by Janna Thompson, 'Land rights and aboriginal sovereignty', pp. 313–46, and by John Bigelow, Robert Pargetter and Robert Young, 'Land, well-being and compensation', pp. 330–46; Susan Dodds, 'Justice and indigenous land rights', *Inquiry* vol. 41 (1998), pp. 187–205; and Rai Gaita, 'Not right', in Peter Craven (ed.), *Best Australian Essays 1998* (Melbourne, Bookman Press, 1998). Forthcoming are Duncan Ivison, Paul Patton and Will Sanders (eds), *Indigenous Rights and Western Political Theory* (Cambridge, Cambridge University Press, forthcoming); and *Australasian Journal of Philosophy* vol. 78 no. 3 (September 2000), Special Issue: *Indigenous Rights* (eds Chandran Kukathas and Ross Poole).

Citizenship

Excellent genealogies of the concept of citizenship are provided by Michael Walzer, 'Citizenship', in Terence Ball *et al.* (eds), *Political*

Innovation and Conceptual Change (Cambridge, Cambridge University Press, 1989), and J.G.A. Pocock, 'The ideal of citizenship since classical times', *Queen's Quarterly* vol. 99 no. 1 (spring 1992), pp. 33–55. An overview of recent discussion is provided by Will Kymlicka and Wayne Norman, 'Return of the citizen: A survey of recent work on citizenship theory', *Ethics* vol. 104 (1994), pp. 352–81*. Jürgen Habermas, 'Citizenship and national identity: Some reflections on the future of Europe', *Praxis International* vol. 12 (1992), pp. 1–19, argues that the connection between citizenship and national identity is a historical accident, which should be overcome. Iris Marion Young, *Justice and the Politics of Difference* (Princeton, Princeton University Press, 1990) provides an influential case for a concept of citizenship which recognises cultural difference. Important collections are Ronald Beiner (ed.), *Theorizing Citizenship* (Albany, State University of New York, 1995) – which includes many of the above; Chandran Kukathas (ed.), *Multicultural Citizens: The Philosophy and Politics of Identity* (St Leonard's, Sydney, Centre for Independent Studies, 1993); and Geoff Andrews (ed.), *Citizenship* (London, Lawrence & Wishart, 1991).

Arguing through the nation

These days, very few English-speaking intellectuals are prepared openly to celebrate their national identity, and enter into debate as to how that identity should be developed. Perhaps not surprisingly, the most notable exceptions to this generalisation are from the United States. See especially Michael Walzer, *What it Means to be an American* (New York, Marsilio, 1992) and Richard Rorty, *Achieving Our Country* (Cambridge, MA and London, Harvard University Press, 1998). It is tempting to read John Rawls, *Political Liberalism* (New York, Columbia University Press, 1993) and Michael J. Sandel, *Democracy's Discontents: America in Search of a Public Philosophy* (Cambridge, MA and London, Harvard University Press, 1996) as arguing for different accounts of American national identity, but this is not the way in which the authors understand their enterprise. Perhaps also the last chapter of David Miller's *On Nationality*, op. cit., is a tentative – and surely too late – step in this direction with regard to Britain.

Final remarks

There are many chastening things about writing a bibliographical essay. One is the discovery of important work which should have been discussed in the body of the text. Another is the awareness that it will be quickly out of date. One way in which a reader might overcome the second limitation is to browse among issues of relevant journals. These include *Ethics, Philosophy and Public Affairs, Political Theory, Political Studies, Radical Philosophy, Canadian Journal of Philosophy, Journal of Applied Philosophy, Critical Inquiry, Representations, Constellations, Nations and Nationalism*, and others. These can be expected to publish articles on most of the topics covered in this essay (and this book), and many of them will also publish reviews of relevant new books – perhaps even this one. The Queen's Forum for Philosophy and Public Policy publishes a quarterly e-mail newsletter on *Citizenship, Democracy and Ethnocultural Diversity*, edited by the indefatigable Will Kymlicka. This provides a listing of publications, research, conferences and Internet resources. To get on the mailing list, contact *philform@qsilver.queensu.ca*

Index

208   *Index*

THE UNIVERSITY OF MICHIGAN

DATE DUE

AUG 1 3 2004